Household Economy and Urban Development

Dellplain Latin American Studies

Household Economy and Urban Development: São Paulo, 1765 to 1836

Elizabeth Anne Kuznesof

Between 1765 and 1836 the household economy of São Paulo was transformed from a subsistence to a market-oriented economy. This transformation was paralleled by dramatic changes within society, existing kinship systems, and the organization of the household. The author suggests that this fundamental change in the mode of production was intentional, engineered by an interested elite of merchants and plantation owners who utilized local government bodies to promote the construction of centralized markets, roads, warehouses, and port facilities. The same group sponsored changes in local administration and land law in order to increase and control the resultant commerce in sugar and coffee. This book, based on household-level census data, looks at economic development at the micro level and analyzes how the change took place at a juncture in history when prior options seemed to disappear.

Elizabeth Anne Kuznesof is associate professor of history at the University of Kansas.

DELLPLAIN LATIN AMERICAN STUDIES

Household Economy and Urban Development

São Paulo, 1765 to 1836

Elizabeth Anne Kuznesof

Dellplain Latin American Studies, No. 18

LONDON AND NEW YORK

First published 1986 by Westview Press

Published 2018 by Routledge
52 Vanderbilt Avenue, New York, NY 10017
2 Park Square, Milton Park, Abingdon, Oxon OX14 4RN

Routledge is an imprint of the Taylor & Francis Group, an informa business

Library of Congress Cataloging-in-Publication Data
Kuznesof, Elizabeth Anne.
Household economy and urban development.
(Dellplain Latin American studies ; 18)
Bibliography: p.
Includes index.
1. São Paulo (Brazil : State)—Economic conditions.
2. Households—Brazil—São Paulo (State)—History.
3. Community development—Brazil—São Paulo (State)—History. I. Title. II. Series: Dellplain Latin American studies ; 18.
HC188.S3K89 1986 307.7'64'098161 85-31491

ISBN 13: 978-0-367-00886-4 (hbk)
ISBN 13: 978-0-367-15873-6 (pbk)

Contents

Figures and Maps

MAPS

FIGURES

Tables

Abbreviations

ACMSP	Actas da camara municipal de São Paulo.
AESP	Arquivo do Estado de São Paulo.
DI	Arquivo do Estado de São Paulo, Publicação official de documentos interessantes para a história e costumes de São Paulo.
HAHR	Hispanic American Historical Review.
RGCMSP	Registro geral da camara municipal de São Paulo.
RIHGB	Revista do Instituto Histórico e Geográfico Brasileiro.
RIHGB/TE	"Catalogo de documentos sobre a história de S. Paulo, existentes no Arquivo Histórico Ultramarino de Lisboa," RIHGB, Tomos Especiais. 15 vols. Rio de Janeiro, 1956-1959).

Preface

This is a book about São Paulo, Brazil and the way in which the extraordinary expansion of the city and the economy in the nineteenth century affected people's jobs, living conditions, the way they organized the running of their households, and even household size and fertility. The legendary resiliency of the Brazilian kinship structure and the way that the Brazilian family as a social, economic, and political unit has pervaded historiography--from the colonial period to the present--made me especially interested to analyze the impact of the industrial revolution and what is known as the "demographic transition" on the Brazilian household and on the family.

Even more important than analyzing the impact of these larger social and economic transformations on the household and family is the determination of the process itself. The means by which the household interacted with the economy, what the patterns of interaction were, and how they were determined in a given time and place are significant questions which are seldom addressed. In this study those interrelationships and the process of their interaction and change are traced diachronically through three manuscript censuses, property inventories, genealogies, and other records in a period of major economic transformation in the community of São Paulo.

It is not possible to acknowledge here everyone who has helped in the development of this book. Dauril Alden has followed this project from the beginning and before the beginning. Rather like the postman--through training, example, and the reading and criticism of many drafts--he has continued to provide assistance and unremitting support. William P. McGreevey, Kingsley Davis, Eduardo Arriaga, Albert Fishlow, Nicia Vilela Luz, Nestor Goulart Reis Filho, Richard Morse, David Brading, Simon Schwartzman, Gary Nigel Howe, and Nelson do Valle Silva have also assisted me with training, advice, or suggestions somewhere along the way. I also wish to acknowledge the guidance and help I received from Ody Siqueira de Noronha and Maria Gloria Martinelli of the Arquivo do Estado de São Paulo. I want to thank Robert J. Oppenheimer and Dauril Alden for reading and making useful suggestions on the final manuscript. The research in Brazil was supported by a Fulbright-Hays pre-doctoral fellowship and a pre-doctoral fellowship from the University of California at Berkeley. The General Research Fund of the University of Kansas also supported supplementary research on this project at the Library of Congress.

Elizabeth Anne Kuznesof

1 Household Economy and Modernization: A Comparative Perspective

The relationship of household and family organization to changes in the larger economy (e.g., commercialization, industrialization) has long fascinated and baffled scholars. Data that specifically link the household and/or family unit to economic change have proved elusive, and most studies do little more than note temporal crosscultural coincidences of demographic and residential characteristics with those of economic development.[1] The means by which the household interacted with the economy, what the patterns of interaction were, and how they were determined in a given time and place are significant questions which are seldom addressed. Even less accessible are the changes in the dynamics of household organization in conjunction with economic development in terms of informal economic and social exchanges and household and family formation.

This book attempts to relate changes in household economy, composition and size to the larger changes in the economy and society of São Paulo in the late eighteenth and nineteenth centuries. My original questions in beginning this study were sparked by studies of the impact of modernization in Western Europe on age at marriage, completed family size, household size and composition.[2] The "Demographic Transition Theory"--based on the experience of England and Wales--states that industrialization was accompanied by a transition from high birth and death rates to low birth and death rates, with a period of accelerated population growth while the declining birth rates lagged behind the declining death rates.[3] This theory has also been extended to suggest that a decline in number of children per ménage and, by extension, of household size, a decline in the extended family and household, and an

[1]There is an enormous literature on this question, much of which is cited in Peter Laslett, ed. Household and Family in Past Time (Cambridge, 1972). A useful crosscultural statistical analysis of household and economy is Thomas Burch, "The Size and Structure of Families, a Comparative Analysis of Census Data," American Sociological Review 32, no. 3 (1967): 347-63.

[2]Most important were Michael Anderson, Family Structure in Nineteenth Century Lancashire (Cambridge, 1971); D.V. Glass and D.E.C. Eversley, eds. Population in History (London, 1965); Louis Henry, Anciennes familles genevoises (Paris, 1960); and Peter Laslett, The World We Have Lost (London, 1965).

[3]The first statement of the theory was Warren S. Thompson, "Population," American Journal of Sociology, Vol. 34 (1929), pp. 959-75. A more recent positive statement of the theory is found in Secretary-General, United Nations, "Population Change and Economic and Social Development," in United Nations, The Population Debate: Dimensions and Perspectives. Papers of the World Population Conference Bucharest 1974 (New York, 1975), Vol. 1, p. 52.

increased proportion of women in the labor force are characteristic of the final phase of the transition as the birth and death rates become more proximate.[4]

I was fascinated by the theory--vague though it continues to be--because it seemed to provide a means to inter-relate macro-economic changes with individual decisions concerning basic life choices--to possibly discern the process and direction or causality which resulted in the new economic and social modes of production and reproduction. The theory has been much criticized particularly because it does not specify in what way or by what means the household and/or individual interacted with the economy and how aggregate changes in individual behavior and household composition resulted from this interaction.[5] Demographers have also suggested that the transition theory may not be applicable to developing countries because of basic differences in the experiences of these countries.[6] They point out that declines in mortality, which were gradual and in step with economic growth in Europe, have occurred suddenly and dramatically in developing countries through the importation of modern medical technology. On the other hand birth rates, which declined in Europe as a response to economic and social changes, remained at a high level in developing countries, as the large bulk of the population remained outside of the development process. For many modernizing countries it is still not obvious whether, or in what way, fertility rates are responding to socio-economic change. Furthermore demographers fear that the continuing rapid growth in population may be detrimental to the development process, another factor which did not enter into the European experience.

The history of political economy in Latin America during modernization also reveals important differences from that of England or Europe. These include population density, the uses of slavery, the frontier experience, the importance of agricultural export crops and mining in development, the predominance of foreign capital in the development process, the structure of imports and exports, the slow development of factories, the patterns of transportation networks, and the significance of basically non-monetary subsistence economies in Latin America as late as the end of the nineteenth century. These contrasts are often linked by scholars to the relationship of Latin America to those economies which preceded her in economic development, especially Great Britain. In Latin America many changes related to the development process took a different form and occurred at a different pace because of the prior existence of a world economy based on a technology and an accumulation of

---

[4]The first statement on this seems to be Ivy Pinchbeck, Women Workers and the Industrial Revolution (New York, 1969). Also see William Goode, World Revolution and Family Patterns (New York, 1963), p. 63; Elizabeth Pleck, "Two Worlds in One: Work and Family," Journal of Social History 10 (Winter 1976): 178-95; Cynthia Lloyd, ed. Sex, Discrimination and the Division of Labor (New York, 1975), p. 9; and Louise A. Tilly and Joan W. Scott, Women, Work and Family (New York, 1978).

[5]Ansley J. Coale, "The Demographic Transition," in United Nations, The Population Debate Vol. 1, pp. 347-55; Michael S. Teitelbaum, "Importancia de la téoria de la transición demográfica para paises en desarrollo," Demografia y Economía, Vol. 10 (1976), pp. 54-67; Kingsley Davis, "The Theory of Change and Response in Modern Demographic History," Population Index (October, 1963), pp. 345-66.

[6]Eduardo E. Arriaga and Kingsley Davis, "The Pattern of Mortality Change in Latin America," Demography, Vol. 6 (1969), pp. 223-42. Samuel H. Preston, "The Changing Relation between Mortality and Level of Economic Development," Population Studies 29 (July, 1975), pp. 231-48. Also see Eduardo Arriaga, "The Nature and Effects of Latin America's Non-Western Trend in Fertility," Demography, Vol. 7 (1970), pp. 483-501.

capital beyond that available anywhere in Latin America. The role of Latin American products and consumers within this world economy was also important to the way these developments occurred. In some cases--as in the creation of commercial urban centers and in changes in land use--the transformation was much more rapid than in Europe in a similar historical period. In other cases--as in the development of factories and an urban proletariat dedicated to manufacturing, or the decline in patronage relationships and the development of an effective government bureaucracy--Latin American societies were slower.

DEPENDENCY

The significance for the history of the family, kinship, or demographic trends of the "historically dependent nature of Latin American nations within the world capitalist system" remains unclear. Cancian, Goodman, and Smith suggest that the dependency situation "concentrates most resources in the international or enclave sector. . . and keeps. . . wages. . . low." As a result "there tends to be a sharp division between the culture of the ruling international sector of the large city and the culture of the rest of the population." (pp. 326-27) Tamara Harevan, responding to this focus on dependency theory as an integrating theoretical framework within which to examine the family in Latin America, pointed out, however, that "dependency theory apart, the patterns of change which they (Cancian, Goodman, and Smith) predict within the Latin American context, especially their emphasis on family adaptation, have many striking parallels in Europe and in the United States.[7]

In spite of these reservations, scholars taking a broader view continue to find "transition theory" relevant for Latin America. Although Nicholás Sánchez Albornóz cautioned that the history of the demographic transition in Latin America must be considered as "qualitatively different" from that which occurred in the United States and Western Europe, his analysis viewed demographic change as closely related to economic change. Robert McCaa, while admitting "problems" with the demographic transition theory, concluded that, based on his study of Chile, "there is a marked interrelationship between marriage, fertility, mortality and both socioeconomic realities and aspirations." In 1975 Kirk and Oeschli suggested that doubts about the applicability of demographic transition theory to developing countries may be based on too narrow an interpretation of the theory. Similarly Merrick and Graham (1979), while advising "caution" in the applicability of the theory to Brazil and suggesting that considerable complexity exists in the Brazilian response to socioeconomic change as compared to the European experience, gear their analysis to the inter-relationship of the development process to demographic change.[8]

The city of São Paulo seemed the ideal testing ground for the theory of demographic transition within a Latin American context especially as it related to household structure and functions. According to generations of Brazilian historians,

---

[7]Francesca M. Cancian, Louis W. Goodman, and Peter H. Smith, "Capitalism, Industrialization and Kinship in Latin America: Major Issues," Journal of Family History 3, no. 4 (Winter 1978): 319-36 and Tamara K. Harevan, "Postscript: The Latin American Essays in the Context of Family History," Ibid. pp. 454-57.

[8]Nicholas Sánchez Albornóz, The Population of Latin America: A History. Translated by W.A.R. Richardson (Berkeley, 1974), pp. 6 and 182-218. Robert McCaa, Marriage and Fertility in Chile (Boulder, 1983), pp. 1-11; Dudley Kirk and Frank Oeschli, "Modernization and the Demographic Transition in Latin America and the Caribbean," in Economic Development and Cultural Change, Vol. 23 (1975), pp. 381-417; Thomas W. Merrick and Douglas H. Graham, Population and Economic Development in Brazil (Baltimore, 1979), p. 276.

the social, economic, and political formation of Brazil was based on the family, and the most famous study of the Latin American family was actually a study of the Brazilian household--Gilberto Freyre's Casa Grande e Senzala (1933). This study pictured the traditional (i.e., pre-nineteenth century) household as very large, extended, and economically self-sufficient with many slaves. I thought that analysis of the impact of economic growth on a family and household structure of such strength and far-reaching functions would be particularly interesting. Furthermore, in São Paulo the process of modernization was a local response to the expansion of a world-wide economic system during the period in which industrial capitalism, tied to the concept of mass production (as opposed to the "limited market" concept of mercantilism), was becoming important in the more developed world.

For São Paulo and many other areas in Latin America the transition from household production for use and neighborhood exchange to an export economy closely tied to the international economy and involving the integration of factory-produced products from industrial nations into their economies often implied abrupt disruption of prior forms of production and exchange. This sudden disruption contrasts strongly with the gradual changes experienced in Europe in a similar historical period. The rapidity of the transformation seemed to make São Paulo an especially good place for study of change in household organization, occupations, marriage patterns, and fertility.

Another factor which made São Paulo an attractive place to study was the existence of a group of almost yearly manuscript census enumerations for the district from 1765 until 1843.[9] The censuses list all inhabitants (except slaves in the censuses between 1765 and 1776) by name, age, marital status, race (only sometimes and categories appear inconsistent), place of birth (the best cite city and captaincy but after 1817 they distinguish little beyond the distinction between Brazilian and other nationalities), relationship to head of household, occupation (most censuses), income (a few censuses after 1797), or property (only the 1765 census), production by household by crop and amount of harvest, distinguished by use for subsistence or sale (most censuses, some in more detail), livestock and other animals owned by the household, other types of household production (rum, quilts, or woven cloth), location of house by street and number (about half the censuses), members added or departed since last census and sometimes the reason for their absence, and empty houses on the street.

The enumerations were instituted by Luis Antônio de Sousa, the Morgado de Matheus and Captain-General of São Paulo from 1765 to 1775, and included the entire captaincy. His motivations were multiple: population available for possible conscription in the southern wars, interest in the development of commercial agriculture and the develoment of exports which meant finding out who could possibly produce for these purposes, and sources of possible tax revenues. Although some people might have wanted to avoid the census, the small, cohesive nature of the neighborhoods ensured relative completeness in the counts. The listing for each household was also confirmed by a separate enumerator who compared this year's listing of each household with last year's.

I developed the data for this study on the basis of the three manuscript censuses of 1765, 1802, and 1836 of the cidade (city)--the three "urban" bairros (neighborhoods) of the city--and the more distant rural bairros of Santana, Nossa Senhora de O, and Nossa Senhora de Penha (listed together with São Miguel). These censuses were chosen for coding and electronic analysis on the basis of completeness (determined through bairros, streets, and numbers of houses listed), characteristics given, consistency, and a desire for a certain periodization in terms of economic

[9]The censuses may be found in the Archivo do Estado de São Paulo (hereafter AESP), Maços de População (Capital).

development. I used the rest of the censuses partially and in an auxiliary fashion, especially to complement the 1765 census which was least satisfactory of the three. Collections of government documents as well as 150 years of property inventories, wills, and land records for the period 1700 to 1850 were also important in the interpretation of economic and social changes in São Paulo in this period.

I analyzed the data on an individual basis for characteristics, such as age-sex structure, population growth, number of children per mother, occupational structure, and income structure. Production (agricultural, livestock, and textiles) was analyzed both aggregating that list for households to give a figure for São Paulo, and differentiating by urban and rural districts and by bairro. Household composition and size were analyzed by looking at the relationship of each household member to the head of household, and by analyzing household heads by type. I also made an effort to look at kinship in a limited way because it was and is clearly a major aspect of the social, economic, and political relations of Brazilians. Unfortunately kinship is a less accessible variable than others, particularly for the popular classes, so this dimension of the study is more partial, more inferential and speculative, and less based on empirical evidence than the work on the household or general population traits. Since the household is the basic unit of analysis for this study, I will begin with a discussion of the implications of that choice.

The household, or co-resident domestic group, has been chosen as the focus of analysis in the belief that the economic situation of the adult individual is most clearly displayed in the context of his relations with his most significant social dependents and, usually, also those others whose productive efforts add to his well-being.[10] That is, the co-resident domestic group is the definable unit which best juxtaposes the economic and social resources of the individual qua individual in a given community. While the household in its totality does not provide the sum of possible contributions to the household economy, or to any given member, the co-resident domestic group is generally the basic unit of production and consumption in Brazil, and certainly the most clearly defined on the individual level. Other related and overlapping units such as the "family" or the "kinship group" lack precision for purposes of analysis, a fact which has led to apparently contradictory results in studies concerning the Brazilian "family."[11] The functional importance of the kinship group or network, as well as ritual kin relations, to the household economy will be discussed in Chapter III. In general these latter relationships can be viewed as occurring between households or household economies, such that the co-resident domestic group works well in analysis even for consideration of kin network.

---

[10]Household and co-resident domestic group are used interchangeably in this chapter to denote those who live together and share some minimum activities. The definitions utilized here are generally those suggested by Laslett, Household and Family, pp. 23-39.

[11]The seemingly contradictory conclusions of those researchers who have affirmed the endogamous and highly extended character of the Brazilian family as opposed to those who have "proven" that the Brazilian family is and always has been "small and confined to the nuclear unit" is largely definitional. The former group concentrate on genealogical sources which emphasize the extensive aspects of the kinship network, while the latter emphasize the characteristics of the co-resident domestic group. Those affirming the extensive aspects of the Brazilian family include Gilberto Freyre, Oliveira Vianna, Raymundo Faoro, and many others. The more recent school emphasizing that the Brazilian residential group was always predominantly composed of members of the nuclear family include Maria-Luiza Marcílio, Oracy Nogueira, and Antonio Cândido.

When I first began to apply the theory of demographic transition to São Paulo by analyzing the 1765 census I was surprised to discover very little correspondence between Freyre's view of the traditional household and the mean or even the elite paulistana household of that period.[12] Household size, type of household headship, number of children, age at marriage, and presence of slaves in the household were all very different than that implied by Freyre's model. My data indicated a much smaller household (mean 4.24) with a high proportion of female headed households, relatively few resident relatives, less than half of the households with any slaves at all, and a relatively high age at marriage for both men and women. Returning to the literature, I found evidence for large, extended, prolific Brazilian families in the inventories of property which were taken when someone died.

The difference between the extensiveness of the Brazilian kinship system and the fertility of the menage as indicated by the inventories and by genealogies compared to household composition as indicated by census analysis is more than a product of class differences. Often elite families had more extensive households but differences in household size and composition were also products of the family cycle, and the mode of production in which the households were involved. Subsistence production was consistent with a small, nuclear-family household in most of Latin America. Indeed Linda Greenow recently suggested that the nuclearity of the domestic unit combined with the traditional significance and functions of kinship in Latin American society means that analysis of the family by domestic unit may be insufficient.[13] We must also be aware of the proximity or non-proximity of kindred and of the functions of even distant kin (both in terms of space and of blood) in the daily lives and basic life decisions of individuals and households. The definition of the Brazilian kinship system and the role kinship has played historically in the development of São Paulo is a necessary part of the context against which this analysis must be viewed.

Cancian, Goodman, and Smith, analyzing the Latin American family from a structural-functionalist perspective, suggested that "economic changes affect the family by: 1) changing the allocation of resources, both within kin groups and between kin groups and other groups; 2) changing the activities performed by kin groups and the location of these activities; and 3) changing cultural conceptions of normal or desirable kin relations."[14] This perspective is, I think, a very useful one to keep in mind when approaching this study with one caveat. That is, that changes in society and economy which involve a move from production for use of the producer to production for the market necessarily involve decisions within individual households to make that kind of transformation. The market may at some point in development acquire autonomy, become an "invisible hand," but the initial stages of the transition from a subsistence to a market economy require considerable effort on the part of some and a minimal kind of cooperation on the part of most households.

Cancian, Goodman, and Smith further argue that kinship be regarded as adaptive, stressing the flexibility of kin relations rather than the usual premise of structural-functionalists that the nuclear family arrangement is best suited for the period of industrialization. Clearly this approach makes a good deal of sense in view

---

[12]Term for resident of the city of São Paulo.

[13]Linda Greenow, "Spatial Dimensions of Household and Family Structure in Eighteenth Century Spanish America." Department of Geography, Syracuse University, Discussion Paper, No. 35 (July 1977) and "Micro-Geographic Analysis as an Index to Family Structure." Paper presented at Latin American Studies Association Meetings in Mexico City, 1983, Sept. 28-Oct. 2.

[14]Cancian, Goodman, and Smith, op. cit., p. 324.

of twentieth century evidence of the continued significance of kinship in modern urban environments.[15]

Between 1765 and 1836 the household economy of São Paulo was transformed from one of production for the use of the producer to one oriented toward the market. This fundamental change in mode of production was paralleled by dramatic changes within the household, the unit that was the locus of production as well as labor in the first phase. I suggest that the development of the market economy and related changes in mode of production had a rapid, direct and profound influence on the organization of households and family formation. Patterns of relationships between modes of production and household composition and headship are identifiable for three different moments in the development process: 1765 (subsistence production), 1802 (simple market exchange), and 1836 (incipient export economy).

São Paulo household organization is revealed in this study as highly flexible, capable of rapid and diverse responses even to short-term changes in social and economic conditions. In the subsistence regime in 1765 the São Paulo household was made up of small, predominantly nuclear family units. This conclusion, while at odds with much of the older literature, does agree with recent studies on the nineteenth-century household in Europe and the United States.[16] Most surprising are the findings related to change in household organization in the period of commercialization. The data show that in 1802 these São Paulo households had become larger and more complex and differed substantially in type of headship, composition, and size, as distinguished both by rural or urban location and by socioeconomic group. The urban area by 1802 was notable for the dramatic increase both in households headed by women and in persons living within the urban household yet unrelated to its head. The continued location of productive activities within the home throughout this period does much to explain the coincidence of the expansion of the economy and the development of specialized production with the increased complexity of the household.

The 1836 census analysis reveals a bimodal household organization in both the urban and the rural <u>bairros</u>. Elite households continued to expand while nonelite households decreased in size after 1802. The ratio of nuclear members within the urban household continued to decline, and members unrelated to the head of household increased to 26 percent of free members. The number of urban households headed by couples declined to 29 percent. In the rural <u>bairros</u> slave and land ownership were becoming increasingly concentrated within a few agricultural establishments where crop specialization for market sale was being developed. These households continued to grow in size and complexity. Poor rural households shrank, had fewer slaves and children (although some children may have been residing with an elite household), and were more dominated by persons over forty-five and especially by widowed heads of households. Many of the poor, who failed to obtain or retain title to their lands, established dependent relations with their more affluent neighbors as sharecroppers, <u>agregados</u> (literally added-on members) or persons living <u>a favor</u> on someone else's land in return for labor.

On the household level the change from a subsistence to a market economy implied a dramatic, even violent, reorientation of social existence as well as of

[15] <u>Ibid</u>., p. 321.

[16] See P. Laslett, ed. <u>Household and Family</u>; Michael Anderson, <u>Family Structure in Nineteenth Century Lancashire</u> (Cambridge, 1971); J. Demos, <u>A Little Commonwealth: Family Life in Plymouth Colony</u> (London, 1971).

productive activities.[17] The household in the subsistence economy was an interdependent unit of production and consumption, locked into wider systems of kinship and neighborhood through which mutual aid flowed and communal action was organized. The advent of an economy based upon market exchange ultimately meant the total disruption of society, both in terms of the structure and functions of the household unit itself and in terms of the political and economic relationships among households in the community.

In 1765 the village of São Paulo was officially made a city, an administrative entity entitled to a bishop, and the capital of the new captaincy by the same name. Nevertheless, São Paulo was not yet an "urban" area, either in terms of population density or of economic activities. Subsistence agriculture and home industry for subsistence purposes were dominant in the center of the city, as well as in the outlying neighborhoods.

Eighteenth-century São Paulo was characterized by seminomadic residence patterns, accompanied by slash-and-burn agriculture--a system of extensive land usage that required land to be freely available. Population in the frontier community fluctuated constantly in the colonial period, reflecting the comings and goings of expeditions into the sertão and the splitting off of large family clans who formed new communities in the sixteenth and seventeenth centuries. Mass migrations followed the mineral discoveries in Minas Gerais in 1695, and in the late eighteenth and early nineteenth centuries paulistas migrated to the interior to establish sugar and coffee plantations.[18] Although migration was clearly an integral aspect of paulista life, the available evidence suggests that changes in the population structure and sex ratio within the community of São Paulo between 1765 and 1836 were principally the result of local economic changes combined with short-range migrations (see Chapter IV).

The sex ratio of the captaincy of São Paulo in 1765, the first year for which data is available, was 110 men for every 100 women, a high ratio for a "normal" population but not high for a frontier area.[19] The sex ratio in the city of São Paulo in the same year was significantly lower--82 men for every 100 women--and can be explained by the tendency of paulista women to maintain a farm that produced basic crops in the village while the men went to the mines, herded cattle, and engaged in other migratory enterprises. From 1765 to 1798 the sex ratio in the captaincy declined to the more "normal" level of 93.3, reflecting the transition from a population strongly affected by migration to one based primarily on natural increase. The decline in the sex ratio in the city of São Paulo to 75 by 1802 can be interpreted as a continuation of a pattern in which women remained in the city while men migrated into the new settlement areas of the captaincy to claim lands. More than that, it represents the migration of women into the city in response to the decline of subsistence agriculture in the rural suburbs and the departure of many young men for the interior. These women came to the city to work in textiles or other types of household industrial production instead of in agriculture and cottage industrial production for home use.

---

[17]Hans Medik, "The Proto-Industrial Family Economy: The Structural Function of Household and Family during the Transition from Peasant Society to Industrial Capitalism," Social History 3 (1976), pp. 291-315.

[18]Residents of the captaincy/province/state of São Paulo.

[19]Sex ratio figures for the district of São Paulo were based on the "maços de população," capital, 1765, 1802, 1836, AESP. Figures on the captaincy of São Paulo were taken from Maria-Luiza Marcílio, "Crescimento demográfico e evolução agrária paulista 1700-1836," Tése de Livre Docência de história na Universidade de São Paulo, 1974, p. 135.

By 1836 the sex ratio for the captaincy was 94.7 while that of the city of São Paulo had increased to 94, in aggregate demographic terms becoming an altogether normal population. The normalization of the sex ratio was not, however, reflected in changes in household composition and headship by 1836. Instead the household headed by a female continued to be the mode, the household headed by a single, never-married male the second most common, and the household headed by a "married" couple the least common (29.2 percent of total urban households). Short-range migration and changes in the sex ratio in São Paulo were associated with substantial alterations in household structure and headship. However, these demographic movements were essentially reactions to larger economic changes of the period. Furthermore, demographic factors alone fail to explain the household patterns emerging in 1802 and remaining prominent in 1836 when the sex ratio returned to normal. It is more important for an understanding of those patterns to look at the three modes of production involved, the relationship of each to the individual household and the patterns of transition from one mode to another on the household level.

II
Political Structure and Economy in São Paulo, 1554–1850

Interior São Paulo in most of the colonial period was an unpoliced, largely unmapped area, with a sparse population and few roads or known mineral resources. Its residents generally adopted the semi-nomadic slash-and- burn culture of the Indians who, along with their Portuguese-Indian descendants, made up the greatest part of the population well into the eighteenth century.[1] The indigenous work party (mutirão) for shared community labor, and other aspects of indigenous culture such as the use of manioc, hammocks and the wattle and daub (pau a pique) mode of house construction were generally adopted by Europeans and mameluco alike.[2] The existence of this type of economy in the interior of Brazil was not predicated upon an ignorance of marketing or a lack of interest in European products. Isolation and a sparse population accounted for the development of a largely self-sufficient subsistence economy. The lack of a good communication system was symptomatic of the lack of domestic capital or of any significant commercial development as well as being directly responsible for the isolation of the area. The road over the steep Serra do Mar to the port of Santos

---

[1]Studies on São Paulo for the colonial period are fairly numerous though uneven. Affonso d'Escragnolle Taunay has produced many volumes including História seiscentista da villa de São Paulo, 4 vols. (São Paulo, 1926-1929); História geral das bandeiras paulistas, 11 vols. (São Paulo, 1924-1950); História da cidade de São Paulo no século xviii, 2 vols. (São Paulo, 1945). Other studies include Alfredo Ellis, Jr., A economia paulista no século XVIII (São Paulo, 1950), Maria Thereza Schorer Petrone, A lavoura canavieira em São Paulo (São Paulo, 1968), Maria Sylvia de Carvalho Franco, Homens livres na ordem escravocrata (São Paulo, 1969), Maria-Luiza Marcílio, La ville de São Paulo (Rouen, 1970). The background section of Richard M. Morse, From Community to Metropolis: A Biography of São Paulo, Brazil (Gainesville, 1958) is also useful.

[2]Antonio Cândido, Os parceiros do Rio Bonito (Rio de Janeiro, 1964) discusses the history and present-day significance of the caípira culture of interior São Paulo.

was a hazardous footpath. Roads to neighboring captaincies were unsafe for horses and too narrow for carts.[3]

As a population these people could be only vaguely defined in a geographic sense. The paulistas wandered from Bahia and the São Francisco Valley to Ceará to Goiás, Mato Grosso, Minas Gerais, to southern Brazil and Uruguay and Paraguay and back again in the sixteenth and seventeenth centuries. Much of this movement was accomplished through expeditions or bandeiras in search of precious metals or Indian slaves.[4] The bandeiras were largely composed of kin-based groups, including women and children, with from eighty to several hundred members. These expeditions often disappeared into the bush (sertão) for several years, living on fish, game, and the manioc which they planted along the way. Gold and slaves were the major forms of property in interior colonial São Paulo. Land--essentially a free good in this period--was not to acquire commercial significance until the second half of the eighteenth century.[5] What was important to the paulista was the proximity of the social group on which he relied for aid and exchange--the family clan. The somewhat precarious economy of subsistence farming was supported and protected through a system of group exchange and mutual aid. These were not market relations, nor relations based upon a specific system of reciprocity, but rather a system of generalized support for all members of the group.[6]

In direct contrast to the society described above was the logic of the royal government structure, designed in and imported from Lisbon.[7] Government was specifically tied to the problem of space; it was territory and persons within those territories who could be governed and taxed. Social control required fixed, sedentary populations--preferably concentrated in urban settlements. The government bodies

---

[3]Studies on the relationship of the road system to the economic development of São Paulo include Petrone, A lavoura canavieira; Caio Prado, Jr., "O fator geográfico na formação e no desenvolvimento da cidade de São Paulo," in Evolução política de Brasil e outros estudos (São Paulo, 1969), Antonio Manoel de Mello Castro e Mendônça, "Memória sobre a communicação da villa de Santos com a cidade de São Paulo," Publicação official de documentos interessantes para a história e costumes de São Paulo (hereafter DI) XXIX (São Paulo, 1895-), pp. 112-13. See also Elizabeth Kuznesof, "The Role of the Merchants in the Economic Development of São Paulo 1765-c1850," HAHR 60, no. 4 (1980): 571-92.

[4]Literature on the bandeirantes is enormous but is mostly episodic and biographical in nature. See Richard M. Morse (ed.), The Bandeirantes: The Historical Role of the Brazilian Pathfinders (New York, 1965); Clodomiro Vianna Moog, Bandeirantes and Pioneers, (trans.) L.L. Barett (New York, 1965); Taunay, Bandeiras paulistas; Francisco de Assis Carvalho Franco, Bandeiras e Bandeirantes de São Paulo (São Paulo, 1940); Alfredo Ellis, Jr., Capítulos da História Social de São Paulo (São Paulo, 1944); Tito Livio Ferreira, Génese Social da Gente Bandeirante (São Paulo, 1944).

[5]For an analysis of wealth in São Paulo in 1765/1767 see Alice P. Canabrava, "Uma economia de decadência: os níveis de riqueza na capitania de São Paulo, 1765/67," Revista Brasileira de Economia 26, no. 4, (1972): 95-123.

[6]See Cândido, Os parceiros, pp. 36-80; Carvalho Franco, Homens livres, pp. 80-81. For a theoretical analysis of these kinds of relations in more modern settings see Marshall Sahlins, Stone Age Economics (Chicago, 1972).

[7]The major works on colonial government are Dauril Alden, Royal Government in Colonial Brazil (Berkeley and Los Angeles, 1968); and Caio Prado, Jr., The Colonial Background of Modern Brazil, (trans.) Suzette Macedo (Berkeley, 1967).

represented the interests of the ruling class of Portugal, intent upon extracting preciosities and selling European goods to the colonists. Of course the fact that local colonial government came to be dominated by the Brazilians meant that the structure and uses of government were modified and adapted to the colonial situation. At the same time colonial society gradually developed modes of structural and spatial modification in conjunction with the larger political reality. The changes within the government structure itself were necessary adaptations to a given social reality. How and why the paulistas were persuaded into a cooperative or even relatively cooperative position with respect to royal government is harder to explain.

In the sixteenth and seventeenth centuries the primary social group--the kinship group or family clan--was defined in terms of its internal social and economic functions and had little real relationship to the formal polity or to a particular geographic area. The economic history of São Paulo until the end of the eighteenth century can be simply viewed as a function of the geographic location of the city combined with a chronic shortage of labor and capital for purposes beyond subsistence production. Lack of any profitable export product, combined with serious communications problems, made the development of trade with Portugal or even the other captaincies very difficult.

The transformation of the economy of the community of São Paulo from a subsistence to an exchange basis was to a large extent dependent upon the construction of a commercial infrastructure which would resolve the geographic barriers to trade. Construction of transport, marketing, and port facilities was, in turn, dependent upon the supply of both labor and capital as well as the existence of a well-organized, politically influential group with strong incentive to see that such construction took place. The crown might conceivably have played the major financial and organizing role in the development of social overhead capital in the paulista area.

Portugal, however, was hard pressed to finance the lucrative sugar endeavors on the coast of northeastern Brazil in the sixteenth century when her economy was relatively strong.[8] Later, with the debilitations of the Spanish occupation (1580-1640), including loss of both the rich oriental colonies and the Dutch commercial alliance, followed by the fatal rise of competitive sugar-producing colonies in the Caribbean, there was even less possibility of significant capital investments in the paulista area originating with the crown. Private investment, on the other hand, had to wait upon the creation of significant capital among the paulistas themselves--which was not to occur until the mining boom (1692-1760).[9]

The gold economy and the subsidiary development of roads, mule transport, and commercial agriculture and livestock to supply the mines, created a new set of commercial opportunities by the last half of the eighteenth century. These commercial opportunities, as well as the cooperation necessarily involved in the early stages of commercialization, made it beneficial for the clan leaders to involve themselves, and thus their clans, in the formal polity.

---

[8]Celso Furtado emphasizes the critical importance of the Dutch contribution to the sixteenth-century sugar production, both in terms of refining and marketing which they dominated, and also in the financing of production facilities in Brazil and in the importing of slave manpower. The Economic Growth of Brazil, translated by Ricardo W. de Aguiar and Eric Charles Drysdale (Berkeley and Los Angeles, 1965), pp. 8-9.

[9]It was unlikely that foreign capital (or even non-paulista capital) would have been attracted to the financing of social overhead capital in São Paulo since the infrastructure needed was both extensive and costly while the productive possibilities of the plateau were largely unexplored. Only residents whose interests were localized in the paulista area were sufficiently motivated to attempt the needed developments prior to the establishment of stronger evidence of potential profits.

The adoption of a more permanent geographic identity by kin groups in the eighteenth century was principally due to economic causes. However, the increased residential stability of the paulistas also improved the effectiveness of government administration and social control. The kinship groups of each bairro were incorporated structurally into the community polity through the mechanism of the bairro militia--the ordenanças. These groups and their officials, who were also clan leaders, became the intermediaries between the royal government organization and the kinship-based paulista society.

This chapter will provide a general history of São Paulo from 1554 until the mid-nineteenth century with emphasis on the evolution of political institutions and interest groups, the impact of external factors such as the discovery of gold and changes in the international market, and the development of a commercial infrastructure and trade.

THE ECONOMIC HISTORY OF SAO PAULO (1554-1695)

São Paulo do Campo de Piratininga was founded in 1554 on a site about forty-five miles from the port of Santos, on the plain of Piratininga, at the confluence of the rivers Tamanduateí and Anhangabaú.[10] It was the first Portuguese inland settlement in Brazil, located opposite the point where the 2400 foot Serra do Mar was most easily traversible. The plain lay on top of a hill, accessible from only one side, and easy to defend in case of Indian attack. The well-organized and hard-working Jesuit founders were able to attract willing Indian laborers from among the friendly Tupinakins. In return, the Jesuits offered protection inside the stockade against the raids of the enemy Tamoyó, help and care in sickness, and the exchange of useful objects. In 1561 São Paulo was officially raised to the status of a town. A 1573 estimate included 120 households (all said to be white) in a population of approximately 1,000 to 1,500, which included Indian slaves and mamelucos (a mixture of Portuguese and Indian).[11] The proportion of slaves in the total population was not given, but it seems clear that most of the slave population was Indian up until the opening of the mines at the beginning of the eighteenth century.[12]

The Portuguese settlers on the plateau had difficulty in developing a means of exchange for the necessary import items of iron utensils, firearms, and salt. Although soil and climate conditions were appropriate to diversified agriculture and stockraising,

---

[10]See Richard M. Morse, From Community to Metropolis: A Biography of São Paulo, Brazil (Gainesville, 1958), pp. 2-19, for a succinct history of São Paulo in this period. Extremely detailed though non-analytical studies on São Paulo from the sixteenth through nineteenth centuries have been written by Affonso d'Escragnolle Taunay. To cite only a few, there are História seiscentista da villa de São Paulo, 4 volumes (São Paulo, 1926-1929); História do cafe no Brasil, 15 volumes (Rio de Janeiro, 1927-1937); História geral das bandeiras paulistas, 11 volumes (São Paulo, 1924-1950).

[11]Presumably some of the "white" households were actually headed by mamelucos since the annexed village of São Andre was headed by the mameluco João Ramalho and was referred to as predominantly "mameluco." See Pierre Monberg, La croissance de la ville de São Paulo (São Paulo, 1953), pp. 12-13; Fernão Cardim, Tratado da terra e da gente do Brasil (São Paulo, 1939), pp. 314-15.

[12]More Negroes entered in the seventeenth century than in the sixteenth century, but even so, according to an estimate made by Bastide and Fernandes, until 1700 there was only one African slave for every 34 Indian slaves. Roger Bastide and Florestan Fernandes, Brancos e negros em São Paulo (São Paulo, 1959), p. 2.

the problems of transport, first across the Serra do Mar, and finally overseas, were discouraging to these kinds of exports.

The first road from the Serra do Mar to the coast was the trilha dos Tupininquím, a footpath of Indian origin.[13] About 1553 a new footpath, the caminho de Padre José, was adopted, probably to avoid problems with the Indians. Throughout the sixteenth and seventeenth centuries repairs to the paths, when they were made, were executed by the volunteer labor of the urban militia companies and their slaves.[14] The road continued to be extremely narrow and dangerous throughout the period and essentially to preclude exports through Santos. Other significant regional problems were sparse European population and lack of labor.[15] São Paulo was initially able to develop only such exports as quince marmalade, wheat flour, and salt meat in the sixteenth century.[16] Ultimately, it was the enslavement and sale of Indians which provided the first stable export activity in the captaincy of São Paulo.[17]

Portuguese municipal organization was transferred to Brazil more or less intact, by means of the Philippine Code of 1603.[18] Most important among town officials were the city council (camara) and the captain-major and the sergeant-major of the urban militia companies (companhia de ordenança). Crown officials who also involved themselves in municipal affairs included the captain-general or governor of

---

[13]See "Povoamento e caminho nos séculos xvi e xvii" in Pasquale Petrone, A baixada paulista (São Paulo, 1965), pp. 51-63.

[14]Ibid., pp. 62-63.

[15]Furtado makes the point that seventeenth-century England had an abundant population surplus with which to occupy her colonies, as compared to Spain and Portugal with their permanent manpower shortages. São Paulo was an interior and economically marginal area within an enormous (sometimes secondary) colony of a European power which itself lacked both capital and manpower. Economic Growth, p. 21.

[16]Morse, From Community to Metropolis, p. 11. See also the interesting article by John D. French, "Wealth, Power and Labor in a Subsistence Economy: São Paulo 1596-1625," Revista do Arquivo Municipal No. 195, 1982, pp. 79-107. French suggests that merchants constituted the most prosperous group, even in a subsistence-oriented economy.

[17]See Furtado, Economic Growth, pp. 44-45, for a discussion of Indian slaving as an economic base.

[18]Edmundo Zenha, O município no Brasil (1552-1700) (São Paulo, 1948), says "As humildes vilas brasileiras. . . tiveram seu nascedouro subordinado a um programa elaborado em Lisboa," p. 25; and ". . . no bojo das naus, mandava tudo para o deserto americano: a população da vila, os animais domésticos, as mudas das especies cultaváveis e a organização municipal encardernada no Livro das Ordenações," p. 23.

the captaincy, and the royal circuit judge (ouvidor) whose jurisdiction extended over a large territory.[19]

Practical implementation of the Portuguese municipal organization within the towns of colonial Brazil was sometimes, and for differing periods of time, incomplete. Positions often went vacant for long periods for lack of anyone qualified or willing to fill them. In other cases, municipal offices were filled by persons without the qualifications specified by law. Expansion in royal officialdom occurred in various towns in the early eighteenth century with the addition of a royal judge to head the city councils, and in the 1760s and 1770s when royal treasury boards were introduced in selected cities.[20]

The city council was originally made up of two justices of the peace (juizes ordinários), three aldermen (vereadores), and one procurator (procurador). Disputes over small property claims and taxes were settled by the justice of the peace. The aldermen were charged with administrative functions such as decisions about road-building, disease, private and public building construction, recommendations concerning commerce, the awarding of municipal contracts, and the appointment of various officials. Public complaints were heard and handled by the procurator or people's lawyer. His other duties included inspecting the public fountains, bridges, roads, and pavements to see they were all in repair, and acting as treasurer for municipal projects.[21]

Municipal council members were chosen yearly through a complicated electoral system designed to avoid the domination of the council by any individual or family group.[22] The electors were chosen every three years in a free meeting of the "men of quality" or homens bons, presided over by the royal circuit judge. The homens bons were formally defined as those who owned property, were educated, had

---

[19]Existing studies on municipal government in colonial Brazil tend to be general and non-analytical. The best available are Zenha, O município; Afonso Ruí, História da camara municipal da cidade do Salvador (Salvador, 1953); C.R. Boxer, Portuguese Society in the Tropics. The Municipal Councils of Goa, Mação, Bahia and Luanda, 1510-1800 (Madison, 1965). See also the few pages in Dauril Alden, Royal Government, pp. 422-30; and Reis Filho, Nestor Goulart, A Evolução urbana do Brasil, 1500-1720 (São Paulo, 1968), pp. 34-38. Donald Ramos, "A Social History of Ouro Preto: Stresses of Dynamic Urbanization in Colonial Brazil, 1695-1726" (Ann Arbor, 1972), pp. 296-384 analyzes the municipal council in Ouro Preto from 1695-1726.

[20]See Alden, "The Reorganization of the Royal Fisc," in Royal Government, pp. 279-311 for a discussion of the late eighteenth-century changes in royal personnel in Brazil.

[21]Zenha, O município, pp. 56-65; Ruí, História, pp. 30-31.

[22]Boxer, Portuguese Society in the Tropics, p. 77, suggested that the colonial Portuguese city council was not a self-perpetuating oligarchy, as compared to cabildos in many Spanish American countries. Alden, Royal Government, p. 427, also studied city council participation in Rio de Janeiro from 1769-79 and discovered that of 37 men who served as aldermen during the period, only 4 served more than once. Alden observed a number of similarities among names of aldermen, however, and cautioned that perpetuation of power was not simply a question of individual domination but also of families and interest groups. In the São Paulo city council there is likewise little evidence for domination by a few individuals, the city councilmen changing every year as prescribed in the election rules. There were, however, family groups which continued to be prominent in the council.

a title of nobility, or were related to someone who had held an office. The criteria were elastic, rigidly excluding only those who were laborers, mechanics, artisans, or of Jewish or non-Portuguese blood.[23] Lists of the homens bons were made up by the justices of the peace and approved by the Crown circuit judge. Thus, in effect, the control over who could gain public office was maintained by those already in public office.

In his discussion of local government in Brazil prior to 1720, Nestor Goulart Reis Filho explained that many city council members who were also clan leaders and often sugar planters (in the North), included within their conception of official municipal privileges those of giving political asylum to criminals, as well as personally meting out justice (including the death sentence) to members of the family clan, subordinates, and slaves.[24]

Effective administration was made difficult by the physical size of the jurisdictional units. Each captaincy was divided into a small number of comarcas or districts.[25] Comarcas were made up of têrmos for each town. Between têrmos there were three kilometers for a village common, and a minimum of 6 leagues or 36 kilometers in circumference to the next town. The têrmo was divided into parishes (frequesias) which were, in turn, divided into bairros. Although bairro may be loosely translated as "neighborhood," many eighteenth-century bairros are cities today. To give an idea of the physical size involved, the têrmo of the city of São Paulo in 1765 was more than 70 kilometers from one end to the other on the northern axis.[26] The municipal council of São Paulo also administered the comarca of which it was part throughout the colonial period, one of a total of three comarcas for the entire captaincy of São Paulo, which at that time included the present state of Paraná. It is easy to understand, considering the distances involved and the primitive level of transport and roads during mmost of the colonial period, why it was sometimes impossible for city council members to attend meetings, and why government orders were difficult to enforce. The urban militia companies or ordenanças, organized on a residential basis by bairro, provided the best available administrative and law enforcement agency in the colonial period for precisely that reason.[27]

Intended originally as an auxiliary force to assist in case of enemy invasion, the territorial militia was never used that way in São Paulo. Instead, by the end of the eighteenth century, the ordenanças became central to the practical administration of both local and captaincy affairs.

In theory all males between the ages of eighteen and sixty, not belonging to other military organizations, nor sick, crippled or blind, were to be automatically enrolled in the urban militia company of the bairro. The positions of captain-major and sergeant-major were to be selected by the governor from a list of three

[23]Zenha, O município, pp. 88-98.

[24]Reis Filho, Evolução urbana, pp. 34-38.

[25]There were four comarcas in Minas Gerais, four in Bahia, three in São Paulo, three in Pernambuco, two in Goiás, and the rest of the captaincies had only one comarca. Caio Prado, Jr., Formação do Brasil contemporáneo (São Paulo, 1973), p. 306.

[26]Maria-Luiza Marcílio, La ville de São Paulo, p. 54. Over time the physical limits of the city decreased, as distant bairros broke off to form their own municipalities.

[27]The companhias de ordenança were created for use in Portugal in 1570 and extended to Brazil. On the early history of the ordenanças see Oliveira Vianna, Populações meridionaes do Brasil (Rio de Janeiro, 1949), pp. 186-93; and Diogo de Vasconcellos, Linhas geraes da administração colonial (n.p., n.d.).

nominations presented by the city council of their jurisdiction. The first captain-major of most bairros was also the original founder. Appointments were made for three years, but were renewable.

From the time of the militia's organization the captain-major was the strongest authority within any bairro.[28] He was chosen on the basis of his "nobility and fortune" and had to be obeyed without question. Washington Luis reports that whenever the captain-major appeared in public in his bairro, "conversations hushed and men took off their hats respectfully."[29]

I have argued elsewhere that the militia was the key to the integration of kinship into the structure of the community polity in the eighteenth century.[30] Essentially it was only through the kinship structure that a political structure reaching to the individual level could have developed in São Paulo in the colonial period. Not only was the territorially based militia the obvious vehicle of the political integration of kin groups, but the power of the clan relative to the state in this period suggests that nomination of other than clan leaders for these positions would have been ineffective. It seems likely that clan leaders were named as militia leaders from the early seventeenth century, but the conflicts between family clans and the geographic instability of clans until the eighteenth century confounded royal efforts to incorporate kinship interests into those of the larger polity.

One clear type of evidence of seventeenth century instability is found in a series of eight community fissions based on family feuds which repeatedly split the population of São Paulo between 1600 and 1675. In each case a large group of kindred moved from São Paulo to another community or to settle a new area because of a quarrel with another clan. The move of most of the Pires clan to Parnaiba in 1625 during their famous feud with the Camargos is the most dramatic example. Another is the migrations of the Ortíz brothers and many of their kinfolk to Jundiaí in 1659 after one of the brothers, Fernando, the "Tiger," killed the illustrious Pedro Taques.[31] These seventeenth-century mass migrations of kin groups from São Paulo were symptomatic of the weakness and non-cohesiveness of the municipal and captaincy

---

[28]Washington Luis, A Capitania de São Paulo: Govêrno de Rodrigo Cesar de Menezes (São Paulo, 1938), pp. 12-14. Ramos, "Ouro Prêto," pp. 163 and 279 views the militia as a vehicle of social mobility into city council positions because many men named alferes (captain) in the militia were elected to the council six to ten years later. He does not examine the records for how many of the city council were never militia officials nor point out the kinship dimension of the militia. However Ramos clearly sees the militia as a dimension of private power (see pp. 170 and 411).

[29]Ibid., p. 14.

[30]See Elizabeth Kuznesof, "Clans, the Militia and Territorial Government: the Articulation of Kinship with Polity in Eighteenth Century São Paulo," in David Robinson (ed.), Social Fabric and Spatial Structure in Colonial Latin America (Ann Arbor, 1979), pp. 181-226.

[31]See Sérgio Buarque de Holanda, "Movimentos da população em São Paulo no século XVIII," Revista do Instituto de Estudos Brasileiros, No. 1 (1966), pp. 98-105. For other examples of quarrels between family clans leading to community splits outside São Paulo, see Maria Isaura Pereira de Queiroz, O mandonismo local na vida política brasileira (São Paulo, 1969), pp. 18-19.

governments of São Paulo in that period as well as of an economic system in which land was neither a scarce nor an economically valuable commodity.[32]

Government at the local level in sixteenth- and seventeenth-century São Paulo represented private family interests more than it did royal authority. Royal decrees which opposed local interests were ignored and royal officials who attempted to oppose the local will sometimes came to fear for their lives.

For example, royal decrees prohibiting slaving expeditions into the sertão were common at the end of the sixteenth and early seventeenth centuries.[33] Other expeditions into the sertão could be organized only with official approval. Disobedience was to be punished with fines and prison. Nevertheless, the city council records in the first decades of the seventeenth century indicate that the movement into the sertão on slaving and other expeditions was enormous. Affonso de Escragnolle Taunay reports that "almost the entire village went on the 1602 expedition of Nicolaú Barreto." When news arrived that the Governor was planning to tax the disobedient bandeirantes one out of every three Indian slaves taken, the São Paulo city council responded that unless the Governor should annul his decree, none of the members of the expedition would return to São Paulo.[34]

The years following witnessed incredible movements of paulistas into the sertão in spite of repeated decrees prohibiting such activity. Nothing was done about the situation since no royal judge (ouvidor) had visited São Paulo in the sixteenth century to rule on these matters. In 1614 the ouvidor finally announced that he would make an official visit to São Paulo, traveling from Rio de Janeiro where he was located. The São Paulo city council suggested that representation from São Paulo instead be made to the ouvidor in Rio de Janeiro since if the ouvidor came to São Paulo, "the people would flee and the land would become dispopulated!"[35] When the ouvidor insisted on coming to São Paulo he was surprised by a flurry of arrows shot through his window one night and left precipitously the next day without passing on the cases concerning illegal expeditions to the sertão. Two royal judges who made visits to São Paulo in 1619 and 1620 limited themselves to general orders to the population against disorder and Indian enslavement. Nevertheless, Taunay reports that the movement to the sertão increased geometrically after 1620.[36]

In 1623 an expedition including many of the best citizens of São Paulo was organized but the city council expressed itself "unable" to stop it. Later that same year the Governor nullified the laws concerning the sertão as being of no effect.[37] In 1628 the bandeira of Antonio Raposo Tavares departed from São Paulo with most of the village, including all members of the city council save one! These records indicate

---

[32]See Robert Carneiro, "Slash and Burn Cultivation among the Kuikurú and its Implications for Cultural Development in the Amazon Basin," in Y. Cohen (ed.), Man in Adaptation: The Cultural Present (Chicago, 1968), p. 136. Carneiro has noted this centrifugal characteristic in primitive subsistence societies today. He argues that fission is not caused by the nature of the economy but rather by factional disputes within the society.

[33]Affonso de E. Taunay, História seiscentista da villa de São Paulo, pp. 11-19.

[34]Ibid., pp. 13-15.

[35]Ibid., pp. 47-50.

[36]Ibid., pp. 50-55.

[37]Ibid., p. 62.

both the effect which the expeditions had on village population and everyday life as well as the helplessness of the royal officials to control the activities of the paulistas.

The paulista population was famous throughout the sixteenth and seventeenth centuries for its geographic instability.[38] The exodus of the able-bodied male population into the sertão in search of a "remedy for poverty" was a constant refrain. Yet, as Sérgio Buarque de Holanda pointed out, those who went into the mato also generally returned to their families within two or three years. Buarque de Holanda further concluded that this type of migration was more or less constant throughout the seventeenth and eighteenth centuries.[39]

An especially strong temptation to the bandeirantes were the Spanish Jesuit missions in what is now the state of Paraná. These Indians were gathered together, conveniently pacified and disciplined, and were therefore ideally suited to the purposes of the bandeirantes. Between the years of 1628 and 1632 the missions were effectively wiped out by slaving parties, forcing the Jesuits to move south to Paraguay. The Jesuits claimed, with probable exaggeration, that the paulista slavers captured 300,000 Indians from the missions in that period.[40] Most of these slaves were sold within the captaincy, about one-third of them being shipped north to the sugar-growing northeast. Nevertheless, the Indian slave trade was only the best of possible alternatives. According to Richard Morse, the profits from it never reached one percent of that accruing to Brazil's major crop, sugar.[41]

The search for precious minerals was an aspect of bandeirante activity from the time of the earliest expeditions. During the seventeenth century, however, the quest became more urgent as persistent rumors of gold circulated. The first important gold strikes were made in the years 1692 to 1695, triggering a rush for the mines from all over Brazil as well as Europe.[42]

FROM THE GOLDEN AGE TO THE SUGAR ECONOMY

The early rush for the mines all but depopulated the city of São Paulo, leaving farms untended and resulting in famines in 1697, 1700, and 1701. Food scarcities and enormous price increases also took place in the mines and many of those who left São Paulo returned quickly. The prosperity of a number of the elite listed in the 1765 census of São Paulo was derived from their stay in the mines.

Almost all of the initial gold discoveries and most of the early claims were made by paulistas, who seriously considered that they were entitled to a monopoly of

---

[38]Sérgio Buarque de Holanda, "Movimentos da população em São Paulo no século xviii," Revista do Instituto de Estudos Brasileiros, No. 1 (1966), pp. 66-68.

[39]Buarque de Holanda, "Movimentos," p. 68.

[40]Dauril Alden, "Black Robes versus White Settlers: The Struggle for Freedom of the Indians in Colonial Brazil" in Peckham and Gibson (eds.), Attitudes of Colonial Powers toward the American Indian (Salt Lake City, 1969), pp. 25-28 on efforts to control Indian slaving activities in São Paulo. On paulista raids of the Jesuit reducciones in Paraguay see Morse, From Community to Metropolis, pp. 14-15 and Ernani Silva Bruno, História do Brazil geral e regional (São Paulo, n.d.), V, pp. 31-47.

[41]Morse, From Community to Metropolis, p. 15.

[42]See C.R. Boxer, The Golden Age of Brazil 1695-1750 (Berkeley, 1962), pp. 35-36, 58-61, for a discussion of the dates and locations of the first gold discoveries.

the mining economy.[43] The paulistas were, however, rapidly outnumbered by migrants from elsewhere in Brazil, and from Portugal. War broke out between the paulistas and the emboabas (as the paulistas referred to the outsiders) in 1708-09, with the royal authorities incapable of controlling the situation and many paulistas driven from the area. The governor of Rio de Janeiro was expelled from the mining area by the emboaba leader, Manuel Nunes Viana, after the governor traveled to Ouro Preto to try to force a reconciliation between the two sides. Manuel Nunes Viana took over the administration of the area and made civil and military appointments, strictly on his own authority. Because Portugal was involved in the Spanish War of Succession, the crown could not respond militarily to the breakdown of order in the mines. Finally peace was arranged in 1709 by Antônio de Albuquerque Coelho de Carvalho, the new governor named to the newly formed captaincy of São Paulo and Minas Gerais, with the capital in São Paulo. Manuel Nunes Viana was persuaded to leave the area, but, according to Charles Boxer, dissension had already developed among the emboaba leaders before Albuquerque's arrival.[44]

Gold was an important source of local wealth in São Paulo in the eighteenth century. Just as significant, however, was the integrating effect which the mining economy had on the previously autonomous subsistence economies of southern Brazil.[45] Mining was highly profitable in the short-term, extremely uncertain in the long-term, such that the rational approach for a miner was to concentrate all resources into the extraction of ore. Food shortages and the need for beasts of burden in an economy with no resources to spare for the production of these commodities automatically produced a profitable market for cattle and food supplies.

Cattlemen of Rio Grande do Sul reoriented production from subsistence use to production for sale in the mining region. Mule breeding for transport purposes also became important. The cattle and mules were brought north to the cattle fairs and fattening areas in São Paulo before being sold to the mines, as well as to adjacent markets in São Paulo and Rio de Janeiro.[46] Provisions were sent to the mining region from the Fluminense area of Guanabara and from Bahia. São Paulo was, however, the most important supplier of food products to the mining area. Smoked salt pork, various kinds of cereals, marmalade, and especially sugar were shipped to the mines in great quantities.[47] The first significant commercial agricultural development in São Paulo occurred in conjunction with the market for provisions which opened up in the mines.[48]

---

[43]In 1700 the city council of São Paulo petitioned the crown asking that all land grants in Minas Gerais be reserved exclusively for paulistas because of their part in the discoveries. Camara municipal de São Paulo a coroa, em 7 de abril de 1700, as cited in Taunay, História geral das bandeiras paulistas, IX, pp. 473-74.

[44]Boxer, The Golden Age, pp. 93-105.

[45]See Furtado, Economic Growth, pp. 84-85, on the integrating effect of the mining discoveries in relation to the south of Brazil.

[46]See Alfredo Ellis, Jr., A ecónomia paulista no século xviii (São Paulo, 1950) for a discussion of the importance of the mule to the economic development of São Paulo.

[47]Myriam Austregesílio Ellis, "Contribuição ao estudo do abastecimento das zonas mineradoras do Brasil no século xviii," Revista de História, XVII (1958), p. 36 and pp. 429-67.

[48]Maria Thereza Schorer Petrone, A lavoura canavieira em São Paulo (São Paulo, 1968), p. 167.

The role of São Paulo as a point of commodity collection and redistribution also began to develop during the mining boom in the first half of the eighteenth century. São Paulo became a center for sale and redistribution of livestock and mules to Minas Gerais, as well as the lesser mines in Cuiabá and Goiás, and to the cities of Rio de Janeiro and Santos. During the period from 1690 to 1702 the three ports of Salvador, Rio de Janeiro and Santos were in competition for the handling of the gold from Minas Gerais. The construction of the new road from Rio de Janeiro to Minas Gerais, completed in 1702, resolved the competition in favor of Rio, but Santos continued to handle all gold exported from the lesser mines of Cuiabá and Goiás, a fact which significantly increased the importance of both the Caminho do Mar and Santos.[49] Map II:1 illustrates the position of São Paulo relative to the mines and the cattle-producing region in the South of Brazil circa 1750.

When gold production began to fall in the 1760s, the demand for pack animals also began to decline. However, the importance of the mule teams as a mode of transport continued to grow. From 1780 to 1800 more than ten thousand mules per year passed through the livestock register at Sorocaba, growing to over thirty thousand a year in the period from 1800 to 1826.[50] The mule teams found alternate employment in the developing sugar trade both in São Paulo and in Guanabara. Large ranchos in the suburbs of the city of São Paulo served as resting and loading areas for the mule teams coming and going from Santos, Itú, Campinas, Piracicaba, the Paraiba Valley, and Rio de Janeiro.[51]

São Paulo suffered a number of administrative changes in the eighteenth century, including its separation from Minas Gerais in 1720, losses of territory in 1738 and 1748 and its annexation to the captaincy of Rio de Janeiro in the latter year. In 1765 autonomous government was restored to São Paulo principally because of the threat of the Spanish in the South. In the eighteenth century there were a number of royal efforts to subjugate the private authority of clan leaders throughout Brazil, many of them with administrative positions. These efforts often took the form of restricting

[49]See the article by Caio Prado, Jr., "O fator geográfico na formação e no desenvolvimento da cidade de São Paulo," Evolução política do Brasil e outros estudos (São Paulo, 1969).

[50]Figures cited in Alfred Ellis, Jr., A ecónomia paulista, with an incomplete reference to a study by F.L. D'Abreu Medeiros on the feira de Sorocaba.

[51]Maria Petrone, A lavoura, pp. 34-53.

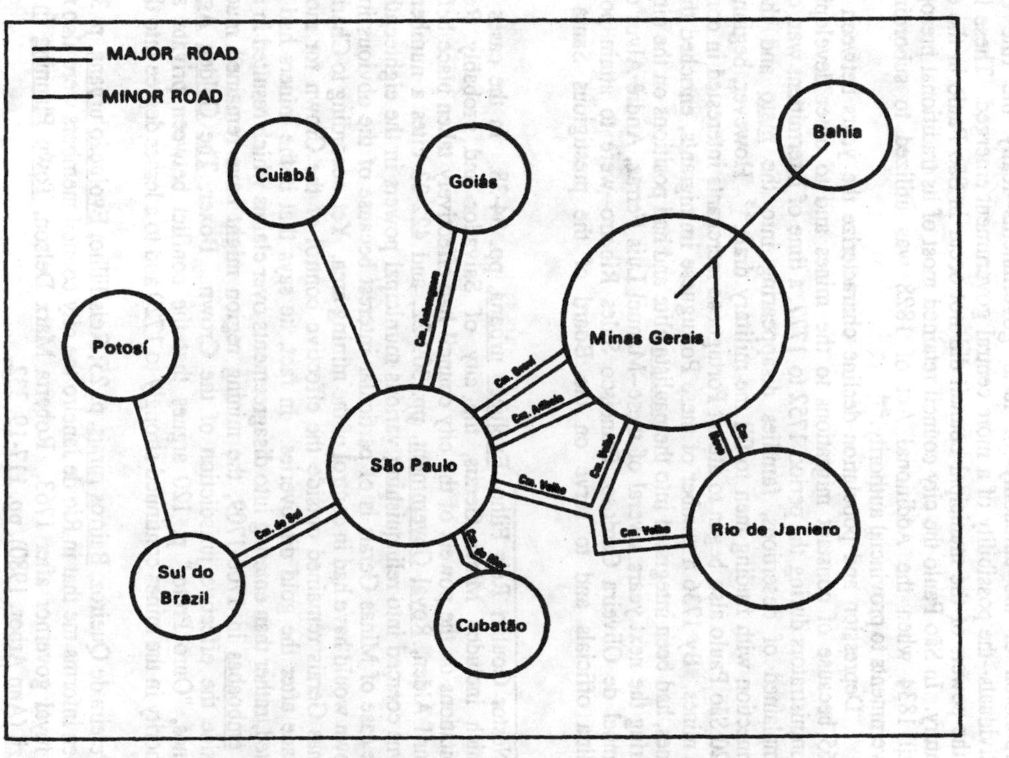

Map II:1 The roads of Southern Brazil by 1750

the powers of the municipal bodies themselves.[52] The privilege of nomination of the officials of the urban militia was taken away; the right of criminal asylum was suppressed; a royal judge (juíz de fora) was appointed to head the local councils of Bahia, Rio de Janeiro, and Pernambuco; in Salvador, Bahia, even the city council members were nominated by the royal governor. In newly formed communities the right to distribute lands was also usurped from the city council.[53] Through the suppression of the autonomy of local governments--really the rule of private individuals--the possibility of a more central government emerged. These limitations of the powers of the municipal council did not occur in São Paulo in the eighteenth century. In São Paulo the city council retained most of its traditional prerogatives up until 1834 when the Additional Act of 1828 was utilized to subordinate local governments to provincial authority.[54]

Depression and population decline characterize the years between 1700 and 1765 because of constant migrations to the mines and to other developing areas. Administrators during the period 1752 to 1777, a time of intermittent war, commonly complained of desertions, families disappearing into the mato and the like in connection with finding men to fill the military draft.[55] However, beginning about 1720 São Paulo also began to attract Portuguese merchants interested in commerce to the mines. By 1736 a number of these Portuguese immigrants, enriched through the mines, had been integrated into the paulista elite and had positions on the city council. During the next years several of these--Manuel Luis Ferraz, Andrê Alves de Crasto, Manoel de Oliveira Cardoso, Francisco Sales Ribeiro--were to attain positions as militia officials and to serve on the Board of the prestigious Santa Casa de

[52]Nestor Goulart Reis Filho, Evolução urbana, pp. 34-38. In the cases discussed (which included Minas Gerais, the city of Salvador and probably Recife) the limitations on the powers of the city council had effectively taken place before 1720. Dauril Alden, Royal Government, pp. 309-22, and 422-23 cites a number of small towns coerced into relinquishing various municipal powers in the eighteenth century. The case of Minas Gerais is of particular interest because of the obvious interest the Crown would have had in control of the mining area. Yet, according to Charles Boxer, Minas Gerais remained outside the effective control of the Crown for more than a decade after the gold discoveries. In fact, he says that if the miners had remained united, rather than entering into disagreements over claims which resulted in the war of the emboabas in 1708-1709, the mining region might have remained much longer outside the effective jurisdiction of the Crown. Boxer, The Golden Age, p. 72. Ramos, "Ouro Preto," p. 120 argues that the conflict between private and royal authority in the mines continued strongly to 1720 and to a lesser degree into the 1730s.

[53]Pereira de Queiroz, Bairros rurais, p. 25; Reis Filho, Evolução urbana, p. 37; Dauril Alden informs me that in Rio de Janeiro the city council members were also named by the royal governor after 1763. Roberta Marx Delson, Town Planning in Colonial Brazil (Ann Arbor, 1980), pp. 117-19, 332.

[54]The royal judge (juíz de fora), officially introduced to Brazil in 1696, did not appear in the São Paulo city council until 1810. At that time the reason given was that "os juízes ordinários eletivos--pelas relações de parentesco e amizades de força, contraídas no país da sua habitação, não practicavam os seus deveres e obrigações do cargo com exatidão e imparcialidade que covem a pública utilidade." Coleção das leis do Brasil, 1810 (Rio de Janeiro, 1880-1946), p. 105.

[55]For a detailed discussion of these military conflicts see Alden, Royal Government, pp. 83-267.

Misericórdia.[56] These men reinvigorated the old family clans through their commercial enterprises and the capital gained in the mines. Nevertheless all of them became slaveholders and agriculturalists by the late eighteenth century.

FROM SUGAR TO THE GENESIS OF THE COFFEE ECONOMY

The gold discoveries resulted in a population shift from the northeast to the center-south in addition to significant foreign immigration to the mining region. The Indian was displaced as the predominant element in the slave population at this time because of the importation of African slaves. The quest for mineral wealth in the interior also reduced the search for Indian slaves as well as driving potential Indian slaves even farther into the mato. The decree liberating the Indians was passed in 1758 at a time when most of the slave population was already Negro.[57] By the end of the eighteenth century the Indian element was largely indistinguishable from the rest of the free population. In spite of the substantial increase in population in this period, according to Dauril Alden, in the period 1772 to 1782 Minas Gerais contained only 20.5 percent of Brazil's total estimated population, with São Paulo, Goiás, and Mato Grosso trailing with 7.5, 3.5, and 1.3 percent of the total population respectively.[58] Alden and Caio Prado Junior agree that approximately 60 percent of the population continued to be located on the Atlantic seaboard in this period.[59]

Lack of sufficient personnel for local administrative positions combined with a continued scarcity of Royal administrators and sources of revenue to make the center-south a difficult area to administer. The scattered nature of settlements and the poor road system made this situation even more difficult. While the gold economy and related economic developments resulted in a dramatic change in regional production and trade, the center-south generally and São Paulo in particular continued to be viewed as an economic backwater isolated from the more "civilized" and "developed" seaboard areas of Brazil.

The captain-general, the Morgado de Matheus, viewed the predominance of the subsistence economy as an important problem in 1765, since he was most interested in extracting some kind of agricultural surplus from the population, both for the purposes of military campaigns and also in order to promote exports between the port of Santos and Portugal. The captain-general wrote sadly in 1766 that the paulistas, through laziness, grew only what they needed for consumption and informal exchange and kept no surpluses for market sale. By way of illustration he recounted that, being in need of two hundred alqueires of corn for a military expedition, he was forced to order somebody to forage through an entire district, buying a little here, a little there, in order to acquire the quantity required. In Portugal, remarked the captain-general, any

[56]Laima Mesgravis, A Santa Casa de Misericórdia de São Paulo, 1599-1884 (São Paulo, 1974), pp. 75-87.

[57]Bastide and Fernandes, Brancos e Negros, p. 12.

[58]Dauril Alden, "The Population of Brazil in the Late Eighteenth Century: A Preliminary Survey," HAHR XLIII, no. 2 (May, 1963): 192.

[59]Caio Prado Junior, Formação do Brasil Contemporáneo (São Paulo, 1973), p. 39 and Alden, "Population of Brazil," p. 192.

poor vicar could sell you two hundred alqueires of corn and you could find it anywhere.[60]

Eighteenth-century city council records are full of complaints about the "laziness" of the farmers who failed to produce surpluses for sale in the city. The municipal council of São Paulo repeatedly asked that surpluses of basic crops be brought to the city and that the farmers increase or even double their planned crops, and passed bills suggesting that a study be done on the crops planted in the vicinity to see what results could be expected in the coming years.[61] These official demands and suggestions were largely ignored by the local population, whose neighborhood economies were, in any case, almost totally self-sufficient. The mode of production was also important because sources of public income were necessarily centered upon the "exchange" aspects of the economy. Taxes on sellers, on rum, and the auction of the municipal meat market were all dependent on the existence of exchange. The building of the municipal marketplace in 1773--financed privately by a São Paulo businessman--had positive effects on municipal income, due to the impulse given to the exchange basis of the economy.[62]

From the viewpoint of both municipal leaders and the crown the production of surpluses was important not only to promote the economic development of São Paulo but also to establish an internal market for goods imported from Europe. The following excerpt from a letter of the Morgado de Matheus to the Marquis de Pombal in 1767 demonstrates that the Captain-General concretely perceived the problem in these terms:

> so that through the convenience of profits it would become attractive for the people to work because in these lands little imported cloth and other goods are purchased because no one has money with which to purchase. If the people had something to sell they would also have the means to buy and the demand would be enormous.[63]

Sugar was to become the first significant agricultural export from the paulista plateau. Although sugar was introduced to the captaincy in the sixteenth century, it was not successfully exported because of transport difficulties and the care necessary in the handling of sugar.[64] The gold boom provided the first significant market for paulista sugar, but as mining production fell sugar producers began to look for other

---

[60]DI, XXIII, pp. 1-10. An alqueire was a grain measure during the colonial period, the measure of which varied from locality to locality. Dauril Alden suggests that an alqueire of rice weighed 72 pounds. In modern Brazil an alqueire is usually a unit of land, corresponding to the land needed to grow an alqueire of grain.

[61]Arquivo Municipal de São Paulo (hereafter AMSP), Regístro geral da Camara municipal de São Paulo (hereafter RGCMSP) (São Paulo, 1919-1941), XI, 9 novembro 1765, AMSP, Actas da camara municipal de São Paulo (hereafter ACMSP) (São Paulo, 1918-1939), XV, 5 de marco 1766, XVI, 4 de janeiro 1772, 17 de junho 1775.

[62]Taunay, História II, no. 1, p. 133; RGCMSP; XI 26 agosto 1780, 23 janeiro 1783, 13 outubro 1783; XII janeiro 1796.

[63]DI XXIII, p. 383.

[64]Petrone, A lavoura, pp. 178-87.

markets, and miners began looking for new areas of investment.[65] Many African slaves brought to the center-south to work in the mines--and their offspring as well--became a source of unemployed capital after 1760 when mining declined. For the first time in paulista history, relatively cheap labor was available for productive use.[66] Although the condition of the roads by the 1770s continued to be poor, the development of mule transport represented a highly significant improvement in the facility of communications. The international market for sugar had begun to improve also, after the decline of the early eighteenth century. In part, the improvement was simply a function of increased population in Europe and a development of the European taste for sugar.[67] In addition, an English law of 1739 gave a monopoly price advantage within England to sugar grown in the British West Indies, a factor which tended to free other markets for the Brazilian product.[68]

In the period following 1765, and especially after 1780, concerted efforts were made to develop the infrastructure necessary to the commercialization of sugar in São Paulo. The possibility of sugar as an export provided an important stimulus to the development of the roads, port facilities, and personnel necessary to the handling and transport of exports. The first important efforts were made, interestingly enough, prior to the great impetus to Brazilian sugar exports taken from the 1789-1792 revolution in the important sugar producing colony of Haiti. That event, along with the market dislocations which accompanied the Napoleonic Wars, resulted in a skyrocketing of sugar prices and at least a ten-fold increase in demand.[69] Prior to 1789, however, market improvements were not significant enough to have alone provided the incentive for the actions taken to develop commercial infrastructure. Although some product with a strong export potential was certainly needed to encourage such developments, it was exports and the development of commerce in the abstract which initially interested the merchants and businessmen involved, rather than the specific case of sugar.[70] Sugar remained the dominant commercial crop in the São Paulo area until 1850, when coffee became more important. The growing areas, the roads, and the transport and commercialization process developed around sugar were utilized for coffee at a later date.

In spite of the impetus to sugar production provided by food shortages during the mining boom, paulista sugar available for export was reported to be nil by 1751.[71] Nevertheless, in 1767 the Morgado de Matheus wrote that rum and sugar from Itú

---

[65]Ibid., p. 10.

[66]See Roger Bastide and Florestan Fernandes, Brancos e negros em São Paulo (São Paulo, 1959), pp. 1-15 for a history of the slave populations in São Paulo.

[67]Caio Prado, Jr., História económica do Brasil (São Paulo, 1974), pp. 79-80.

[68]Furtado, Economic Growth, p. 95.

[69]Ibid., pp. 98-99.

[70]This point is supported by the fact that attempts were made to develop several crops--namely cotton, rice, and indigo--with a view to exports. Even the Regístro geral da camara municipal of São Paulo included recipes for the production of indigo in its records. XI, 23 de dezembro 1785. See Alden, Royal Government Chapter XIII, on Viceroy Lavradio's efforts to introduce new crops.

[71]Field Marshal Diogo de Toledo Lara stated in 1751 that the captaincy of São Paulo had not even one arroba of sugar available for export. AESP, TC, Livro 106, Ofícios do General Mendonça aõs Vice-Reis e Ministérios (1797-1802), pp. 104-05.

were among the possible commodities for export.[72] Construction of sugar engenhos reportedly became common in São Paulo about 1776.[73] During the administration of Bernardo José de Lorena (1788-1797) sugar clearly became the outstanding export of the captaincy. Lorena's trade policies and especially the termination and paving of the Santos road as far as Cubatão were a great stimulus to the development of sugar cultivation of the paulista plateau. Undoubtedly the collapse of the sugar colony of Haiti in 1789 provided extra incentive for the work on the road at this time. Governor Antônio Manoel de Mello Castro e Mendonça (1797-1802) referred to sugar as the crop which "without a doubt best occupies a large part of the population to a good advantage."[74]

The production and export figures on sugar in the period between 1797 (the first available statistics), and 1846, when coffee began to supersede sugar as the most important export, are not entirely reliable and come from diverse sources. However, there does seem to be consistency in the figures and implied trends. In her closely researched monograph, A lavoura canavieira em São Paulo, Maria Thereza Schorer Petrone discusses data gleaned from a plethora of contemporary observers and every possible official source. For the purposes of this discussion I have chosen statistics for a number of apparently average years. This data is intended simply to give a notion of the magnitude, rate of change and general trends in the exports of sugar. Excepting 1797 and 1807, the figures refer only to sugar exported through Santos. Clearly, as far as the development of the entrepôt function of the city of São Paulo is concerned, this is the most relevant statistic.[75]

Year	arrobas [32 lbs]	index:1797=100
1797	114,550	100
1807	183,660	160
1818	294,267	257
1824	450,000	393
1826	600,000	524
1830	443,619	387
1836	433,268	378
1840	533,142	465
1842	194,504	170

Cane sugar cultivation was located in three major areas within São Paulo.[76] The first and initially the most prosperous was the coastal area between Santos and Rio de Janeiro--principally Ubatuba, São Sebastião, and Ilha Bela. The sugar produced there was more saleable in the beginning because there were no difficult transit problems nor the likelihood of damage to the sugar which so frequently occurred on the trip down the Serra. A second area of cultivation was the Paraiba Valley. There sugar had some importance but was never the principal crop. Production was

[72]RIHGB, TE, VI, p. 55; Maria Petrone, A lavoura, p. 9.

[73]Daniel Pedro Muller, Ensaio d' um quadro estatístico da província de São Paulo (São Paulo, 1923), p. 238.

[74]Antônio Manoel de Mello Castro e Mendonça, "Memória sobre a communicação da villa de Santos com a cidade de São Paulo," DI, XXIX, pp. 112-13.

[75]Petrone, A lavoura, pp. 152-67.

[76]Ibid., pp. 24-47.

relatively small and the exports of this area were almost always sent out through Rio de Janeiro or one of the small ports in the north such as Paratí. The third and, by 1797, the most important area of sugar cultivation was on the inland plateau in the area comprised by the communities of Moji-Guacú, Jundiaí, Porto Feliz and Piracicaba, including these populations and also those of Itú, Campinas, and Capivari. Sugar production from this area was sent out through São Paulo to the port of Santos.

The development of commercial agriculture, the expansion in communication facilities and the expansion of exports were the accomplishments of a local group of merchant/businessmen (many of them immigrants) in alliance with traditional elite families and with the crown.[77] The way in which this happened necessarily involved the utilization of local governing bodies, kinship groups, and capital acquired by the elite during the mining era as well as the efforts, resources, and commercial connections of particular merchants and merchant associations. Portuguese merchants in Portugal and in Brazil constituted a network of credit and trade information and could influence ship's captains in their choice of merchandise and ports of call. The traditional elite provided financial contributions, but at least as important was the control this group exerted over local governing bodies as well as the labor and materials of the family clans--the only available means of public support of community projects. The specific contributions of the crown to this effort included tools from the Royal warehouse and the labor of two royal engineers between 1788 and 1792.

The interest of the governors of São Paulo in the development of exports was facilitated after 1765 by important modifications in Portuguese crown policy with respect to Brazilian commerce. In 1766 the fleet system which had handled all trade with Portugal through the ports of Recife, Salvador, and Rio de Janeiro was abolished and Portuguese ships were permitted to trade at any and all ports along the Brazilian seaboard.[78] Portuguese ships were also allowed to engage in trade between Brazilian ports. The Morgado de Matheus--Captain-General of São Paulo from 1765 to 1775--was the first to make a serious attempt to reconstruct the Santos Road to facilitate the passage of mules and carts. Initially it was difficult to induce ships to come to Santos because of the lack of goods for export and the Morgado also took a variety of measures to improve agricultural production and to encourage the accumulation of produce for export from Santos. In 1767 he wrote to the sergeant-major of Santos that the ships could carry "sugar from Itú, rum, rice, cotton, and wood."[79] The captain-general complained repeatedly that ships would not stop at Santos and often when they did the space on ship had already been committed. Furthermore, traders in Santos were few and relatively poor compared to those of Rio de Janeiro. Also the consumer market for imports in São Paulo was weak compared to that of Rio de Janeiro or Salvador.

A successful drive to reconstruct the caminho do mar began in 1780. Captain-General Martím Lopes Lobo de Saldanha wrote to the São Paulo city council that the Santos road was indispensable to the interests of the royal treasury and to all of the peoples of the captaincy since Santos was its principal port. He pointed out that the

---

[77]For an elaboration of this argument see Kuznesof, "The Role of the Merchants in the Economic Development of São Paulo: 1765-c 1850," HAHR (November 1980): 571-92.

[78]DI, XXIII, pp. 193-96.

[79]DI, XXIII, pp. 193-96, 4 junho 1767; 154, carta de 27 de marco 1767; pp. 383-85, considerações de 2 de janeiro 1768. DI, LXVIII, pp. 19-20, carta de 10 de novembro 1767.

road had not been repaired for many years and that the merchants of many captaincies were no longer dealing with the plateau because of the transport costs.[80]

The municipal council collected donations and then made each bairro militia company responsible for the work on a specific section of the road. Two members of each company were put in charge of organizing laborers and supervising the work. In some cases households donated slaves or paid day laborers for their particular contribution to the project. Members of less prosperous households contributed their own labor. By the end of 1781 the road bed had been completed and hardwood bridges constructed within a few kilometers of Cubatão.[81] Reports that occasional ships with cargoes sailed from Santos for Portugal beginning in the period 1782-86 indicate that even this partially completed road had tangible effects.[82] The last stretch of the road bed plus bridges to Cubatão was finished during the administration of Marechal do Campo Frei José Raymundo Chichorro de Gama Lobo (1786-1788).[83]

Pavement from São Paulo to Cubatão was laid under the supervision of Captain-General Bernardo José de Lorena (1788-1797). Financing included new solicitations of funds requested through the urban militia companies, plus a loan of 400 mil reis from the coffers of the Orphans and Absent Persons.[84] Lorena put two royal engineers and two mathematicians to work on the road--the greatest royal contribution to the entire project. The "calçada de Lorena," as it was called, completed from São Paulo to Cubatão in 1792, was wide enough so that "two mule teams meeting on the road (could) pass each other without stopping."[85] Ships bound for Portugal began to make regular stops in Santos for cargoes of sugar, rice, leather, and cotton during the period 1788-97. By 1797 sugar exported from Santos totaled 114,550 arrobas.

São Paulo and Santos merchants were finally able to bring together enough produce in Santos in the 1790s that ships sailing for Portugal found it worthwhile to make regular stops in the port. The expansion of the São Paulo export trade was continuous after the completion of the road to Cubatão, first with the development of sugar production, and later with coffee. By 1824 exports of sugar had increased to 450,000 arrobas; by 1826, when the final section of the road from Cubatão to Santos was complete, sugar exports had expanded to 600,000 arrobas.[86] The completion of a road fit for mule teams from São Paulo to Cubatão was sufficient to substantially reorient production on the plateau toward an export market. The unusual international demand for sugar during the Napoleonic Wars gave further stimulus to production,

---

[80]AMSP, Registro geral, XI, 7 de abril 1780.

[81]Taunay, História, II, no. 1, p. 155.

[82]Maria Petrone, A lavoura, p. 12.

[83]Mendonça, "Memória sobre a comunicação," pp. 112-13.

[84]AESP, Registro geral, XIV, 18 julio 1812. The loan was made in 1791. On the source of funds see Taunay, História, II, no. 1, p. 155.

[85]DI,XLV, p. 70. Additional funds were promised annually from São Paulo, Parnaíba, Itú, Sorocaba, Jundiaí, Mogi das Cruzes, Jacareí, and Atibaia for conservation costs. Taunay, História, I, no. 1, p. 159. It was also agreed that a tax of 40 reis for each mule and 120 reis for each head of cattle be paid for the use of the new road to be used for upkeep. There is, however, no clear evidence that this tax was implemented.

[86]RIHGB, XXXVI, p. 256.

though the development of the road itself preceded the increase in international demand for sugar.

Continued efforts by merchants and governors to complete the final twenty-mile stretch between Cubatão and Santos, and to otherwise improve the commercial infrastructure, marked the period from 1797 to 1826. The land route from Cubatão to Santos required an immense amount of land fill and numerous bridges, making the work especially difficult and costly. In the interim, merchandise was transported from Cubatão to Santos by canoe, a procedure which resulted in considerable water damage, especially to sugar.[87] Frequently mule team drivers had to wait as long as two weeks before being able to cross to Santos, because of winds, bad weather, or simply a matter of too few ferries.

In 1797 the merchants of the city of São Paulo sent a petition to Captain-General Antonio Manoel de Mello Castro e Mendonça (1797-1802) asking that the work be initiated on the land route from Cubatão to Santos. The merchants offered to pay twenty reis for each arroba of merchandise transported to Santos, beyond the usual costs, in order to help finance the road.[88] The suggestion was followed, the extra contributions being paid by merchants of Itú, São Paulo, and Santos and was the major source of financing for the Cubatão-Santos land route.[89] Only in 1826, however, after numerous letters and petitions attesting to the urgent need to finish the road to Santos, was the road finally completed and paved, fifty-six years after the first fund was set up for the building of the road.

The São Paulo-Santos road was clearly intended for mule trains and was constructed as such. One of the major concerns came to be the development of a system of shelters or ranchos at each end of the road and also at intervals along the road for tending the mules and protection of produce from inclement weather. These, too, were built with the labor of the urban militia companies during the years between 1797 and 1808.[90] Evidence exists that the size of mule teams increased with the improvement of the road. A 1775 reference by the Morgado de Matheus seems to refer to teams of about 20 mules each; Hercules Florence in 1825 mentioned teams of from 40 to 80 pack animals; Kidder claimed that the teams he met on the caminho do mar included from 100 to 300 mules.[91]

Governor Mello Castro e Mendonça reported in 1799 that ranchos for the shelter of mule trains and the sugar they carried had been built on the roads to Itú, Sorocaba, Jundiaí, and São Carlos (Campinas). The letters of Governor França e Horta (1802-1811) also show his concern for the upkeep of the "estradas de açucar" and his interest in building new roads to Campinas and Piracicaba. The roads most

[87]Maria Petrone, A lavoura, pp. 194-98. AESP, Ofícios dos engenheiros sobre estradas e jardins, no. ordem 241, no. caixa 14, includes an enormous file concerning the financing and work on the road from Cubatão to Santos.

[88]RIHGB/TE, IX, p. 361.

[89]Maria Petrone, A lavoura, pp. 196-98. AESP, Ofícios dos engenheiros, includes a letter from the merchants of São Paulo in 1815 complaining that they had been paying the special tax since 1797, a total of over 200,000,000 mil reis, and the road had yet to be finished. See also Mendonça, "Memória sobre a comunicação," pp. 115-20.

[90]Mendonça, "Memória económico-política," p. 114.

[91]DI, LXIV, p. 310; Hercules Florence, Viagem fluvial do Tieté ão Amazonas de 1825 a 1829 (São Paulo, n.d.), p. 5; Daniel P. Kidder, Reminiscencias de viagens e permanencia no Brasil, translated by Moacir N. Vasconcelos (São Paulo, 1972), p. 181.

affected by the sugar trade were 1) the old road to Goiás which led from São Paulo to Jundiaí, Campinas, Mogi Mirím, Mogi Guacú and finally to França and Goiás; 2) the road from São Paulo to Itú and Porto Feliz; 3) the caminho do sul to Sorocaba and the southern captaincies; 4) the road from São Paulo to Mogi das Cruzes, the Paraiba Valley, and Rio de Janeiro. These roads were improved and conserved in the period after 1797 to facilitate the commerce first in sugar and later in coffee.[92]

By 1820 there was already discussion of the construction of a new road which would allow vehicular traffic. The new highway, averaging four to seven meters in width, opened in 1846. Mule teams, however, continued to use the older São Paulo-Santos road which had been constructed for that purpose.

Trade policies of captains-generals in the period 1765-1808 also had an influence on the expansion of commercial agriculture and export. In 1789 Governor Bernardo José de Lorena prohibited coast-wide trade within the captaincy and all exports except those to Portugal.[93] All trade between São Paulo and Portugal was to go through Santos. Even local sale of sugar, starch, and rum was permissible only with a license. These measures were intended to foster direct trade with the kingdom and the results were dramatic. Sugar cane producers of the northern coastal communities such as Ubatuba and São Sebastião suffered drastically from the prohibition of coastwide trade. But the inland communities of the plateau--Itú, Piracicaba, Campinas, and Sorocaba--benefited enormously from these measures. In addition, both the community of São Paulo and the port of Santos were strongly advantaged. In effect, the measure served as a protectionist device of the inland against the coastal producers. Since all <u>paulista</u> sugar had to be carried to Santos overland, all growers were facing equivalent market prices and similar transport problems. Lorena also channeled all surplus production for export into the Santos port, thus ideally increasing the effective quantity of produce available for export in one place. Apparently the hoped-for result was realized, for by 1797 Governor Lorena claimed that twelve ships per year were loaded for Portugal in Santos.[94]

Regardless of Lorena's apparent success, his successor, Mello Castro e Mendonça believed that Lorena's trade policy was misguided.[95] He suspended all the restrictions on trade in effect during the previous ten years. This policy, too, had beneficial results, giving a strong stimulus to internal commerce. Santos developed as a port and commercial agriculture was directed towards the export market under Lorena's protectionist regulations. With the liberalization of trade after 1798 the internal market again became available and the result was a general expansion of production. This was most dramatic in sugar cultivation, but rice production also increased significantly. Sugar production rose from 114,550 <u>arrobas</u> in 1797 to 198,483 in 1799.[96] The next governor, Antonio Jose de França e Horta (1802-1811) returned to a protectionist policy with similarly controversial results.

After King Don João VI arrived in Rio de Janeiro in 1808, free trade with friendly nations was decreed and there were no more trade prohibitions. By that time Santos had been established as an international port and improvements had been made in the roads as well as the construction of <u>ranchos</u> to protect the transport of cargo. The agricultural exports of the inland plateau had been stimulated and developed

[92]Maria Petrone, <u>A lavoura</u>, pp. 24-47.

[93]<u>DI</u>, XXXI, pp. 192-93, 28 de dezembro 1789.

[94]<u>DI</u>, XLV, pp. 208-09, Relatório de 28 de junho de 1797.

[95]Antônio Manoel de Mello Castro e Mendonça, "Memória económico-política da capitania de São Paulo," <u>Anaes do Museu Paulista</u>, XV (1961), p. 205.

[96]Maria Petrone, <u>A lavoura</u>, pp. 146-47.

through almost twenty years of what amounted to a protectionist policy. Similarly, all policies which benefited Santos as a port also benefited São Paulo to handle the transport of merchandise to port. Business of all kinds improved with the increased traffic to bring goods to the major distribution center. The greater volume of business also implied improved municipal and royal revenues, the ultimate professional goal of all colonial administrators.

CONCLUSION

São Paulo was founded at the lowest point of the Serra do Mar on the edge of a plateau overlooking the port of Santos. The broad interior plateau was well suited to diversified agriculture but the caminho do mar was in such poor condition until about 1781 that it was generally used only by travelers. The primitive condition of the roads and lack of a reasonable mode of transport would not permit any kinds of perishable exports. Furthermore, the level of both the free and the slave populations was very low in the paulista area prior to the eighteenth century. As a result, commercial agriculture was inhibited and trade, such as it was, was carried on with the interior and through Rio de Janeiro. Commerce in Indian slaves was an important mainstay of the paulista economy during the seventeenth century. After the gold strikes of 1695 the communications networks began to be developed throughout the south of Brazil. Santos increased in importance as a port. Agricultural surpluses began to be produced in response to the interior market for foodstuffs in the mining areas.

In 1766 the Portuguese fleet system which had only stopped at Recife, Salvador, and Rio de Janeiro was abolished. All Brazilian ports were allowed direct trade with Portugal and coastwise trade was permitted. Efforts were made to develop exports from the São Paulo area as well as to improve the Santos port facilities and to improve communications. The emergence of the mule team as the basic mode of transport greatly improved the speed and care with which products could be transferred. These changes plus a protective trade policy favoring plateau agriculture facilitated the development of a sugar economy in the São Paulo region. The economic infra-structure developed around that trade was to benefit all kinds of commerce and the later development of coffee exports. The roads emanating from the major areas of agricultural production on the plateau all converged on the city of São Paulo, likewise all of the goods imported from Portugal, and later other countries, came from Santos to São Paulo. Thus the importance and size of São Paulo as an entrepôt grew along with expansion in exports.

III
Kinship, Marriage, Birth, Death, and Inheritance

The basic demographic characteristics of fertility and mortality both reflect and respond to social and economic changes as well as medical and technological advances. However, it is insufficient to know how "advanced" a society is economically or technologically to predict such characteristics as age of marriage or proportions marrying and size of completed family. Cultural characteristics imbedded in the kinship structure and reflected in patterns of marriage, household formation, child-rearing, and inheritance have highly significant implications for fertility patterns.[1]

In this chapter I will define the kinship system as it existed in the mid-eighteenth century as well as its operational importance for the subsistence-based economy in São Paulo at that time. Inheritance as a factor in fertility, property distribution, and marriage patterns will be discussed as well as the marriage practices and statistics on marriage over the period. Finally I will look at data on fertility, illegitimacy, and number of births per woman, and at major causes of death and death statistics for the period.

KINSHIP AND THE DOMESTIC MODE OF PRODUCTION IN PAULISTA HISTORY

The domestic or subsistence mode of production was dominant in the captaincy and the district of the city of São Paulo in the seventeenth and eighteenth centuries. Within this mode social relations--kinship, ritual kinship and community membership--were the basis for exchanges of goods and services. Exchanges of work or bounty between neighbors and kinfolks were not necessarily equivalent (an exchange of one day of labor on your farm for one day of work on mine), even though an approximate balance was expected to eventually occur. Moreover, those households unable to survive on their own labor were commonly supported by assistance from other households within the community, and the burden of "extra" children (those who could not be cared for by their own family) was also frequently assumed by other households.[2] Clearly these exchanges were predominantly based on the general needs of the community and the ability of particular households to give needed assistance.

[1]Raymond Smith, "The Family and the Modern World System: Some Observations from the Caribbean," Journal of Family History 3, no. 4 (1979):337-57.

[2]Antônio Cândido, Os parceiros do Rio Bonito (Rio de Janeiro, 1964), pp. 36-80. Maria Sylvia de Carvalho Franco, Homens livres na ordem escravocrata (São Paulo, 1969), pp. 80-81.

Marshall Sahlins has pointed out that this "altruistic" characteristic, which is common to subsistence societies, makes sense because wealth has no use value within a subsistence economy--that is, it does not function as capital. The accumulation of wealth has a relatively low priority, except as it leads to the development of personal power within the community, and then the purpose becomes redistribution for community benefit. The "chiefs" or leaders of such communities organize such activities as wars, cooperative work parties, church festivals, and the construction of public buildings and roads, as did the bairro leaders in São Paulo in 1765. Such leaders have little or no coercive power in terms of sustaining leadership or forcing tribute or contributions from community households. Each household continues to control the means of its own subsistence and therefore has no real dependence on any particular chief.[3] In a more important sense, however, the social interdependence of household units in the subsistence economy was extreme. The absence of market production meant that it was only through social ties that goods were shared and assistance rendered.

The household unit was the effective labor force in the paulista subsistence economy, with women and children over ten years of age contributing substantially. Besides the domestic chores which the adult men normally did not share, women and children produced certain household utensils, took care of most food-processing tasks (such as flour-making), wove cloth, and also worked in the fields with the menfolk.[4] Slaves were another source of labor but an indirect estimate suggests that while approximately 50 percent of households possessed at least one slave in 1765, less than ten percent had as many as four slaves.[5] In São Paulo in this period it was common for family members to work alongside their two or three slaves in the fields. Wealthy rural households sometimes also managed to acquire slaves skilled as cobblers, carpenters, and blacksmiths, making their households even more self-sufficient.[6]

---

[3]Marshall Sahlins, Stone Age Economics (Chicago, 1972), pp. 130-43.

[4]Cândido, Os parceiros, pp. 37-41 provides a useful summary of contemporary evidence for the eighteenth and nineteenth centuries on home-made utensils and manufactured goods. The role of women and children in the eighteenth-century household as presented here is partly assumed on the basis of structural similarities to present-day subsistence slash-and-burn cultures as described especially in Lia Freitas Garcia Fukuí, "Parentesco e família entre sitiantes tradicionais," (doctoral thesis in ciencias socias at Universidade de São Paulo, 1972) and Maria Isaura Pereira de Queiroz, Bairros rurais paulistas (São Paulo, 1972). Fukuí, Pereira de Queiroz, and Cândido also present historical evidence suggesting ways in which present practice is or is not the same as that common in the eighteenth and nineteenth centuries. Other evidence is found in Carvalho Franco, Homens livres.

[5]This estimate is based on the assumption that the slave population in 1765 was equivalent to that of 1767, and also that 50 percent of households had at least one slave. Note that 43.6 percent of households owned slaves in 1778. An assumption that a higher proportion of households possessed slaves would result in an estimate of a lesser proportion of households with over four slaves. The 1767 slave census is found in Archivo do Estado de São Paulo (hereafter AESP), Publicação oficial de documentos interessantes para a história e costumes de São Paulo, 82 volumes (São Paulo, 1895-), hereafter cited as DI, XIX, p. 285ff.

[6]Slaves are frequently described in terms of special skills in the property inventory of Maria de Araújo, 1756, caixa 56, where a dispute is recorded over the disposition of a slave named Antonio who was apparently a very skilled cobbler.

The work role of the child in the subsistence household was of great importance.[7] By the age of six or seven the child was expected to help with domestic tasks and was allowed access to the household tools.[8] Assimilation into the household work force was gradual, paralleling the development of the child's strength and skills.[9] Since the necessary skills were rudimentary, the child had only to imitate his elders. Working beside his parents, he learned how to plant beans, corn, and manioc, how to work the soil, how to care for the animals. More subtle knowledge concerning the appropriate times for the planting of different crops, how to choose the best soils, and how to manufacture domestic utensils was also acquired by age nine or ten.[10] The importance of child labor within the household of the poor subsistence farmer in eighteenth- and nineteenth-century São Paulo was potentially high. It was, in these terms, very rational for a subsistence farmer to want numerous children in the household, particularly with high levels of mortality, and when there were already children present to alleviate the difficulties of caring for the next.

The position of the paulista woman in the subsistence household was one of helpmate and collaborator. The woman's work was as important as that of the man and frequently overlapped. In general, tasks connected with household manufacture of utensils, clothing, soap, oil for fuel and light, and firewood, water and the jobs connected with cooking, cleaning, and childcare were and are the principal responsibility of the women and children. Both men and women worked the fields with the divisions in types of labor as much dependent on age and strength as on sex.[11] Relationships with the market, on the other hand, were the sphere of the male. Sale of any surplus as well as the purchase of the few necessities not produced nor grown within the household were handled exclusively by the man. If the head of household were female (as 26.55 percent

---

[7]The following evidence of the probable role of household members in specific areas of the domestic economy is based on recent anthropological studies of subsistence farmers in São Paulo. Most important were Lia Fukuí, "Parentesco e familia"; Cândido, Os parceiros do Rio Bonito; Pereira de Queiroz, Bairros rurais paulistas. In part this procedure is justified by the fact that a number of these studies present historical evidence suggesting ways in which present practice is or is not the same as that common in the eighteenth and nineteenth centuries. To a large degree, however, it is the environmental constants connected with subsistence farming and the exclusive use of the members of the household as work force, along with the persistence of cultural characteristics such as the identical type of housing and a very similar diet which justify the use of recent materials as evidence for past practice. On diet see Cândido, Os parceiros do Rio Bonito. Chapter 10 for a discussion on alimentary changes in the paulista subsistence farmer's diet since the eighteenth century.

[8]A knife was ritually given to the child at about this age, symbolic of the transition from infant to useful member of the household. Fukuí, "Parentesco e familia," p. 237.

[9]Sidney Mintz, Worker in the Cane (New Haven, 1964) discusses the gradual integration of the child into the family labor force in Puerto Rico.

[10]By the same age a young boy would also know how to use firearms, how to hunt and to defend himself against physical attack. A girl that age knew how to make soap, how to produce brown sugar, flour or land, as well as the arts of basket weaving, spinning and ceramics. Cândido, Os parceiros do Rio Bonito, pp. 117-18.

[11]Fukuí, "Parentesco e família," 232; Cândido, Ibid., p. 126.

of rural heads were in 1765), either a male relative or compadre handled these matters for her, or she might have to do them for herself.[12]

The agricultural work year was divided into the cold months from March to September and the hot months from October to February. During the cold months food was plentiful, and the work day short (except during harvest), while in the hot months food was scarce, and the work on the farm was long, intense and difficult. Jose Arouche de Toledo Rendon estimated in 1788 that the paulista subsistence farmer worked no more than two or three months in the year.[13] Usually a day was dedicated to one task, the hours worked depending upon the difficulty of the task, and the entire family participating. Some jobs, such as the production of manioc flour, were commonly executed with neighborhood assistance, beginning at day break and working into the night.[14] To some degree, the isolation of small domestic units was compensated for by the cooperative work projects of the bairros, as well as assistance between kindred. While marrying children could easily mark out their own land where they wished in the eighteenth century, it was common to both marry and settle within the bairro where the new couple could count on the assistance of relatives and compadres, and where they could continue to help their parents.

The most important basis of social exchanges in seventeenth and eighteenth century São Paulo was kinship. The Brazilian kinship structure is normally described as patriarchal in rule, bilateral in structure, extensive in the upper-class, and less so for less well-off families.[15] Brazilian kinship terminology includes terms for ten generations of levels of kin, from great-great-great grandfather (tetravô) to great-great-great grandson (tetraneto). No difference exists in nomenclature between relatives of the same degree from the maternal or the paternal side, nor is there any terminological distinction between blood relations and affines.[16] The existence of kinship terms for ten generations implies

---

[12]Fukuí, "Parentesco e família."

[13]"Reflexões sobre o estado em que se acha a agricultura na capitania de São Paulo" (1788), DI, XLIV, p. 196.

[14]José Arouche de Toledo Rendon describes the utilization of neighborhood help for farm work as the "norm" in 1788. He says, "O que pretende fazer a sua roçҫada ou derrubada de matto convoca os seus visinhos para certo dia em que, despois de comer muito e beber melhor, pegam nos machados e nas fouças, mais animados do espírito da canninha do que do amor do trabalho. Acabada aquella funcção convocam-se para outras, e este vem a ser unicamente o tempo em que trabalham, com interpolação de dias." Ibid.

[15]Studies specifically dealing with the Brazilian "family" (which is variously defined, if at all) include: Gilberto Freyre, Casa grande e senzala (Rio de Janeiro, 1933), and Sobrados e mocambos, 2 vols. (Rio de Janeiro, 1961); Antônio Cândido Mello e Souza, "The Brazilian Family," in Brazil, Portrait of Half a Continent (New York, 1947); Emílio Willems, "The Structure of the Brazilian Family," Social Forces, XXXI, no. 4 (1953); Charles Wagley, "Kinship Patterns in Brazil: The Persistence of a Cultural Tradition," in The Latin American Tradition (New York, 1959); Thales de Azevedo, "Família, casamento e divórcio no Brasil," in Cultura e Situção Racial no Brasil (Rio de Janeiro, 1966). It is impossible to cite here all those works which touch on the Brazilian family in one way or the other.

[16]The material on kinship terminology has been drawn from the unpublished analysis of Fukuí, "Parentesco e família," pp. 47-86, though the implications drawn about the material are my own responsibility. There is no detailed analysis of Brazilian kinship in print.

the recognition of kin at all those levels. Similarly, the lack of difference in terminology between the maternal and paternal sides, as well as between blood relatives and affines, suggests that there was an equal recognition of kinship obligations and exchanges across all of these groups. Thus the Brazilian kinship group was and is, at least in ideal or theoretical terms, about as broadly based generationally and laterally as is possible within a monogamous system.

Marriages in Brazil were governed entirely by canon law until 1916, a system whereby nuptial prohibitions for relatives were relatively severe. All direct blood relatives, siblings, cousins, uncle or aunt and niece or nephew to the third degree and direct-line affines--the primary blood relatives of a married pair--were forbidden to marry. Canon law also prohibited marriage between the primary pairs in ritual kinship relations--ritual father and ritual daughter (padrinho and afilhada) and ritual mother and ritual son (madrinha and afilhado). In spite of these stringent church laws, the frequency of ecclesiastical dispensations demonstrates that marriages of these prohibited endogamous categories were very common.[17] Cousin marriage and especially cross-cousin marriage (sister's son with brother's daughter) was in fact a preferred kind of marriage. This type of kinship structure and marriage customs implies that almost any traceable relationship would be viewed as a kinship relationship by the Brazilians affected.

Kinship links were significantly reinforced and supplemented in the eighteenth century by compadrío or ritual kinship. Compadrío, a chosen relationship, as compared to kinship, a given relationship, was even more closely linked to the practical aspects of everyday life. Lia Fukuí affirms, for example, that in Laranjeiras, a rural bairro of the municipality of Itapecerica da Serra in São Paulo, there was a definite preference for choosing kin as compadres. More important than kin, however, was the criteria of proximity of residence of the prospective compadre. If there were no appropriate kin in the neighborhood, the tendency was to choose as compadre someone who lived close enough to help out in times of need.[18] A further criteria--especially important in urban areas--was the economic and/or political situation of the person selected.[19] Obviously the idea was to develop strong links of mutual assistance with those persons with the greatest capacity to help in critical life situations.

In quantitative terms each child had two compadres of baptism, one of christening and usually the persons selected to stand up with the bride and groom at their wedding were considered compadres. Parents were also ritual kin to the compadres of each child.

---

[17]Independent evidence of the importance of endogamy or inbreeding is provided in the studies of levels of inbreeding on a comparative basis, by a group of geneticists, who found endogamy to be the most significant in Brazil of the twenty-one countries studied. These studies were based on parish marriage records combined with records of church dispensations for disallowed categories of marriages, in the nineteenth and twentieth centuries. These studies were discussed in Fukuí, Ibid., pp. 58-59.

[18]Robert W. Shirley, The End of a Tradition: Culture Change and Development in the Município of Cunha (New York, 1971), pp. 39-40. Fukuí, "Parentesco e familia," pp. 250-54. As a widow of Laranjeiras explained, "He who has compadres is never alone. Clothes are given to me; I always have food and everyone gives me work. Why should I leave here if I will lack the necessities of life in other places. I'm fine here. I'm alone in the world and the important thing is that I have compadres." p. 253.

[19]Pereira de Queiroz, Bairros rurais, pp. 39-40. For a discussion of the relative social position of ritual kin in eighteenth century Minas Gerais see Donald Ramos, "A Social History of Ouro Preto: Stresses of Dynamic Urbanization in Colonial Brazil, 1695-1726" (University Microfilms, Florida, 1972), pp. 242-54.

It was thus possible for any given household to be linked to a majority of the households in the bairro in this way.[20]

Compadrío functioned as a means of developing bonds of trust and political, economic, and social exchange patterns within the bairro. Kinship links within the bairro were reinforced through compadrío, the term "compadre" frequently replacing the kin term as a form of address.[21] In the same way compadrío integrated unrelated persons in the bairro and newcomers into neighborhood patterns of mutual assistance.[22] In essence, compadrío acted as a kind of amalgam between kinship (a blood connection) and neighbor (a place connection), combining the level of trust and the sense of obligation and expectation of kinship with the practical convenience of locational proximity, for the satisfaction of day-to-day needs for ready and easily available help.

In addition to ties of kinship and compadrío, Brazilian neighborhoods were frequently organized for more generalized mutual help projects, particularly in rural areas.[23] The classical form of the neighborhood mutual aid organization was the mutirão, an example of which was observed by Luis D'Alincourt in 1818 somewhere between Jundiaí and Campinas:

> ...in a house, in which, in that occasion there was a large number of people of both sexes; which by custom came together for work, which they called "muchiron" in the Indian language; and in this way they went from house to house, as they finished the tasks: the work consisted of preparing and spinning cotton, and making gardens for the plantings. The poor people employ themselves this way in the months of September, October, and November, and they pass the nights gayly with music and games.[24]

No direct pay was given for this work, but reciprocation--viewed as a definite bairro obligation--was expected.[25] Besides the more or less formally organized mutirão, there were casual reunions to help somebody behind in their work,[26] to trade "days of

---

[20]See Donald Pierson, Cruz das Almas (Rio de Janeiro, 1966), pp. 280-82 for data on the extent of compadrío linkages in that village.

[21]Pierson, Cruz das Almas, p. 280.

[22]Pereira de Queiroz, Bairros rurais, p. 40.

[23]Antônio Cândido has suggested that a good definition for a bairro would be "A territorial settlement, more or less dense, the limits of which are traced by the participation of the residents in projects of mutual assistance." Os parceiros, p. 67.

[24]Luis d'Alincourt, "Memória sobre a viagem do Porto de Santos a cidade de Cuiabá," Anais do Museu Paulista (São Paulo, 1950), XIV, p. 281.

[25]The importance of the mutirão custom undoubtedly varied among bairros in the eighteenth and nineteenth centuries, as is true today. Most scholars affirm that the custom was more important in the past than it is today. See Pierson, Cruz das Almas, p. 144; Pereira de Queiroz, Bairros rurais, p. 27; Cândido, Os parceiros, p. 68; Shirley, Cunha, p. 137. Pierson (p. 145) and Pereira de Queiroz (p. 27) have suggested that the appearance of fazendeiros willing to pay for labor has had a disorganizing effect on the mutirão system in some areas.

[26]Cândido, Os parceiros, p. 69.

work" with neighbors,[27] to assist with house and farm work as well as expenses in times of sickness and/or death,[28] to fix a bridge,[29], or to put out a fire which threatened the crops.[30] These types of exchanges between households were undoubtedly of importance in at least the rural bairros of São Paulo in the period between 1765 and 1836. It is difficult to say how important such customs were in the urban environment, though it is known that a system of neighborhood help was used in cases of fire in early nineteenth-century São Paulo.[31]

Morgado de Matheus, captain-general of São Paulo in 1765, described the domestic mode of production of the captaincy of São Paulo in that year, as did Coronel Jose Arouche de Toledo Rendon in 1788.[32] The characteristics they noted bear a fundamental resemblance to those described in more recent ethnographic accounts of traditional Brazilian cultures as well as those described by Marshall Sahlins in his stimulating work on subsistence economies, Stone Age Economics.[33] The basic characteristics for all of these cultures are: 1) labor is organized around small households based on the nuclear family; 2) production is primarily for use by the domestic group and secondarily for group functions or exchanges with neighborhood or kin; 3)both actual amount of production and the time spent working are very low compared to potential production per land area or labor force, and potential working hours, and 4) frequently there is little centralized formal political control of the population, personal social relations being much more important for the organization of collective action and the maintenance of public order.[34]

Exchange of goods and services within neighborhoods (bairros) and between kinfolk were an integral part of the domestic economy in eighteenth-century São Paulo. Indeed, Colonel Jose Arouche de Toledo Rendon, in his "Reflexões," characterized the agriicultural practices of the captaincy of São Paulo in 1788 as being one work party (mutirão) after another, separated by parties with an abundance of food and even more

---

[27]Pereira de Queiroz, Bairros rurais, p. 35; Pierson, Cruz das Almas, p. 146; Shirley, Cunha, p. 37.

[28]Fukuí, "Parentesco e família," p. 277.

[29]Ibid., p. 257.

[30]Cândido, Os parceiros, p. 69.

[31]Richard Morse, From Community to Metropolis, p. 28.

[32]Morgado de Matheus, "Cartas escriptas a S. Mage. pelo seu conselho ultramarino no anno de 1767," DI, XIII, pp. 1-10.

[33]Fukuí, "Parentesco e família"; Pereira de Queiroz, Bairros rurais; Sahlins, Stone Age Economics.

[34]Sahlins points out, "...But no one is thereby rendered dependent, and this respect will have to compete with all the other kinds of deference that can be accorded in face-to-face relations. Hence the economic is not necessarily the dominant basis of authority in the simpler societies: by comparison with generational status, or with personal attributes, and capacities from the mystical to the oratorical, it may be politically negligible." Ibid., p. 139. The Morgado de Matheus attributed the difficulties in dealing with the local populace to their dispersed residence patterns, but he also stated that paulistas deliberately avoided (and successfully) any contacts with the authorities, DI, XIII, pp. 1-10.

rum (pinga), as well as long periods of absolute indolence.[35] "Work parties" were the common practice for building houses or roads, clearing land, harvesting crops, butchering livestock, making corn or manioc flour, spinning and weaving cloth, and quilting, among other tasks.

These work exchanges occurred because some tasks were more easily executed by a number of persons larger than the household, which is the case of the mutirão in colonial Brazil. Another example of exchange, the division of hunting bounty, can be explained by the lack of cold storage which, combined with the unspoken agreement that future bounty of neighbors would be similarly shared, resulted in a relatively constant supply of meat commonly provided for all. Exchanges of work and goods in the domestic mode of production were not paid for but rather reciprocated.

The importance of inter-bairro household relationships can be demonstrated for the rural bairro of Nossa Senhora da Penha e França in 1765 through an analysis of name links, as shown in Figure III:1. The basic assumption behind this analysis is that multiple linkages between households, as suggested by common last names, correlated with frequent cooperation or exchange relationships between the related households. The possession of a common last name does not necessarily denote kinship. However, confirmation of the high probability that many of these links were kin links is provided by the case of the Captain-Major of Penha, Manuel Dias Bueno (household 864) for whom a genealogical search was done. He was related through kinship or affines to at least one-third of the households in the bairro, indicating a strong family basis for his political power. Some of these connections were detectable through name analysis; others were not. It is notable that the wealthiest household of the bairro was that of the Captain-Major's father-in-law (household 863; 500 mil reis) while Manuel Dias Bueno's property was matched only by that of household 895 at 300 mil reis.

[35]Jose Arouche de Toledo Rendon, "Reflexões sobre o estado em que se acha a agricultura na capitania de São Paulo (1788)," DI, XIII, p. 196.

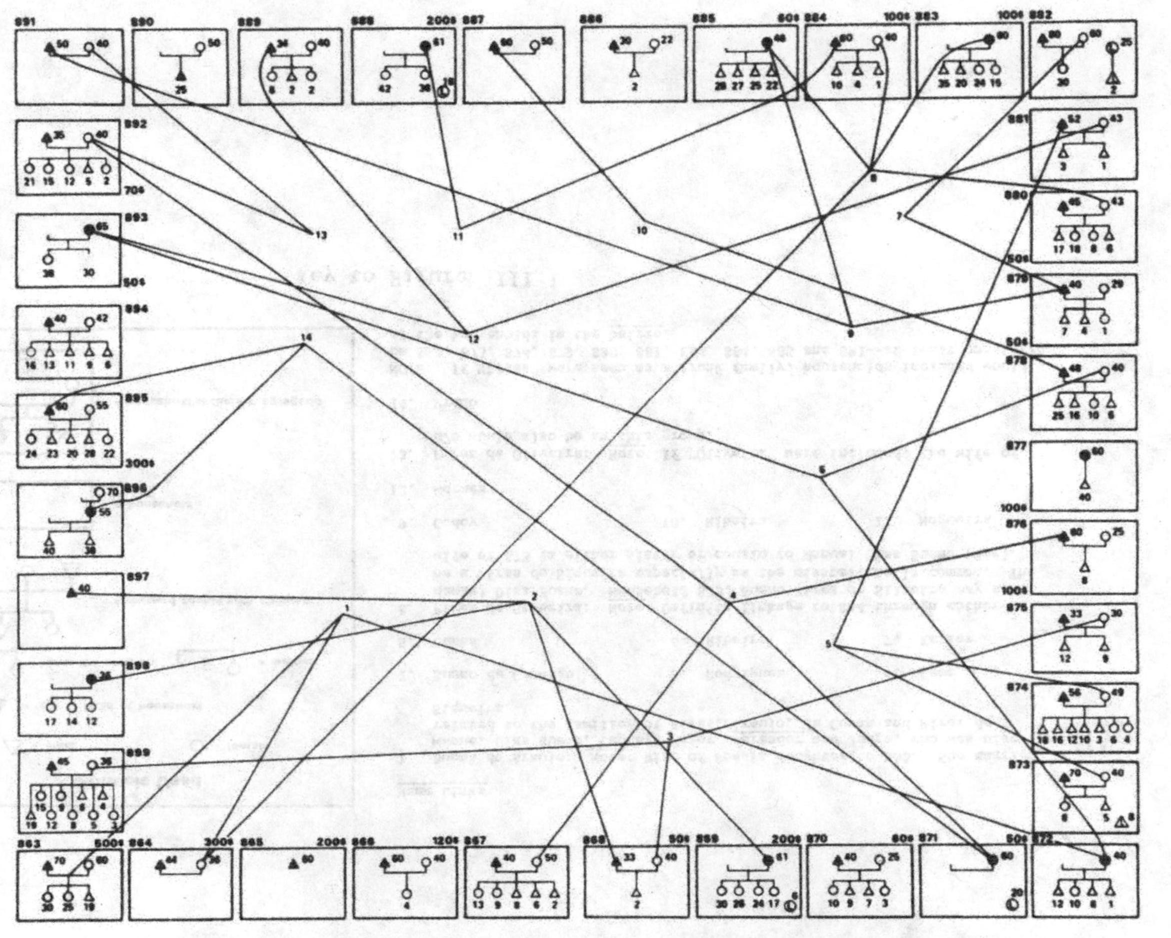

Figure III:1 Households in Nossa Senhora da Penha e França in 1765

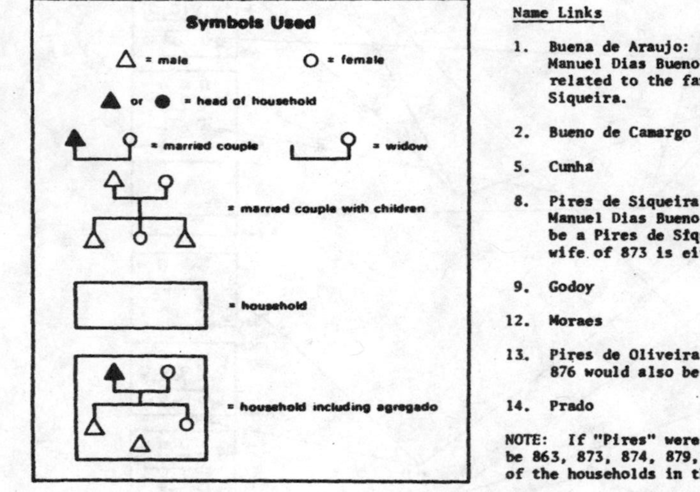

Name Links

1. Buena de Araujo: Note: Wife of 864 is daughter to 863. She married Manuel Dias Bueno, Captain-Major, *vereador* and Judge, who was also related to the families of Pires, Araujo, da Cunha and Pires de Siqueira.

2. Bueno de Camargo 3. Rodriguez 4. Leme

5. Cunha 6. Ribeira 7. Xavier

8. Pires de Siqueira: Note: Definite linkage to 864 through mother of Manuel Dias Bueno. Household 873, Bueno Pires de Silveira may also be a Pires de Siqueira especially as the misspelling is common. The wife of 873 is either sister or cousin to Manuel Dias Bueno (864).

9. Godoy 10. Ribeira 11. Nogueira

12. Moraes

13. Pires de Oliveira: Note: If "Oliveira" were included, the wife of 876 would also be in this group.

14. Prado

NOTE: If "Pires" were seen as a trunk family, households included would be 863, 873, 874, 879, 880, 881, 883, 884, 885 and 891--at least one-third of the households in the *bairro*.

Key to Figure III:1

The matrilocal tendency in Brazilian residence patterns is also illustrated in the pictograph. Most traceable kinship connections and name links within Penha were on the female side in 1765. Name links were specifically traced to 25 out of 35 female heads of households or wives of heads in the bairro. By comparison only 13 of the 26 male heads of households had these specific connections. Such evidence confirms the popular Brazilian belief that daughters remain closer to their families of origin after marriage--both physically and in terms of effective involvement--than sons. It seems probable that marriage of daughters within the bairro was a means of continuing to protect their property (the daughters' and indirectly the kindred's) as well as taking best advantage of whatever political or commercial advantages the new son-in-law and his kindred brought for the daughters' households of origin. If the daughter migrated much of the advantage of the marriage alliance was lost. Sons, who were better able to defend themselves and their interests, migrated or stayed near home, depending upon available opportunities. The result was, and still is today, that any given kinship network was often preserved and even controlled through the female line.

While day-to-day life in São Paulo was extremely affected by community relations, kinship, ritual kinship bonds, and mutual aid, the inheritance system combined with the colonial property laws influenced paulista society in longer-term, structural ways.

INHERITANCE LAWS AND PRACTICE

Inheritance has been generally recognized in the literature as having an important, if not critical, influence on population growth, family size, household structure and composition and economic development.[36] H.J. Habakkuk suggests that primogeniture was conducive to very large households which included the non-inheriting relatives, as well as the many off-spring of the inheriting oldest son. Theoretically, the system of primogeniture encouraged the family heir to have many children--as he did not have to fear the division of his property--and also fostered life-long celibacy among non-inheriting brothers. Equal division of property, on the other hand, tended to promote universal marriage but might have been an influence against unrestrained fertility because of the fear of property division.[37] The situation in São Paulo in the eighteenth and nineteenth centuries, while analyzable in these terms, was complicated by the effects of changing external variables, such as the development of markets and the changing value of land. A discussion of the Brazilian inheritance system and its level of practical implementation must precede analysis of possible effects.[38]

---

[36]See especially the classic article by H.J. Habakkuk, "Family Structure and Economic Change in Nineteenth-Century Europe," reprinted in Norman W. Bell and Ezra F. Vogel (eds.), A Modern Introduction to the Family (Glencoe, 1960), pp. 163-72.

[37]Habakkuk, "Family Structure," p. 167. Kingsley Davis points out that equal division does not necessarily lead to "early" marriage. It depends on when the division takes place, the supply of land, and the expectation of life in late adult ages. Equal division can be conducive to late marriage. Personal communication.

[38]The Brazilian inheritance system in force throughout the colonial period and up to 1916 has been repeatedly misunderstood and misrepresented in historical studies. The emphasis generally given to the power of the male and particularly the husband and father over the women has probably been the reason for this persistent error.

Colonial inheritance law was derived from the Phillipine Code of 1603 and remained basically unchanged until the publication of the Civil Code of 1916.[39] The following discussion is based directly on these laws, on secondary sources discussing the implementation of inheritance laws, and on wills and property inventories written during the period.[40]

Community ownership of all property, whether acquired prior to or during the marriage, was established from the point of consummation of the marriage.[41] Although dowry is normally associated with women, both spouses actually entered the marriage with a dowry. The bride's dowry was, in fact, her legitimate inheritance from her parents plus, occasionally, some extra portion given from the non-committed part of the father's or mother's estate. It is clear that the dowry was equivalent to the inheritance portion because the dowry, as well as any other property given prior to the death of the parent, had to be included in the parent's estate, and deducted from the heir's legitimate inheritance.[42]

---

[39]Sources for the following discussion include Repertório das ordenações e leis do reino do Portugal (Coimbra, 1795), 4 volumes, hereafter called Ordenações; Nicanor Penteado, Reformas e innovações feitas pelo código civil (São Paulo, 1918); Pontes de Miranda, Fontes e evolução do direito civil brasileiro (Rio de Janeiro, 1928); Cesar Tripoli, História do direito brasileiro (Sáo Paulo, 1936), 3 volumes; Martinho Garcêz, Dos testamentos e successões (Rio de Janeiro, 1917). These inheritance laws passed unchanged from the Code of Affonso to the Code of Manuel to the Phillipine Code.

[40]Wills, property inventories and related litigation for the captaincy and province of São Paulo through the year 1822 are available at the AESP. For this study documentation from about 1700 to 1822 was utilized. Published materials are available for the sixteenth and part of the seventeenth centuries in limited numbers in the series Inventários e Testamentos, published by the archive.

[41]"Mulher he meeira em todos os bens, tanto que o matrimónio he consummado por cópula," Ordenações, livro 4, titulo 95. The exceptions to this included 1) property included in morgadia--a particular kind of property in a family qualified by social status to have a morgado, in which certain specified items continued to be passed on indivisibly, usually through the eldest son. There were few morgados in Brazil and the institution was abolished altogether in 1835; 2) property inherited under special conditions as to use or to whom it should next be willed, for example. There is a notable contrast with Spanish colonial law as discussed by Asuncion Lavrin and Edith Couturier, "Dowries and Wills: a View of Women's Socioeconomic Role in Colonial Guadalajara and Puebla 1640-1790," HAHR, 59, no. 2 (1979):280-304. Spanish law distinguished between property gained during the marriage, the individual property of each spouse and the dowry, pp. 284-85.

[42]The property origin of each daughter's dowry was normally specified in the parent's will. Part of the dowry sometimes came from one of the parent's uncommitted property, or the entire dowry may have come from the daughter's rightful inheritance. These distinctions were important in determining how much additional property the daughter should acquire. For a concrete demonstration of this see the property inventory of Marianna Pães de Oliveira, 1782, Inventários não publicados, Caixa 79, AESP. New findings on historical changes in the use of the dowry in São Paulo were presented in Muriel Nazzari, "Women and Property in the Transition to Capitalism: Decline of the Dowry in São Paulo, Brazil (1640-1870)." Paper presented at the 1984 American Historical Association Meeting, December 30, in Chicago.

At the death of either spouse an inventory of property had to be taken within two months. The total value of the estate was divided into two equal halves, to be distributed to the legitimate heirs of each spouse at the time of their respective deaths. The half of the property pertaining to the dead spouse's estate was then divided into thirds. One of those thirds could be disposed of according to the wishes of the deceased, as specified in his or her will.[43] The other two-thirds rightfully belonged to the legally defined heirs. The order of succession was as follows: 1) all children of the current marriage had rights to equal portions, regardless of sex or order of birth.[44] 2) The grandchildren inherited if their parent, legitimate offspring of the deceased, had died. In that case the deceased son's or daughter's portion was divided equally between his or her children. 3) The ascendants--parents followed by grandparents to the tenth generation--inherited if there were no grandchildren to the tenth generation.[45] 4) Lacking any of the aforementioned heirs, the deceased had the right to name any person or persons as heirs. If no one had been named, the line of succession continued laterally--from siblings and their children--through the tenth degree of kinship. If no legitimate heir could be found, the state inherited the property of the deceased. It is important to note that the spouse was never listed as legal heir, although the deceased could name the spouse as heir in number four above.[46] Of course it was also possible for the spouse to inherit through kinship. Marriage between relatives within three degrees of kinship was prohibited by canon law but dispensations were frequently requested and granted.

This system of inheritance is indicative of the existence of a specific approach to family organization and property ownership--an approach or concept which preceded the discovery of Brazil. While interesting in terms of historical roots and basic royal legal policy, the important questions relating to these laws in terms of the current study have to do with the interest of the _paulistas_ in carrying them out. _Paulista_ indifference to royal orders in other spheres (such as laws against Indian enslavement) has often been explained by the inability of the crown to enforce specific regulations in a region and at a distance only reached with great difficulty, and where royal representatives were few. The faithful enactment of legal provisions of property division and inheritance demonstrates not so much the force of law in itself (which could not have been that strong), nor moral principles (even less trustworthy), but rather the private concern of the colonists in seeing that the law was enforced.

[43]If no will was made, the third was divided among the legitimate heirs in the same way as the remainder of the property.

[44]When a widow with children remarried, she was obliged to separate the two-thirds of her estate to which her children were heirs and enter the new marriage solely with the third of her property whose disposition was to be according to her wishes. _Ordenações_, livro 4, titulo 95. The civil code of 1916 corrected what was apparently an inequity in the old system by including the child of the first marriage as half an heir (i.e. to receive an amount equal to half the inheritance of a child of the current marriage) in the subsequent estate. Nicanor Penteado, _Reformas_, p. 266. Illegitimate children had no right to inherit but could be named as heirs for a portion of the third whose disposition was determined by the deceased.

[45]Degree of kinship is equivalent to level, and is determined by generation. The civil code of 1916 has changed the recognition of kinship for purposes of inheritance to only include relations to the sixth degree.

[46]The civil code of 1916 changed this law in that the spouse was made heir following the ascendants, with collateral relatives inheriting after the spouse.

A good example of this concern was the initiation of the inventory of property taken at the death of either spouse--the first step to the division of property. Some interested party had to officially initiate the taking of the inventory, but the surviving spouse obviously would have little interest in doing this--a problem recognized within the legislation. The law stipulated that "a relative or grandparent who fails to initiate a property inventory within two months (of the death of the spouse or son or daughter-in-law) loses the right to usufruct of the spouses, child's or grandchild's property."[47] Beyond these legal threats to the surviving spouse, the fact that the legal heirs of the deceased were strongly advantaged by an early inventory meant that pressure--including the possibility of a denunciation to the judiciary--would likely come from these quarters. The danger was that the surviving spouse might attempt to conceal, misuse, or alienate some part of the estate of the deceased. The extreme care evident in the process of making the property inventory, including a multiplicity of witnesses and the separate appraisal of each possession by an official of the judiciary, functioned as a means of protecting the heirs from the self-interest of the surviving spouse.[48]

Repeated references in the law code concern the problem of the power of the surviving parent, and especially the father, over the property of minor children, inherited from the other parent. The law stated that the father should have usufruct of the patrimony of minor children living in his power.[49] However, it was further stated that the father could not alienate, mortgage or misuse the property of his children. Whatever gains accrued to that property were likewise to be reserved for them. Furthermore, the administration of the children's property could be turned over to someone besides the father, especially if his wife had so specified in her will, or if the father opposed the particular way in which the property was distributed at the time of the inventory.[50] In any case a minor child was considered to be an orphan if one parent had died, meaning that the juizado dos orphãos could assume control of the child's inheritance if the judge thought that would best serve the child's interests.[51]

The practical implementation of all of the above depended, of course, upon the relative wealth and political influence of the two families. The fact is that property inventories were taken throughout the colonial period and the nineteenth century in elaborate detail, and with care to see that all property was included and all heirs accounted for. Often the inventories included massive litigation concerning conflicting rights, allegations of property already received, debt payments demanded, and claims that the deceased had promised to leave particular persons something in the will. Paulista

---

[47]Ordenações, livro 4, título 82, parágrafo 8.

[48]A related problem was that of the abuse of the wife's property by the husband during the marriage. In theory, wives could complain against any sales of property for excessive "gifts or donations" which her husband might make. Ordenações, livro 3, titulo 47; livro 4, titulo 66. One safeguard must have been, however, that the husband could not diminish his wife's property without also diminishing his own. See Pontes de Miranda, Fontes, p. 202.

[49]Ordenações, livro 4, titulo 98, parágrafo 1.

[50]Ordenações, livro 4, titulo 98.

[51]Pontes de Miranda, Fontes, p. 202.

wills and property inventories examined for the years 1750 to 1850 give every appearance of having been executed according to the provisions outlined above.[52]

One further characteristic of Brazilian inheritance law is of great significance to the question of household economy. That is the fact that inheritance laws were generally not applied to unimproved land throughout the colonial period. Until 1802 land was usually acquired through the free granting of tracts of land or sesmarias which were awarded for specified uses (cattle ranching, farming, residence) stated in the petition. If the property had not been improved and was not in use within one year the land was supposed to revert to the municipality. In practice unimproved property commonly remained in the grantees hands until his death at which time it was returned to the municipality for redistribution.[53]

The major effects of the inheritance system on the paulista family and household organization in the eighteenth and nineteenth centuries, according to Habbakuk's mode of analysis, were the following: Since inheritance was relatively equal, marriage was seemingly a possibility for everybody. Since land was readily available, the fear of morselization of land could not have been a restraint on fertility, at least before the nineteenth century. There may have been, however, a fear of too much division of other property--slaves in particular. Furthermore, the combination of community property in marriage with the separation of the spouses' estates at death to be passed on to the particular heirs of each meant that the respective families retained a permanent interest in the estate. In effect, the members of a kin group acted as caretakers of a segmented family patrimony. It was reasonable, then, that marriage within the propertied class was the most serious of propositions--the business of the entire kin group--and involved, in part for this reason, an extremely complicated set of bureaucratic and legal procedures. Although inheritance was basically egalitarian, each individual was not thereby provided the freedom to marry. Formal marriage was by no means universally contracted nor individualistically determined in eighteenth- and nineteenth-century São Paulo. In fact, it appears that any restraint related to property division was exercised not as fertility control, but rather as marriage prohibition.

Community ownership of property from the time of marriage obviously implied that a desirable spouse must possess property equal or greater than that of the prospective husband or wife, or else be closely enough related to insure that property remain within the kinship group. Marriage under other circumstances was usually not advantageous although sometimes marriages were contracted which implied an exchange of wealth for prestige or political power. The contribution of the bride to a marriage consisted of her inheritance (dowry) plus whatever politically advantageous kinship connections she might have, and the possibility of sharing or participating in business with her brothers or father. Sometimes the father of the bride would add some portion of the uncommitted third of his estate to her legitimate inheritance in order to win a particularly desirable son-

---

[52]This assertion is based on unpublished property inventories (Caixas 50-94, 1740-1820). Extreme regularity was encountered in the observance of these laws, even when heirs were not physically present to defend their interests. I received invaluable assistance in the reading of these wills from Dona Maria Gloria Martinelli of the Archivo do Estado de São Paulo, who also transcribed most of the published property inventories.

[53]On the sesmaria see Alberto Passos Guimarães, Quatro séculos de latifúndio (Rio de Janeiro, 1968), pp. 41-59.

in-law.[54] From the point of view of the bride's father, who generally chose the groom, the marriage of his daughter was like making a capital investment in a business for an ultimate 50 percent of the value of the business. The son-in-law was valued in terms of his estate, his family connections, and the potential of his career, both politically and economically.

Frequently the interests of wealth and kinship combined for the most advantageous marriage, in spite of the necessity for a church dispensation. A good example of this was a petition of 1710 to the Bishop of São Paulo asking for dispensation to allow the marriage of the orphan Anna Ribeiro de Almeida, and José de Goés e Morães, son of Captain-Major Pedro Taques de Almeida. She was the grand-daughter of the latter's brother and, as her parents and grandparents were dead and she had no brothers, her closest relatives were her prospective husband and his father. The statement of the bishop sheds light on the community view of this union:

> It has been shown that the petitioner is an orphan and, since all of the principal families of the village (São Paulo) are closely tied by kinship, among all of them the petitioner has chosen the aforementioned co-petitioner for help in her orphanhood because of finding in him more than in others all of the necessary attributes, with a dowry (inheritance) of eighty thousand mil reis, which the co-petitioner offers, together with the twenty thousand mil reis, which the petitioner has as dowry, they can increase their house and, being of equivalent social standing, it will be to the liking of the principal families. Besides which the ascendants of both of them have greatly served the Catholic Church both socially and with their wealth, with which they conserve and increase their houses and consolidate their families.[55]

It is particularly important in a case like the one above that since the bride's dowry was much lower than the groom's (though she probably had the highest dowry of the possible choices), she was also closely enough related, and did not have close heirs of her own, that her half of the joint estate would inevitably go either to their children, or back to her husband's family.

In addition to the problem of keeping the fortune within the kinship group, there was the related problem of maintaining the integrity of certain kinds of wealth which, divided, became less valuable. In general, some of the heirs would sell their inheritance (if it consisted of some part of an engenho or sugar mill, for example) to co-heirs, and

[54]Property inventory of Domingos José Vieira I, Itapetininga, São Paulo, 1799, cited by Oracy Nogueira, Família e comunidade (Um estudo sociológico de Itapetininga) (Rio de Janeiro, 1962), p. 251. Nine shares were given out, six as dowries during Domingos José Vieira's lifetime and three to sons at his death. One dowry totaled 25 percent of the estate, 7.4 percent from the legitimate inheritance and 17.6 percent from the father's third. Five of the six daughters had dowries larger than any of those of the three sons, all of the father's third being used for this purpose. The marriages served their purposes, uniting the richest and most powerful families in the region, dominant in the next generation within the community. As a sidelight it is interesting to note that Domingos José Vieira owed money to two of his son-in-laws at the time of his death. Ibid., p. 244.

[55]AESP, Inventários e testamentos, XXVII, "Autuação de uma petição de José de Goés e Morães e Anna Ribeiro de Almeida, anno de 1710." The two petitioners were told to live three days on bread and water and pay 240 mil reis for their dispensation.

would purchase or construct other properties with the proceeds. It was also common that certain sons or daughters would ultimately be more favored because of having made an especially advantageous marriage, and receiving extra dowry from one of the parents' thirds in order to facilitate that marriage. Less fortunate sons or daughters often became small property holders or public employees. Thus the increasing wealth of certain members of a kinship group might be partially at the expense of others within the group, the choice of which child was favored being more or less at the discretion of the father.[56]

In middle-income families, it was often difficult for a father to provide a dowry for even one of his daughters during his lifetime, though each child would of course receive an inheritance portion at his death.[57] Furthermore, the slaves and goods of middle-income families seemed in particular danger of being divided in such a way as to impoverish the whole family due to the inability of heirs to buy from each other. After land began to be treated as part of the inheritance after 1822, this problem was noticeable in the progressive fragmentation of land.[58] Ultimately it was the elite who benefited from the property division of the middle-income groups, as the elite were able to purchase these plots to enlarge their own holdings. Sometimes previous owners ended up as tenants on what had been their own lands. It is possible that the fear of fragmentation of property may have had some effect on fertility for middle-income families. However, the latter concern would surely have been counter-balanced by the high rate of infant mortality which created an even greater fear of having no children to care for the couple in their old age.

In lower-income families the question of inheritance cannot have had much effect on fertility. The possessions were so few that undoubtedly the use value of children on the farm and in domestic industry was more important than any other consideration. Formal marriage was less widespread among the poor, consensual unions were common, and less parental control was exercised over the choice of mate. The work partnership of everyday life was the focus of thinking, rather than political connections or property.[59]

The net effect of the factors discussed above in terms of household size and composition differed according to socio-economic level. For the elite, an extended household composition which included unmarried siblings and other relatives whose fortune (inheritance) was of interest to the kin group developed around members of the group who had made advantageous marriages. Unmarried daughters stayed in the paternal home as long as their parents lived and then went to reside with a married brother

---

[56]Nogueira, Família, pp. 250-52.

[57]It was not uncommon for a father to petition the city council for a dowry with which to marry his daughter, though I have encountered no case in which the petition was granted.

[58]Lucila Herrmann, "Evolução da estrutura social de Guaratinguetá num período de trezentos anos," Revista de Administração (Marco-Junho 1948), p. 123. Herrmann mistakenly believed the Brazilian inheritance system to be based on morgadia prior to 1835 when morgadia became illegal. See footnote 32. She attributed the morselization of property to the ending of the morgadia in 1835 when property previously passed on to the morgado (usually the first son) was supposed to be divided according to the general inheritance law. However, since the morgadia itself was insignificant within Brazil, the law abolishing it must have likewise had little effect. The fact is that under the morgadia during the colonial period, unimproved land was likewise not treated as property and was not inherited.

[59]Even for the poor, marriage or informal unions were preferably with kin or ritually related persons, but this was because of the importance of exchange relationships between households, rather than because of inheritance considerations.

or sister, or even with an unmarried brother living alone. Single but well-off males sometimes lived alone with slaves or agregados or with unmarried or widowed brothers or sisters. Widows tended to marry--if they remarried--the closest possible relative of their late husbands, because of the danger of otherwise losing usufruct of their children's paternal inheritance. Marriage to someone outside of the kin group of a widow's husband was very likely to result in a guardian being named for her children and their property because of the assumed interest that she and her new husband had in expropriating the property of her children.[60] It was more difficult in practice to deprive a widower of guardianship of his children and usufruct of their goods on his marriage to someone outside of his late wife's kin group. However, depending upon the political strength of the latter, this too could happen and did provide incentive for remarriage within the same family.[61]

Household size in middle-income families was somewhat smaller due, possibly, to restraints on fertility and lesser interest in control over the property of kin since effective inheritances were smaller. Actual division of property as opposed to sales between co-heirs (common in the elite) was the usual pattern, reinforcing the tendency to a less-extended household because of less space (i.e. less drawing power for prospective residents) and a smaller productive unit in agricultural areas. Unmarried daughters remained in the parental home as long as parents were alive, afterwards living with married siblings or in a group of unmarried sisters. Occasionally such single, genteel, but somewhat impoverished, females have subsisted on the income from hiring out one or two slaves received as their inheritance. Single males often lived alone or with one or two agregados.

Household size and composition for poor families whose limitations centered on housing space and the size of available farming land (in the nineteenth century) tended towards a small nuclear household. Marrying children or those setting up an informal union tried to find new land on which to build a house. The informality and economic instability of many of these unions led to the frequent abandonment of the woman and her children producing a highly prevalent so-called anomalous household made up of a single

[60]On this point see Penteado, Reformas, p. 100.

[61]A clear example is Ana Vicência Rodrigues de Almeida, of the Camargo family, who first married Antônio da Silva Prado in 1786, having three children. Her second marriage was to Eleutério da Silva Prado, brother of her first husband. Any other choice would have probably resulted in an action to deprive her of guardianship of her children and usufruct of their inheritance. Another case is that of Margarida de Oliveira (Oliveiras family) who first married Antônio Alves Rosa (Portuguese) who died in 1722, at which time she married his brother. Her third marriage was to José dos Santos Rosa (cousin to her first two husbands) in 1754. A third example was the merchant and several times councilman Bernardino Antônio Vieira Barbosa who married Anna Prestes Martíns (Taques Pompeus family) in 1798 and had two daughters, still minor when Anna Prestes died. He then married her cousin Gertrudes Miguelina Martíns, there being no eligible sister. The issue of the rights of the surviving parent--and especially the mother--with respect to the patria potestad or control over the actions as well as the property of the children provides another contrast with Spanish law. According to Edith Couturier, although mothers were often named guardians of their children, under Spanish law they had no particular right to this position and, furthermore, remarriage disqualified them for guardianship. See Edith Couturier, "Women and the Family in Eighteenth Century Mexico: Law and Practice," Journal of Family History 10: 3 (Fall 1985). Also see Silvia Arrom, "Changes in Mexican Family Law in the Nineteenth Century: The Civil Codes of 1870 and 1884," in the same issue, for a discussion of changes in rights of patria potestad in nineteenth-century Mexico.

woman and her children. Commonly, at least one child in a poor family would continue to reside with the parents until the latter's death, taking over the household afterwards.[62] Size of household was determined more by short-run productive needs and benefits than by interest in property control.

PATTERNS OF MARRIAGE, CONSENSUAL UNIONS, AND CELIBACY

The proportions of the population marrying and the age at marriage have generally been regarded in demographic studies as major social factors influencing fertility prior to the widespread use of contraceptives. Malthus in his classic essay theorized that "delay of the marriage union" was a fundamental reason for the lower birth rates of Europe. John Hajnal picked up this theme for a series of articles focused on marriage and its linkages to economic circumstances to explain fertility changes.[63]

Complete restriction of childbirth and family formation to the bounds of the marital context provides the societal circumstances in which these "marriage variables" have most explanatory power. Consensual unions and the practice of concubinage, both common in eighteenth and nineteenth-century São Paulo, reduce the potency of nuptiality as a fertility indicator. Nevertheless, marriage, and particularly age at marriage, has a potentially much stronger effect on fertility than either the proportion of a population never marrying or the rate of illegitimacy, because of the high relative frequency of marriage as a context for childbirth.[64] Each of the factors mentioned--age at marriage, proportions marrying, illegitimacy and fertility performance--has importance for the discussion of demographic change in São Paulo over the period 1765 to 1836. It seems clear from the mere fact of so much change in marital and fertility patterns over the period that this was a time of social tumult in the sense that profound accommodations in personal life were necessary.

Marriage in eighteenth- and early nineteenth-century São Paulo was not by any means a universal practice. The non-marrying habits of paulistas were commented upon by governors and travelers to the area, suggesting everything from poverty to vagabondage and love of the easy life as reasons why the men "don't get themselves caught in the ties of matrimony."[65] Formal and bureaucratic difficulties were cited by Captain General Luíz Antonio de Souza in 1768 and again by Captain General Antonio de Mello Castro e Mendonça in 1800 as the major barriers preventing large proportions of the population from marrying. Both governors also specified that the expenses connected

[62]See Michael Anderson, Family Structure in Nineteenth Century Lancashire (London, 1974), pp. 92-98 for an analysis of the "holding power" of the paternal homesite, depending upon inheritance rules and the income level of the household.

[63]"European Marriage Patterns in Perspective," Population in History; "Age at Marriage and Proportions Marrying," Population Studies, 7, no. 12 (November 1953):111-32.

[64]See Kingsley Davis and Judith Blake, "Social Structure and Fertility; An Analytic Framework," Economic Development and Cultural Change, IV, no. 3 (April, 1956): 211-35 for a discussion of the possible relative importance of various cultural variables for fertility.

[65]J. Mawe, Viagens aõ interior do Brasil principalmente aős distritos do ouro e dos diamentes (Rio de Janeiro, 1944), first published in 1812, p. 7 says, "Além de pobres, acontece que os brasileiros, cujas amáveis qualidades são tão características, encontram inclinados como são ãos prazeres, nas mulheres do pais, facilidades de costumes, e em geral não pensam en se deixar prender nos laços do matrimónio."

with the taking of the marriage vows were practically prohibitive for the poor.[66] Statistical analysis confirms contemporary reports of the frequency of non-marriage. Table III:1 indicates the proportion of single persons between 20 and 59 for the years 1765, 1798, and 1827 for the district of the city of São Paulo. Both the unusually high proportion of single persons for both sexes throughout the period and the increase over time in the proportion of single persons for ages 40-49 and 50-59, particularly for females, are apparent in these data. In the captaincy/province of São Paulo, on the other hand, the proportion of the population single at ages 40-49 for both males and females declined substantially from 1798 to 1828.[67]

These opposite changes in proportions probably never-marrying for the captaincy/province compared with the district of the city of São Paulo were accompanied by a significant decline in the age of marriage for both geographic units.[68] For males in the city of São Paulo the trend toward a decline in the age at marriage is most evident in the decline in proportion single for ages 20-39. These are the ages most affected by new socio-economic conditions, at times when marriage was frequent. Average years spent single (the singulate age at marriage) for the district of the city of São Paulo for females declined from 23.95 in 1765 to 21.98 in 1798, to 20.53 in 1827. The corresponding figures for males were 28.33, 23.87 and 22.24.[69] In terms of the captaincy the nineteen percent decline in proportions of single males 40 to 49 in the period 1798 to 1808 (from 29.8 to 11.1 percent) is a dramatic indicator of the effect the economy can have on personal life.

Captaincy-wide nuptiality changes from 1765 to 1808, including decline in proportions single and decline in the age at marriage, can be most reasonably interpreted as an indication of an increasing standard of living. Men were finding the prospect of supporting a wife and family economically more feasible in this period due to

[66]DI, XXIII, p. 380, Carta de Luíz Antônio de Souza a Conte de Oeyras, 31 janeiro 1768. Castro e Mendonça, "Memória," pp. 95-96. See also Donald Ramos, "Marriage and the Family in Colonial Vila Rica," HAHR, 55, no. 2 (May 1975):200-25 for a discussion of marriage in a neighboring captaincy in 1804. For an excellent discussion of marriage in nineteenth century Chile see Robert McCaa, Marriage and Fertility in Chile, pp. 41-74.

[67]Captaincy/province figures from Maria-Luiza Marcílio, "Crescimento demográfico e evolução agraria paulista, 1700-1836," Tése de livre docencia no história na universidade de São Paulo (São Paulo, 1974), pp. 157-83. In the captaincy/province the proportion single for females 40-49 declined from 38.3 in 1798 to 24.7 in 1808 to 20.3 in 1820. For males the figures were 29.8, 11.1 and 8.8. Marcílio suggests no explanation for these changes.

[68]An increase in proportions single most commonly has occurred simultaneously with an increase in the average age at marriage. See Hajnal, "European Marriage Patterns in Perspective," pp. 101-03.

[69]1798 figures calculated from AESP, no. ordem 32, caixa 32, População, Capital, "Mapa dos habitantes que existem na cidade de São Paulo e seos destritos no anno de 1798." 1827 figures calculated from AESP, no. ordem 36, caixa 36, População, Capital, "Mappa geral dos habitantes que existem nesta imperial cidade de São Paulo e seus destritos de suas occupações, cazamentos annuaes, nascimentos e mortes, que haverão nas parochias respectivas em o anno de 1827." The methodology involved in the calculation of the singulate age at marriage is explained in Hajnal, "Age at Marriage and Proportions Marrying," Appendix III. The 1836 census tables include no statistics on marriage.

TABLE III:1

The Proportion Single (10-59) Male and Female Population of the District of the City of São Paulo in 1765, 1798, and 1827

Male				Female		
1765	1798	1827		1765	1798	1827
99.4	88.32	89.73	10-19	93.61	89.65	80.84
69.2	48.66	48.75	20-29	56.67	61.00	50.16
36.27	30.72	22.45	30-39	28.19	41.86	37.42
21.13	26.48	24.28	40-49	23.68	35.96	34.27
18.32	27.46	20.96	50-59	24.41	32.76	31.81

SOURCE: 1765 figures calculated directly from census figures. Data for 1798 calculation taken from AESP, no. ordem. 32, caixa 32, População, Capital, "Mapa dos habitantes que existem no cidade de São Paulo e seos distritos no anno de 1798." The 1827 calculation was based on AESP, no. ordem 36, caixa 36, População, Capital, "Mappa geral dos habitantes que existem nesta imperial cidade de Sm. Paulo, e seus distritos, de suas occupações, cazamentos annuaes, nascimentos e mortes, que haverão nas parochias respectivas en o anno de 1827."

NOTE: Marital status here is based on the actual category reported for the person in the census. Comparing these figures to data presented in later chapters on household organization in which co-residence in the consensual union pattern was defined as marriage, many of the couples so defined are included here in the single population.

improvements in communications, trade, and market conditions.[70] After 1808 the changes in nuptiality were quantitatively important. Similarly, improvements in the quality of life for the population as a whole had probably diminished.[71]

Within the city of São Paulo, the apparently contradictory trends of an increase in proportion single combined with a declining age at marriage requires explanation. An obvious factor was that migrants to the city in this period increasingly were unmarried and looking for nonagricultural employment. Compared to earlier periods in which the urban-rural nexus was fluid and relatively undifferentiated in terms of occupations and household structure, by 1802 agriculture had virtually disappeared from the city of São Paulo and domestic industry and commerce were the principal occupations (see Chapter V). These occupations were especially attractive to unmarried, landless, and unemployed persons, particularly women, who made up a large proportion of the urban population and increased the ranks of the unmarried. From 1765 to 1802 the considerable decline in number of men per 100 women beyond that experienced by the captaincy as a whole suggests that changes in the marriage market may partially account for the increase in proportion single in the city of São Paulo.

From the point of view of female marriageability it may be relevant that paulistas seem to have preferred marriages between young women and older men, with a range of five to twenty-five years difference in age, as indicated in the household censuses. The changes in the age/sex structure over the period 1765 to 1836 combined with these kind of marriage preferences meant that the marriageability of women over 20 declined substantially in 1802 as compared to 1765. By 1836, however, the market improved for women from 20-29 but worsened even more for those who were 30 or older. On the other hand, the marriageability of women 15 to 24 improved throughout the period, possibly constituting one reason for the decline in the age of marriage for women over the period.

Economic explanations for decline in the age of marriage or a change in proportions marrying are meaningful principally for males, even though fertility, the most important effect of such changes, is modified through a decline in the age of females marrying or the proportion of females who never marry. Since males are more directly linked to the public economic sphere than are most females, it is basically their behavior which is modified by economic change. For males, then, it is interesting to note that the decline in the age at marrying was much more significant than for females. It is probably reasonable to conclude that most of the increase in proportions single among females was due to the difference in the sex ratio, the marriage market and the effects of migration. For men the decline in age at marriage between 1765 and 1798 from 28.33 to 23.87 in the city of São Paulo may be partially attributable to the availability of women in highly preferred ages. The economic quickening after 1790 also undoubtedly encouraged an earlier marriage (for those marrying) in the capital as in the captaincy/province. The increase in the proportion never married is much less understandable for the male population of the city of São Paulo than for the female. In fact, the proportion single for males in the 1798 and 1827 distributions were lower than in 1765 for every age group up

---

[70]This interpretation follows the line of recent studies emphasizing conscious fertility limitation as a means of population control in pre-modern societies. Other studies following this kind of interpretation in terms of marriage and marital fertility are D.E. Eversley, "Population, Economy and Society," in Population in History; H.J. Habakkuk, "Family Structure"; K.H. Connell, The Population of Ireland, 1750-1845 (Oxford, 1950); Edward E. McKenna, "Marriage and Fertility in Postfamine Ireland: A Multivariate Analysis," American Journal of Sociology, 80, no. 3 (November, 1974): 688-705; the articles by John Hajnal already cited and others which there is not room to mention.

[71]See Chapters IV and V for a discussion of changes in the quality of life in São Paulo in the early nineteenth century.

to the 40-49 age groups (See Table III:1). Some of the apparent increase in proportions of the population never marrying may be related to the increasingly urban character of the capital city which generally tends to attract single population.

Other factors such as the scarcity of housing in the city by 1836, and the increasing cost of slaves may have had independent effects on the propensity to marry. Single males may have wanted marriage as a means to acquire either a residence or a woman to care for them. As geographical mobility increased, this kind of explanation becomes more plausible. Clearly no explanation can suit the situation of all the economic and social groups of the captaincy/province and/or the capital city in this period. Not only is it true that while living conditions for some were improving, circumstances and life chances for others were declining, but in addition, over 20 percent of the population never did marry legally. For this latter group, nuptiality has little meaning since many who never married did enter into informal unions and raise families. For these reasons, the data on fertility is probably a better indicator of popular response to economic change.

So far in this chapter most of the discussion is based on historical-ethnographical materials, legal documents, wills, and contemporary comment concerning the attitudes and practices of families in late colonial São Paulo. The rest of the chapter will be oriented toward quantitative questions concerning numbers of births, deaths, migrants, children born per women. The conclusions which derive from this discussion will not be in the form of specific numerical values or rates but rather will suggest that certain trends, patterns, or orders of magnitude in specific indexes existed in São Paulo during the period. Such conclusions may be unsatisfactory for demographers but they nevertheless tell us much about the imperatives of everyday life in eighteenth- and nineteenth-century São Paulo.

BIRTH, DEATH, AND MIGRATION

In the eighteenth and nineteenth centuries baptisms, deaths, and marriages were registered (when they were registered) with the parish priest until the beginning of civil registration in 1889.[72] In her study La Ville de São Paulo: Peuplement et Population for the period 1730 to 1850, Maria-Luiza Marcílio presented yearly aggregate statistics of the parish registers of the urban center of São Paulo (the Sé). The total number of births registered in the Sé averaged 136 per year from 1740 to 1759 and then began gradually to increase in the 1760s until the last decade of the eighteenth century when the average was 328 births a year. Marcílio's crude data indicate a decline in births from 1810 to 1818 averaging about 200 per year in that period. After 1818 the alterations in the administrative size of the district of São Paulo make the use of the data incomprehensible. These records are consistent with an increased birth rate and an increase in marriages in the late eighteenth century, followed in the early nineteenth century by a decline in both the birth rate and marriages.

The study of fertility based on the manuscript household censuses is problematical because of the under-enumeration of small children and faulty age reporting. Any index utilized automatically will include the effects of infant mortality. Therefore, I chose a measure of the surviving children of individual women in particular age groups. All mothers up to age 54 listed in each of the three censuses were tabulated according to age, number of resident children, color and marital status. By analyzing the data according to age groups, it is possible to segregate most of the effects of child mortality and children leaving home to the mothers over 39.

Table III:2 compares mother's ages 15-54 with female population in those ages for each census year. The percent of women in these ages who were mothers declined

[72] Ibid., p. 170. Maria-Luiza Marcílio, La ville de São Paulo (Rouen, 1968).

almost 10 percent from 1802 to 1836--a strong indication of a possible fertility decline. Mean number of children of grouped ages of mothers for the three census years is presented in Table III:3. Supplementary Table III:4 indicates the proportional distribution of mothers by five year age groups.

Table III:3 suggests that fertility changes included a period of increased fertility in the late eighteenth century over that of 1765 (indicated by the high fertility of women 25 and over in the 1802 data). The lower means for mothers under age 24 in 1802 may mean that a tendency to restrict births had begun sometime after 1795. The 1836 fertility figures are all consistently lower than those of both the 1765 and the 1802 distributions, in particular for mothers 25 and over. Significantly, in 1765 only 6.02 percent of the mothers were unmarried as compared to 34.3 percent unmarried in 1836. This increase in unmarried mothers probably had a negative effect on the mean number of children since illegitimate fertility is almost invariably lower than that of marital fertility.[73] That the increase in illegitimacy does not imply an increased number of fertile women is clearly demonstrated by the decline in women 15-54 who were mothers. Rather, the rise in unmarried mothers was a function of the increase in proportion of single females. These figures do not of course include children abandoned at birth.

The evidence from the household census analysis on fertility thus corroborates that of the trends indicated by data from the parish registers. Further, analysis of the age-sex pyramids over the period indicates a decline in the population under ten, evidence that also supports the hypothesis of a fertility decline in the early nineteenth century.

Contemporary information on mortality and the contribution of specific causes of death to the level of mortality in eighteenth- century São Paulo is also sparse and inconclusive. Epidemics were occasionally remarked upon in city council records or in government reports along with an infrequent mention of the number of deaths from a particular disease. Travelers also discussed health and disease from time to time. Parish records of deaths excluded children under seven until 1796 and it was only in 1798 that the cause of death was given in less than half the cases.

For the period 1799 to 1809 Marcílio recorded a total of 2,406 deaths, of which 1,036 specified cause. These 512 male deaths and 524 female deaths can be viewed as a kind of cross-section of the major causes of mortality at the time.[74] The major and preponderant cause of mortality for both sexes (622.2 out of 1,000) was infectious diseases. Most important among these were round worms (lombrigas), "fevers" (fievre intermittente), which included malaria, measles (sarampo), and smallpox (variola, bexigas). "Fevers" and smallpox killed more women than men, while the latter were more affected by measles and round worms.

Marcílio gives no indications of the age characteristics of those who died from infectious diseases. However, historically the incidence of death from infectious diseases has been highest for infants and young adults. Furthermore the decrease in this source of mortality through improvements in hygiene and nutrition has been the first step in the demographic transition in several societies, significantly improving the mortality of young age groups. It is likely that the deaths from infectious diseases in Marcílio's sample were underrepresented, in spite of being the most frequently listed. The deaths of infants and young children were not commonly reported in the eighteenth century, a factor which would tend to decrease the reported deaths by infectious diseases. In addition, the fact that as many female deaths as male deaths were registered in this

[73]See Judith Blake, "Family Instability and Reproductive Behavior in Jamaica," Current Research in Human Fertility, Milbank Memorial Fund (New York, 1955), pp. 39-40 for a discussion of the effect of illegitimacy on fertility in Jamaica.

[74]Marcílio, La ville de São Paulo, pp. 204-05.

TABLE III:2

Proportion of Mothers in the Female Population 15-54 in the City of São Paulo in 1765, 1802, and 1836

	1765	1802	1836
Females	1,134	2,283	2,470[1]
Mothers 15-54	490	992	838
Percent Mothers	43.2	43.45	33.93

[1]The parish of Brás was excluded from this calculation as the records were not available for the tabulation of mothers.

TABLE III:3

Mean Number of Children Per Mother by Five Year Age Groups (15-54) in the City of São Paulo in 1765, 1802, and 1836

	1765	1802	1836
15-19	1.56	1.45	1.38
20-24	2.43	2.17	1.99
25-29	2.55	3.58	2.65
30-34	3.95	3.84	2.87
35-39	4.61	4.69	3.54
40-44	3.61	4.40	3.56
45-49	4.65	3.91	3.21
50-54	3.10	4.08	2.94
15-54	(3.51)	(3.75)	(2.87)

SOURCE: Figures based on tabulation made of all mothers listed in the Census manuscripts for 1765, 1802, and 1836. The Parish of Brás was excluded from the 1836 calculation, because of being absent from the census collection.

TABLE III:4

Proportions of Mothers in Five Year Age Groups (15-54) in the City of São Paulo in 1765, 1802, and 1836

	1765	1802	1836
15-19	3.3	2.34	5.01
20-24	10.0	12.74	12.53
25-29	13.27	18.26	17.18
30-34	19.8	23.57	18.62
35-39	12.65	15.29	12.29
40-44	19.18	13.38	16.11
45-49	9.39	6.79	7.88
50-54	12.45	7.64	10.38
	100.00	100.00	100.00

Source: Census manuscripts for 1765, 1802, and 1836 (excluding Brás).

category, when male mortality was higher at younger ages also supports this hypothesis.[75]

The three next most important mortality categories listed by Marcílio were deaths related to the process of giving birth (154.4 out of 1,000), diseases of the digestive tract (95.6 out of 1,000), and skin diseases (69.5 out of 1,000).[76] The remainder (57.9 out of 1,000) was made up of tumors, diseases of the nervous system, diseases of the respiratory system, urinary and genital disorders, and violent deaths.

Syphilis was not included in the list as a cause of death, although it was known to be virulent and widespread in this period. Marcílio suggests that either the deaths from syphilis were undeclared, or else they were listed under another name such as cancer, abcesses, or itching sores.[77] Lycurgo Santos Filho considered syphilis to have been a major public concern of the late eighteenth and early nineteenth centuries. He mentioned that the colonial authorities sometimes took severe measures, expelling syphilitic persons from the towns or imprisoning them for indeterminate periods of time. Captain-general França e Horta recommended to all of the captains-major of the towns of São Paulo in 1808 that they take into custody and send in chains to the capital all of the "flirtatious," vagrant, or disrespectful young men, especially those who had venereal diseases.[78]

Malnutrition, also unrepresented in Marcílio's listing, must have been a major, if not the principal, cause of death in the period as it is today. Much of the incidence of infectious diseases was indirectly attributable to malnutrition. According to Lycurgo Santos Filho, goiter (papo or bocío), an enlargement of the thyroid due to lack of iodine, and general malnutrition was endemic among the poor population in nineteenth-century São Paulo.[79] Beriberi, caused by a deficiency of vitamin B, was also common in São Paulo in the eighteenth and nineteenth centuries.[80]

Incidence of death by age and sex is, again, virtually unknown for eighteenth- and nineteenth-century São Paulo. Marcílio made an estimate of infant mortality based on the aggregations she established for the period 1796 to 1809. Registered deaths of infants under one year of age were 239 per 1,000 births.[81] A separate estimate, based on a unique document listing deaths by age in 1798, suggests an infant mortality rate of 288

---

[75]Female infanticide would also explain this equivalence though I have found no concrete evidence that this practice was common in the eighteenth century.

[76]Dropsy (hidropsia) was the most numerous cause of death among diseases of the digestive tract. Lycurgo Santos Filho has suggested that the so-called "hidropsia" was really a liver problem. História da medicina no Brasil (São Paulo, 1947), II, p. 159. Of the deaths in the digestive category, almost 62 percent were female. Skin diseases included boils or abcesses (apostema), scabies or itching sores (sarnas), gangrene (féridas engangrenadas), and leprosy (mal de São Lazaro).

[77]Marcílio, La ville de São Paulo, p. 205.

[78]Santos Filho, História da medicina, II, pp. 84-87.

[79]Ibid., p. 104.

[80]Ibid., p. 122.

[81]Marcílio, La ville de São Paulo, p. 200.

per 1,000.[82] The two estimates are similar enough to be able to conclude that the rate of infant mortality was well over two hundred deaths in the first year of life per thousand births.

Beyond the preceding general considerations of mortality, the further issues of exceptional mortality levels in times of epidemics or famines must be considered in terms of effects on age-sex structure and rate of growth.

Contemporary accounts and city council records of the eighteenth century frequently mention cases and outbreaks of smallpox, leprosy, and yellow fever during the eighteenth century.[83] In the years 1720, 1724, 1726, 1730, 1731, 1737, 1744, 1746, 1749, 1762, 1768, 1770, 1775, 1777, 1780, 1784, 1785, 1790, 1798, and 1808 epidemics of uncertain proportions are known to have visited the community of São Paulo, though historians seem to agree that these were less destructive to the São Paulo population than were epidemics in other parts of Brazil. Buarque de Holanda points out the fact that epidemics were most commonly introduced by newly arrived slaves and that the latter were less often sent directly to São Paulo.[84]

Numbers of deaths were seldom mentioned, though Captain-General Bernardo de Lorena did specify that more than six hundred deaths occurred from smallpox in the epidemic of 1798.[85] The epidemic years of 1768, 1780, and 1798 are most perceptible in Marcílio's mortality curve, so that the "six hundred," which could not have exceeded 15 percent of the population, may have been unusually high, even for an epidemic. As Marcílio concludes in a later work, "not one epidemic was catastrophic for the population of the city (São Paulo) in the entire century from 1750 to 1850."[86] She further argues that epidemics did not cause sufficient numbers of deaths to alter the rate of growth.[87]

There appears to be no agreement on the importance of famine as a cause of death in eighteenth-century São Paulo. Marcílio believes that famine was an insignificant cause of death prior to 1850. Sérgio Buarque de Holanda, on the other hand, hypothesized that famines as a result of crop failures, insects, climate, and isolated circumstances probably did have a limiting effect on the rate of growth of São Paulo throughout the colonial period.[88] Concrete data related to this problem is lacking. If, however, we accept Marcílio's aggregative data on mortality for the period (1730-1850), it appears that whatever the causes of mortality, they were fairly regular or constant, and not catastrophic. Possibly the improvements in transportation may have resulted in lower mortality related to starvation or malnutrition after 1780.

---

[82]Ibid., The 1798 age distribution of deaths can be found in AESP, no. ordem 32, caixa 32, "Mappa dos nacimentos, mortos e cazamentos anuais da cidade de São Paulo e seos destrictos no anno de 1798."

[83]For a detailed account on epidemics see Affonso de Escragnolle Taunay, História da cidade de São Paulo no séculio xviii (Sáo Paulo, 1949), II, no. 2:237-45. Other sources are ACMSP; Marcílio, La ville de São Paulo, p. 166; and Sérgio Buarque de Holanda, "Movimentos da população em São Paulo no século xviii," Revista do Instituto de Estudos Brasileiros, No. 1 (1966), pp. 68-78.

[84]Buarque de Holanda, "Movimentos da população," p. 74.

[85]Taunay, História, II, no. 2:237.

[86]Maria-Luiza Marcílio, "Crescimento demográfico," p. 128.

[87]Ibid.

[88]Buarque de Holanda, "Movimentos da população," pp. 78-79.

Marcílio's data on numbers of burials registered from 1765 to 1850 indicate that registered burials increased from about 50 per year in 1765 to about 300 per year in 1800 and declined to about 200 per year by 1805, maintaining that level until 1850. Baptisms exceeded burials by approximately 100 per year by 1775; by 1800 the margin had decreased to about 25 and from about 1810 to 1850 burials usually exceeded the number of baptisms.[89] Marcílio suggests that this anomaly--since São Paulo was growing from 1810 to 1850--can perhaps be accounted for by persons registering burials in the principal cathedral of São Paulo--the Sé--even when they were living in other areas. That explanation would only make sense if those who registered burials at the main cathedral did not, also, register baptisms there. The comparison of the baptism and burial records emphasizes the need to rely on indirect methods for estimates of vital rates for São Paulo in this period. A quasi-stable population model will be applied for this purpose, following the discussion of migration.

Migration has already entered considerably into our discussion of the economic history of São Paulo in the colonial period. The exodus of a large proportion of the population into the sertão and in most cases their return within two or three years was a constant pattern throughout the seventeenth and eighteenth centuries.[90] Judging from the literature of the period, there were no unusual migrations in the São Paulo region between 1765 and 1836. Furthermore, an analysis of data on the origins of persons registering for marriage in the parish of the Sé revealed little difference in the distribution of places of birth of those registering between the period 1730-1739 as opposed to 1780-1809. The changes encountered tend to support the idea that a larger proportion of the population was born closer to the city of São Paulo in the later period.[91]

The importance of immigrant population within the city can be shown through the 1802 census data (Table III:5). Unfortunately change over time cannot be estimated because the other censuses utilized did not provide precise information on origin. Over eighty percent of the free population was born within the district of the city of São Paulo, and over ninety percent was born within the captaincy. Column two, on place of birth of heads of household, demonstrates that migrants from other parts of the captaincy and Portuguese immigrants were particularly conspicuous in the adult population. In effect, migration was a factor in the demographic development of São Paulo since the sixteenth century. For the purposes of this analysis, migration will be treated as a constant, with full knowledge of the weakness of that assumption.

A final factor which must be considered in this section is that of the demographic effects of war efforts and related issues from about 1752 to 1777, and again in 1808, 1814, and 1817. While the entire period was not by any means one of ongoing conflict, the climate of war and militarism was consistently strong in São Paulo, especially after 1762.

War was an important consideration in the restoration of the captaincy of São Paulo in 1765 as is very clear from the correspondence of the captains-general. More

[89]Marcílio, La ville de São Paulo, pp. 162-72.

[90]Buarque de Holanda, "Movimentos da população," pp. 66-68.

[91]The most important changes for the make-up of the groom population in the period 1730-1779 as opposed to 1780-1809 are the following: First of all 18.69 percent were Portuguese-born in the earlier period as compared to only 5.49 percent in the later period. Secondly, the percentage of grooms who originated from villages within 100 kilometers of the district of São Paulo increased from 12.98 to 18.72 from the first to the second period. Marrying males native to the district of São Paulo increased as a proportion of total grooms from 58 to 64 percent. Marcílio, La ville de São Paulo, Tableau 34 provided the raw data for these calculations.

than one historian has considered conscription to be an important depopulating factor in São Paulo in the 1760s and '70s.[92] Nevertheless, neither the São Paulo urban militia nor the auxiliary troops were utilized in the war effort. A local group organized by a local fazendeiro called the Legion of Royal Volunteers did belatedly join the war in 1777. In all, Marcílio estimated that only five percent of the population of the captaincy were ever involved in the war efforts of the period 1762-1777.[93] However, it may be that secondary factors such as the desire to avoid the draft resulted in the exodus of a certain proportion of adult males from the area. The decline in the already low sex ratio from 1765 to 1802 provides support for this hypothesis. Furthermore, contemporary opinion in the early nineteenth century also apparently blamed the fear of conscription for the labor shortage in the captaincy of São Paulo at that time.[94]

Age-sex population pyramids based on the censuses of 1765, 1802, and 1836 provide another basis for the demographic study of São Paulo. The quasi-stable population model--as developed by Lotka and modified by Coale, depends upon a constant birth rate and either constant mortality or a decline in mortality which does not affect age distribution.[95] A usual third condition is that of no migration, but Coale has demonstrated that the analysis is feasible for an open population as long as net migration rates are constant at each age.[96] In such a case a combined decrement for migration and mortality replaces that for mortality alone. This estimation method is one of approximation with multiple possibilities for error, and therefore should be viewed as establishing an "order of magnitude" estimate, rather than anything more precise. The

[92]Paulo Prado da Silva, "A Decadencia," in Paulística (Rio de Janeiro, 1934) and Caio Jardím, "São Paulo no século xviii," Revista do Arquivo Municipal, XLI, pp. 149-80 are two historians who emphasize this factor.

[93]Marcílio, "Crescimento demográfico," p. 131.

[94]J.F. de Almeida Prado, D. Joao VI e o início da classe dirigente do Brasil, 1818-1889 (São Paulo, 1968), p. 41. M.F.R. de Andrada, "Jornais das viagens pela capitania de São Paulo," RIHGB, XLV (1882), pp. 5-47.

[95]Much has been written on the use of indirect techniques for estimating basic fertility and mortality rates. A few of the more important are the following: Ansley J. Coale, "How the Age Distribution of a Human Population is Determined," Cold Springs Harbor Symposia on Quantitative Biology, XXII (1957), pp. 83-89; Ansley J. Coale and Paul Demeny, Regional Model Life Tables and Stable Populations (Princeton, 1966); Ansley J. Coale, Methods of Estimating Basic Demographic Measures from Incomplete Data, United Nations Organization, Manuals on Methods of Estimating Populations, ST/SOA/Series A/42 (New York, 1962); W. Brass, "Methods of Obtaining Basic Demographic Measures where Data are Lacking or Defective," World Population Conference, 1965 (New York, U.N. Organization, 1967).

[96]See Coale, Methods. Alse see Peter R. Cox, Demography (Cambridge, 1970), pp. 287-88, which discusses the "open population" variation of the Lotka analysis.

TABLE III:5

Place of Birth of the Free Population of the City of São Paulo, and of the Heads of Households of the City of São Paulo, in 1802

Place of Birth	Percent Free Pop.	Percent Heads H.
District of City of São Paulo	81.7	57.3
Captaincy of São Paulo	11.8	26.4
Minas Gerais	3.0	4.3
Rio de Janeiro	.7	1.8
Bahia	.5	.5
Portugal	1.9	7.5
Spain, Italy	.5	.7
Africa[1]	--	1.5
TOTAL	100.0	100.0

[1]There were 23 slaves who were also heads of households.

SOURCE: AESP, Maços de população, Capital, 1802.

degree of possible error is increased according to the aberrations of the actual population from the conditions inherent to the model.

The absolutely necessary assumption that the population have a constant birth rate is quite safe in utilizing the method for a population in which high mortality conditions are known to have existed. Even should a short-term fertility increase have occurred, the high rate of infant mortality along with other balancing factors would probably have eliminated any possible modification in the age structure. Only an increase in fertility which occurs as a secondary effect of a decline in mortality is likely to effect a change in the age structure, which is the critical factor for both long-term fertility and long-term mortality considerations.[97] Evidence that mortality in eighteenth-century São Paulo was high is strong, so that the fertility assumption appears reasonable.

The assumption that any decline in mortality would occur in such a way as not to affect the age structure is more problematical. Depending upon the reason for a given mortality decline, the age structure may or may not be uniformly affected. Improvements in nutrition, for example, would improve mortality principally for infants and young children, by reducing susceptibility to infectious diseases.[98] The migration assumption (which essentially includes migration in the age-specific mortality decrements) is even more risky, since migration depends upon circumstances and individual preferences, while death is usually externally determined by physiological factors. In effect, although the calculation of vital rates directly is unsatisfactory in this period, the use of a quasi-stable model population for this purpose will also include some margin of error. In spite of drawbacks, the latter technique promises a more valid estimate than the direct approach.

Graphs III:2, III:3, and III:4 present the age-sex distribution for the free population of the urban and rural bairros of the city of São Paulo in 1765, 1802, and 1836.[99] The three population pyramids are strikingly similar. Although there were modifications over time, it is clear both from inspection and testing that the pyramids come from the same population.[100] Given the rate of growth, average age and the proportion between ages 15 and 44, the choice of possible model populations was highly

---

[97]Thomas McKeown and R.G. Brown, "Medical Evidence Related to English Population Changes in the Eighteenth Century," Population in History (Chicago, 1965), pp. 294-95 discusses this question at length.

[98]Ibid., pp. 304-06.

[99]The 1765 age distribution was smoothed from an initial distribution of five year age groups through the use of a weighted three year moving average. The 1802 distribution was smoothed from an initial single-year age distribution through the use of a weighted five year moving average. The 1836 distribution was taken as it stood from the data presented in Daniel P. Muller, Ensaio d'um quadro estatístico da província de São Paulo (São Paulo, 1923).

[100]The chi-square test of goodness of fit was used to determine the correspondence of the São Paulo data to general demographic patterns of normal populations and to the selected model populations. The expected values used in the test were those of the stable population models. These latter were chosen on the basis of average age, over-all age structure, growth rate, and a life expectancy below 27 years. Life expectancy was based on Eduardo Arriaga's estimate of E= 27.08 for males and 27.61 for females in 1879. It should be pointed out that changes in E make little difference in age-sex structure as long as the effects of declining mortality are uniform for all age groups. See Eduardo Arriaga, New Life Tables for Latin American Populations in the Nineteenth and Twentieth Centuries, Population Monograph Series No. 3 (Berkeley, 1968), pp. 29-30.

restricted and the difference between the major characteristics of reasonable choices was minimal. Tables III:6 and III:7 provide observed major characteristics of the three censuses and Tables III:6.1 and III:7.1 the major characteristics of the model populations selected, indicating the range in terms of possible vital rates.

The best fit for the free male populations was the North group of model populations. Mortality Level I was clearly indicated for the 1765 census at a five percent growth rate. The choices for the 1802 and the 1836 pyramids were less obvious. Mortality Level II at five percent growth rate provides a slightly better fit for the 1802 distribution while Mortality Level I at five percent is somewhat closer for 1836. It seems safe to conclude that the male population had vital rates well above 50 per thousand throughout the period, with perhaps some decline in both rates by 1802. Certainly no improvement in mortality occurred from 1802 to 1836 and there may have been a return to the earlier and higher mortality rates of 1765 in the early nineteenth century. Effects of migration are included in mortality rates and could, therefore, contort the results. Lessened out-migration might have given the effect of improved mortality in 1802. While a change in migration patterns could have possibly influenced the results for the 1802 distribution, it would not account for the difference between 1802 and 1836.

The West group of stable populations corresponded best to the observed female populations. In general the fit was closer for the female populations, probably because of lesser effects of migration as compared with the males. The "best fit" model populations for the three census distributions were West Mortality Level I at five percent growth rate for 1765, West Mortality Level II at five percent for 1802, and Mortality Level II at zero percent growth rate for 1836 (see Table III:7.1). The results of this analysis suggest vital rates of about 50 per thousand in 1765, the classic ancién regime population with a very young age structure. Mortality declined from approximately 51 deaths per thousand in 1765 to about 45 deaths per thousand in 1802.[101] No mortality decline occurred from 1802 to 1836 but fertility may have decreased from 50 births per thousand in 1802 to about 45 births per thousand in 1836. The hypothesis of a fertility change is supported by age specific data on mean children per mother to be presented in the final section of this chapter.

[101]Marcílio, "Crescimento demográfico," p. 150 also estimated a crude birth rate of above 50 per thousand for the captaincy/province of São Paulo in the period 1798 to 1836 based on the Coale-Demeny stable population models. Her estimate of the crude death rate as 23 per thousand in 1798 and 29.5 per thousand in 1836 seems unlikely based on my analysis and on Eduardo Arriaga's estimate of 42 per thousand for Brazil as a whole in 1872. Nevertheless, on the basis of this study I would concur that the direction of the mortality rate from 1798 to 1836 was probably positive.

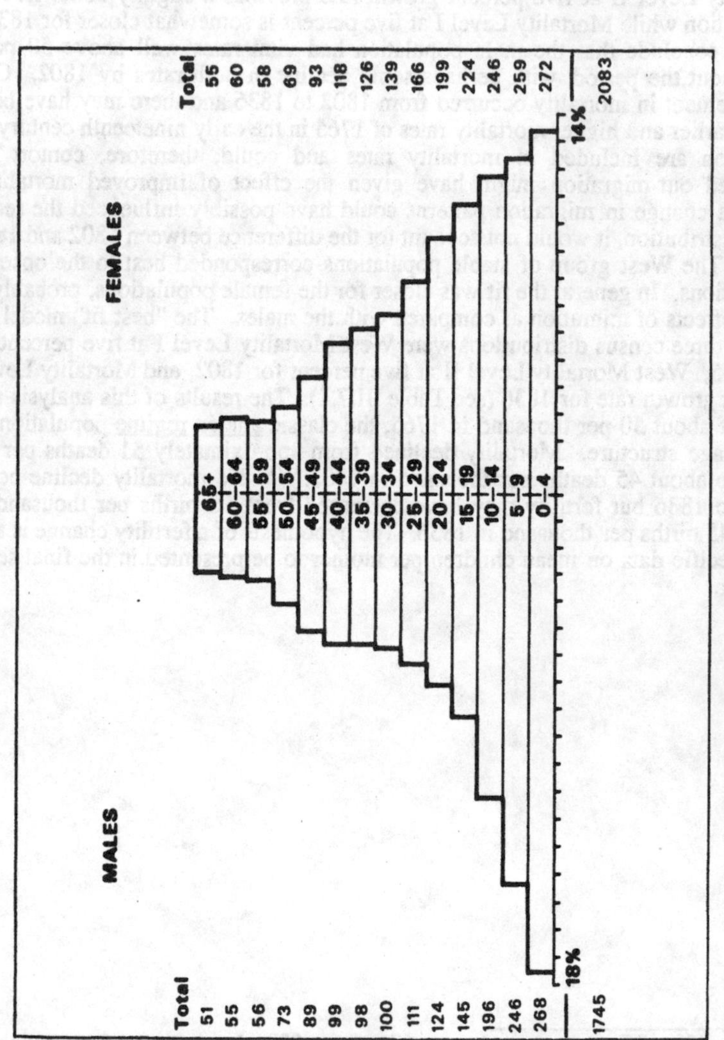

Graph III:2 Age-Sex Distribution of the Free Population of the City of São Paulo in 1765

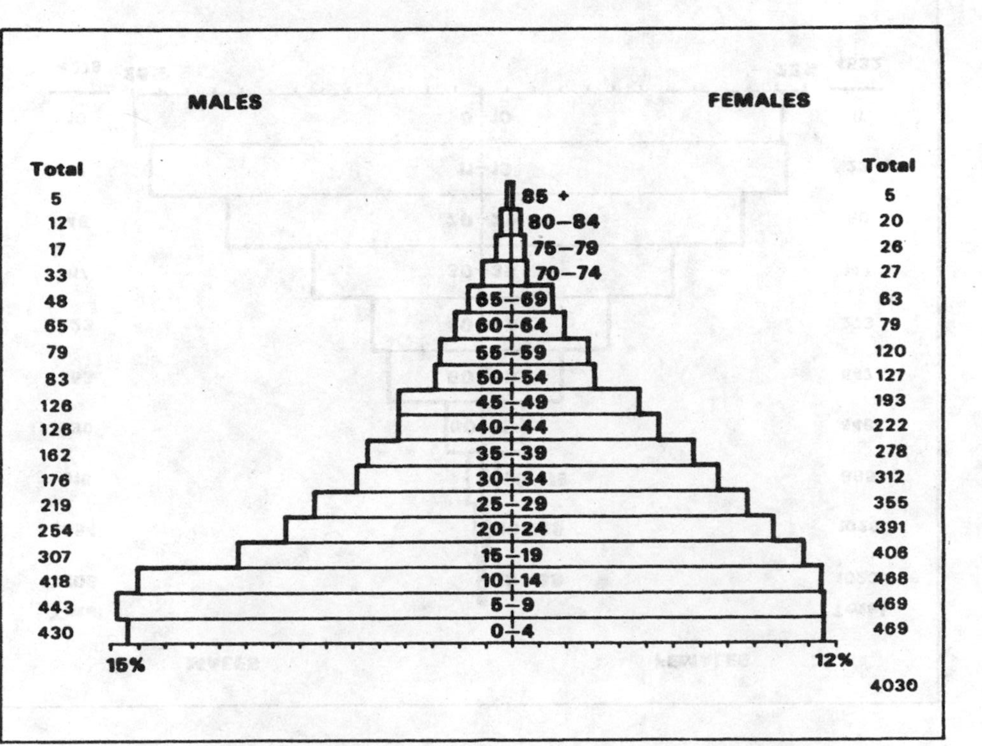

Graph III:3 Age-Sex Distribution of the Free Population of the City of São Paulo in 1802

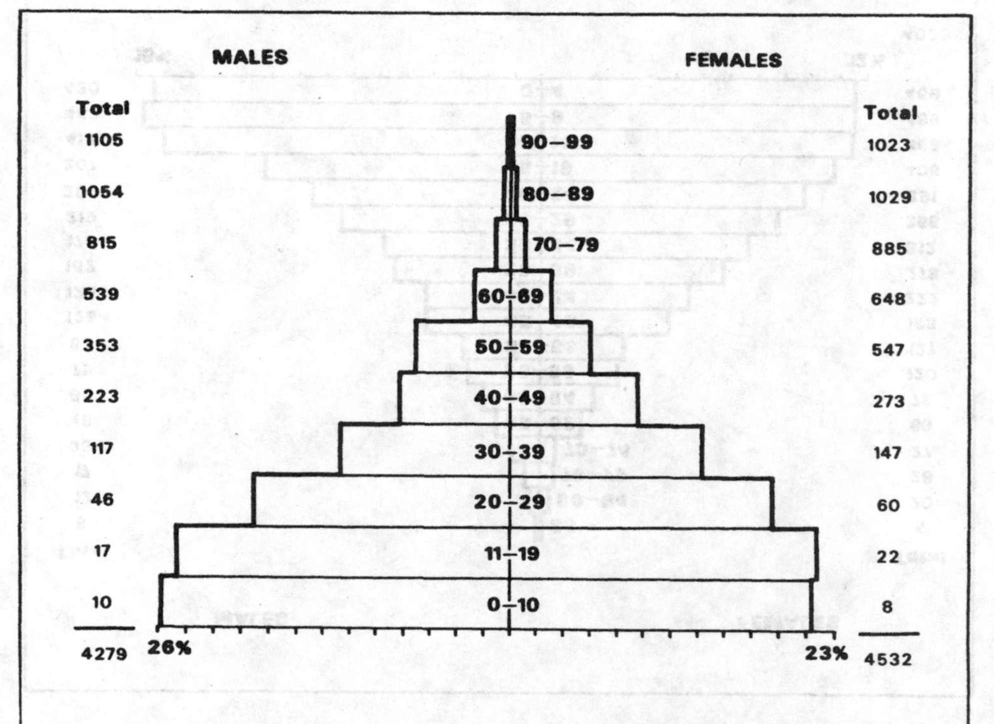

Graph III: 4 Age-Sex Distribution of the Free Population of the City of São Paulo in 1836

Source: Daniel Muller, <u>São Paulo em 1836</u> (São Paulo, 1923)

TABLE III:6

Major Population Characteristics of the Free Male Population of the City of São Paulo in 1765, 1802, and 1836

	1765	1802	1836
Average Age	22.93	23.2	23.87
Proportion 15-44	38.93	41.44	47.15
Dependency Ratio[1]	.94	.96	.70

[1]Dependency Ratio is the sum of the population 0-14 plus population 60 and over, divided by population 15-59.

SOURCE: Calculated from the smoothed population distributions presented in Graphs III:1, III:2, and III:3.

TABLE III:6.1

Major Population Characteristics of Male (North) Stable Population Models Selected for São Paulo City Estimates for 1765, 1802, and 1836

	R = 5 Mortality I	R = 5 Mortality II
Crude Birth Rate	64.16	56.72
Crude Death Rate	59.16	51.72
G.R.R. (27)	3.96	3.49
Average Age	22.93	23.80
Proportion 15-44	45.13	45.44
Dependency Ratio	.81	.78
Ave. Age Death	14.99	17.06
Ave. Age Death Over 5	34.74	38.42

SOURCE: Ansley J. Coale and Paul Demeny, Regional Model Life Tables and Stable Populations (Princeton, 1966).

TABLE III:7

Major Population Characteristics of the Free Female Population of the City of São Paulo in 1765, 1802, and 1836

	1765	1802	1836
Average Age	24.77	25.35	25.75
Proportion 15-44	46.46	48.71	48.83
Dependency Ratio[1]	.74	.68	.68

[1]Dependency Ratio is the sum of the population 0-14 plus population 60 and over, divided by population 15-59.
SOURCE: Calculated from the smoothed population distribution presented in Graphs III:1, III:2, and III:3.

TABLE III:7.1

Major Population Characteristics of Female (West) Stable Population Models Selected for São Paulo City Estimates for 1765, 1802, and 1836

	R = 5 Mortality I	R = 5 Mortality II	R = 0 Mortality II
Crude Birth Rate	56.57	50.50	44.4
Crude Death Rate	51.57	45.40	44.44
G.R.R. (27)	3.45	3.09	2.71
Average Age	23.84	24.69	26.45
Proportion 15-44	45.56	45.71	46.35
Dependency Ratio	.78	.76	.69
Ave. Age Death	17.11	19.3	22.5
Ave. Age Death OVER 5	39.35	41.03	43.31

SOURCE: Ansley J. Coale and Paul Demeny, Regional Model Life Tables and Stable Populations (Princeton, 1966).

CONCLUSION

In late eighteenth-century São Paulo, the combination of the political importance of the clan structure, the extensive bilateral kinship system, the predominance of the domestic mode of production and an inheritance system which preserved property for the family of origin had an enormous impact on marriage customs and practices. Of course the impact varied substantially according to class and to the productive activity of the kindred involved. Nevertheless endogamy within politically or economically allied kindreds, neighborhoods bonded through ritual kinship and common labor activities, and marriage alliances within occupational groups such as merchants were common results of these circumstances.

Proportions marrying and age at marriage, on the other hand, varied more with circumstances and mode of production. The domestic mode of production common in São Paulo in 1765 demanded both male and female labor and either marriage or consensual union was predominantly the rule in that period. The decline of that mode with the development of an exchange economy by 1802 and the establishment of urban markets seems also to have meant the dissolution of many consensual unions leaving a large proportion of households headed by single mothers. By 1802 the proportion of both adult males and adult females who did not marry by age 40 had risen substantially. At the same time those who did marry in urban São Paulo married younger--probably in response to improved economic conditions for the commercial class.

The material on fertility provides strong evidence of a society in substantial tumult. The aggregate data from the parish records, the analysis of children per mother by age, and the changes in the age-sex pyramid all support the hypothesis that fertility increased in the late eighteenth century along with numbers of marriages, and then declined in the early nineteenth century. The decline in fertility in the early nineteenth century was coupled with a dramatic increase in illegitimate births and with numerous official complaints after 1806 of child abandonment. Although an analysis of parish baptismal registers of the Sé for the years 1800 to 1824 reveals that from 17 to 25 percent of baptisms were of abandoned children, contemporary estimates placed the proportion of abandonments at the unbelievable level of two out of three births. The establishment of the "wheel" (roda) of the Santa Casa de Misericórdia in 1824 was the institutional response to this difficult problem but it was well-known in the period that the majority of children left to the care of the city generally died within a short time.[102] Infanticide, increase in infant mortality, and a decline in fertility are all consistent with this evidence.

The increased number of households headed by single women in 1802 and 1836, the decline in marriage and proportions marrying, the decline in fertility, and the increase in child abandonment all lead us to ask what had become of the resilient kinship system and the significance of marriage and inheritance within that system. These are questions which can only be approached through a systematic analysis of the process of urbanization, occupational change, changes in household economy, and the fortunes of the elite.

[102]See Laima Mesgravis, A Santa Casa de Misericórdia de São Paulo (1599? - 1884) (São Paulo, 1974), pp. 171-73. Contemporary estimates were discussed in her "A roda de Santa Casa de São Paulo: a assistencia social aõs enjeitados no século xix" (paper presented at the I Congresso de História de São Paulo, Campinas, Universidade Catolica, July 1972). Governor Antonio Manoel de Mello Castro e Mendonça, "Memória economico-política da capitania de São Paulo," Anais do Museu Paulista, XV (1961), pp. 103-04 in 1800 spoke of illegitimate children as follows: "A falta de providencias a respeito daquellas innocentes cujo nascimento ás circumstancias de suas mays obriga occultar, he cauza não só de muitos infanticídios, que ordinariamente acontecem, mas também de ficar a sociedade privada do bem, que he rezultaria de os fazer educar, sendo muito poucos os que o má trato dos particulares, a cujas portas são lancados, deixa viver...."

IV
From Mud Houses to Town Houses: Rural-Urban Differentiation and Community Development in São Paulo: 1765, 1802, and 1836

The transformation from an essentially "subsistence" economy to one in which "exchange" is the distinguishing characteristic implies a division of labor in society so that exchanges can be profitably made. The division of labor has historically manifested itself in the appearance of urban centers--a progressive economic differentiation along spatial lines where one geographic area (that containing the local administrative buildings, the church, and the marketplace) becomes the city or urban area, and the rest (less densely settled, occupied with primary activities, especially agriculture) is the countryside or rural area.[1]

What has been called the "process of urbanization" can be viewed as the increasing economic differentiation of the community from the countryside, with a

---

[1]The idea of "urbanism" and the "city" encompasses a wide range of characteristics and theories in the literature of sociology. For the most part these ideas are associated with theories of economic development and modernization. Definitions of an urban population include those of Louis Wirth, "Urbanism as a Way of Life," American Journal of Sociology, 44 (July 1938), pp. 1-24; Ralph E. Turner, "The Industrial City: Center of Cultural Change," in Caroline Ware, ed., The Cultural Approach to History, pp. 228-42; Kingsley Davis, "The Urbanization of the Human Population," Cities (New York, 1965), pp. 3-24; Bert F. Hoselitz, "The Role of Urbanization in Economic Development: Some International Comparisons," in R. Turner, ed., India's Urban Future (Berkeley, 1962), pp. 157-81, as well as many others. The most common and generally accepted of the criteria for urbanism has been that of size, both because of the apparent market requirements implicit in a division of labor and because of the ease in measurement. See Eduardo E. Arriaga, "A New Approach to the Measurements of Urbanization," Economic Development and Cultural Change, 18, no. 2 (January, 1970):206-18 for a definition and discussion of this method.

parallel development of inter-dependence between the "urban" and "rural" areas.[2] The way in which and the reasons why this differentiation should take place varies with the unique historical and ecological circumstances of the area.[3]

Many Latin Americanists feel that dependency--political, economic, and social effects within Latin America resulting from incursions of external advanced economies--explains the characteristics of urbanization in Latin America which differ from European or North American experience. However, a few scholars are now suggesting that these differences must be looked at in terms of the internal development of productive forces, and the resolution of contradictions between conflicting modes of production and conflicting political structures.[4] For São Paulo even in the late twentieth century Richard Morse wrote, ". . . the whole of urban society is permeated with vigorous survivals from the agro-commercial regime of the past (status ascription, hierarchical patterns of deference, . . . clientage systems, forms of primary-group organization) which have been reworked in answer to structural and psychological requirements of industrialism and

---

[2]In this study I am most interested in defining the process through which an area becomes "urban" as well as the social meanings of "urbanization." Paul Singer, Economia Política da Urbanização (São Paulo, 1973) emphasizes that the relations of mutual determination between city and countryside are created through the economic system and the political relations between classes. Richard Morse, "Trends and Patterns of Latin American Urbanization 1750-1920," Comparative Studies in Society and History 16, no. 4 (Sept. 1974):434 also points out that cities can only be analyzed in relation to the countryside and that, however important external economies are in general, the working out of social relations within an area is internally determined. Both Marvin Harris, Town and Country in Brazil (New York, 1956) and Nestor Goulart Reis Filho, A Evolução urbana do Brasil, 1500-1720 (São Paulo, 1968) have argued that Brazilian towns were created by a group interested in developing trade and a monetarized economy. Thus, there was strong motivation for the development of institutions which would foster these transformations.

[3]E.E. Lampard, "The History of Cities in the Economically Advanced Areas," Economic Development and Cultural Change III, no. 2 (January 1955):84, states, "Each city, in fact, serves a variety of social purposes and meets an array of human needs. Yet no two are exactly alike in every respect of their functions: each is a more or less unique product of its individual history and circumstances. A city is a concrete manifestation of general social forces; but its identity stems from being a particular accommodation to them. Each city population attempts to reconcile its needs and purposes with the specific limitations of its culture and environment; limitations of size, resources, position, site and technique."

[4]Dependency theorists include Andre Gunder Frank, Capitalism and Underdevelopment in Latin America (New York, 1969); Fernando Henrique Cardoso and E. Faletto, Dependencia e desenvolvimento na América Latina (Rio de Janeiro, 1970); Manual Castells, "La urbanización dependiente en América Latina," in Castells (ed.), Imperialismo y urbanización en América Latina (Barcelona, 1972), pp. 7-26; Samir Amin, Accumulation on a World Scale (New York, 1974); and Harold Brookfield, Interdependent Development (London, 1975). Recent criticisms of the uses of dependency theory in urban history include Singer, Economía Política, pp. 63-113; Marcos Kaplan, "La ciudad latinoamericana como factor de transmisión de control socioeconómico y político externo durante el período contemporaneo." Paper presented at the 39th Congress of Americanists, Aug. 2-9, 1970, Lima; Richard M. Morse, "Trends and Issues in Latin America Urban Research (Part II), 1965-1970," Latin American Research Review VI, no. 2 (Summer 1971):50-55 and Anibal Quijano, "The Urbanization of Latin American Society," in Jorge E. Hardoy (ed.), Urbanization in Latin America: Approaches and Issues (Garden City, 1975), pp. 109-53.

urbanization."[5] In this chapter I will describe the process of population and residential growth and the development of urban institutions and services for São Paulo in the years 1765, 1802, and 1836. In Chapter V I will analyze data on occupational differentiation and crop specialization over the period. The separate analysis of the urban center of São Paulo from the more distant and dispersed bairros, jurisdictionally still within the limits of São Paulo, will serve to emphasize that the process was general, taking place in both city and countryside, although the type of specialization was different.

The population of an urban community in a frontier area--a type of social structure as yet poorly studied--has a fluid relationship with the frontier and yet has astable identity as a base of social relations, supplies, and contact with the outer world for permanent as well as transient members of the community. The resident frontier community of São Paulo in 1765 produced subsistence goods but did not produce a marketable surplus; the "remedy" for poverty was looked for in the hidden gold and diamonds of the frontier itself. The adjustment to a normal population demonstrated in the 1802 and 1836 censuses involved a greater concentration of production within the community, an increase in population, especially through the migration of adult men into the community and its hinterland, and the construction of more permanent and better homes, public buildings, and roads. At the same time the transition from a subsistence to a market economy restructured both productive relationships within households and the composition of households themselves and was accompanied by a concentration of property which likewise had demographic repercussions. Clearly the coincidence of these two transitions was not accidental; the shift of acquisitive focus from the sertão to the profits of commercial agriculture as the locus of prosperity explains a great deal. For São Paulo the political, economic, and social transformations of this period can be viewed on a continuum with the frontier community, important for private and social relations and subsistence, at the beginning and the commercial town, centered around political organization, production, and productive relations, at the end. The process of these transformations and their interrelationships can be traced in the demographic patterns of the community itself.

Tables IV;1, IV:2, IV:3, and IV:4 describe the relative population growth of the district of São Paulo, the region of São Paulo (present-day São Paulo and Paraná) and of Brazil as a whole from 1772 until 1872. These tables will provide a general reference base for the following discussion of São Paulo's urban development from 1765 to 1836.

The sex ratio of the captaincy of São Paulo in 1765--the first year for which data are available--was 110 men for every 100 women (see Table IV:5), a high ratio relative to "normal" populations but not high for a frontier area. The sex ratio current in the city of São Paulo in the same year was significantly lower--82 men for every 100 women. This "low" sex ratio can be understood in terms of the tendency for paulista women to maintain a farm producing basic crops in the village while the men went to the mines, herded cattle, and engaged in other migratory enterprises. In the period from 1765 to 1798 the sex ratio in the captaincy declined from 110.2 to the more "normal" level of 93.3, a change which reflected the transition from a population strongly affected by migration to one based primarily on natural increase.

---

[5]Richard Morse, "São Paulo: Case Study of a Latin American Metropolis," Latin American Urban Research I, eds. Francine F. Rabinovitz and Felicity M. Trueblood (Beverly Hills, 1971), p. 169.

TABLE IV:1

Relative Population Development of the São Paulo Region (Present-Day São Paulo and Paraná, and the whole of Brazil, From 1772 to 1872

Year	São Paulo	Brazil	Percent
1772	100,537	2,566,000	3.92
1778	124,825	2,770,000	4.50
1788	130,586	3,144,000	4.15
1798	162,345	3,569,000	4.55
1800	169,544	3,660,000	4.63
1808	196,206	4,051,000	4.84
1818	221,634	4,599,000	4.82
1822	244,405	4,838,000	5.05
1836	326,902	5,867,000	5.57
1854	480,608	7,711,000	6.23
1872	964,076	9,930,478	9.71

Source: Maria-Luiza Marcílio, "Crescimento demográfico," Tabela I. The population estimates for Brazil from 1772 to 1854 were made by Giorgio Mortara. Marcílio's figures for São Paulo from 1772 to 1836 are based upon the aggregate mapas of the original maços de população.

TABLE IV:2

The Population of the District of São Paulo as a Proportion of the Paulista Region (Present-Day São Paulo and Paraná) and Brazil as a Whole, From 1772 to 1872

Years	District S.P.	Percent Region	Percent Brazil
1772	21,272	21.15	.83
1798	21,304	13.44	.60
1822	24,311	9.95	.50
1836	21,933	6.70	.37
1872	31,385	3.75	.32

NOTE: Territorial changes in the size of the district of São Paulo account for the decline in population until 1836.

SOURCE: Figures for the district of São Paulo taken from Maria-Luiza Marcílio, La ville de São Paulo, p. 119. Base figures for the region of São Paulo and for Brazil as a whole are from Table 1.

TABLE IV:3

The Rate of Total Population Growth of the City of São Paulo, the District of São Paulo and the Captaincy/ Province of São Paulo from 1765 to 1920

Period	S. Paulo City	District S.P.	Region S.P.
1777 - 1802	2.0% (2.5% per yr. free pop.)	.06%[1]	1.2%[2]
1802 - 1836	.75% (1.01% per yr. free pop.)	.50% (1798-1822)	1.45% (1805-1818)
		.95% (1822-1827)	2.75% (1818-1836)
1836 - 1872	2.05%	--	2.65%
1872 - 1920	7.00%	--	3.6%

[1] 1727-1798
[2] 1776-1805

RATE OF GROWTH: The formula utilized for calculation of growth rates was $\underline{P} = (1+r)^n$ where P_1 is total population at Time 1, P_2 is total population at Time 2, n is the period between Time 1 and Time 2 and r is the rate of growth.

SOURCES: The population figures for the city of São Paulo for 1777, 1802, and 1836 were taken from the maços de população as described in Appendix IV:1. Total population figures were 4,409 in 1777, 7,260 in 1802, 9,391 in 1836, 19,337 in 1872, and 580,000 in 1920. The latter two figures were taken from the official census figures for equivalent bairros. For the district of São Paulo the 1772 and 1798 figures were derived from Marcílio, La ville de São Paulo, p. 119. The 1882 and 1827 figures were taken from district census mapas produced in those years and found in AESP, caixa 36, no. ordem 36, população, capital. For the district, the total population figures were 21,272 in 1772, 21,304 in 1798, 24,311 in 1822, 25,466 in 1827, and 31,385 in 1836. After 1836, the city of São Paulo and the district of São Paulo (present-day São Paulo and Paraná) the figures for 1776, 1805, and 1818 were found in Alice Canabrava, "A repartição da terra na capitania de São Paulo, 1818," Estudos Economicas II, no. 6 (1972):77-130.

TABLE IV:4

Age Distribution by Sex of the Free Population of the City of São Paulo in 1765, 1802, and 1836

Male				Female		
1765	1802	1836		1765	1802	1836
31.8	29.06	25.82	(0- 9)	25.83	23.3	22.57
19.5	24.13	24.63	(10-19)	22.45	21.71	22.7
13.4	15.76	19.05	(20-29)	17.44	18.5	19.53
11.3	11.27	12.6	(30-39)	12.66	14.63	14.3
10.7	8.4	8.25	(40-49)	10.08	10.28	9.64
7.3	5.41	5.62	(50-59)	6.06	6.12	6.02
6.0	5.76	4.44	(60+)	5.48	5.48	5.23

SOURCE: Calculated from AESP, maços de população, 1765, 1802, and 1836.

TABLE IV:5

Sex Ratio of the Free and Slave Populations of the Captaincy/Province and the City of São Paulo in 1765, 1802, and 1836

	São Paulo City		Captaincy/Province	
	Free	Slave	Free	Slave
1765	83.77	--	110.2	--
1798	--	--	93.3	117.27
1802	74.52	100.2	--	--
1818	--	--	88.89	144.57
1828	--	--	91.55	154.05
1836	94.42	108.4	94.71	132.11

NOTE: Males per 100 females.

SOURCE: Captaincy/province figures taken from Maria-Luiza Marcílio, "Crescimento demográfico," p. 135. São Paulo city figures were calculated from AESP, Maços de população, 1765, 1802, and 1836.

TABLE IV:6

Dependency Ratio of the Free and Slave Populations of the City of São Paulo in 1765, 1802, and 1836

	Free	Slave
1765	50.06	--
1802	45.85	31.58
1836	37.54	46.19

NOTE: Dependent Population (0-10; 60+) per 100 persons of productive ages (11-59).

SOURCE: Calculated from AESP, Maços de população, 1765, 1802, and 1836.

The decline in the sex ratio in the city of São Paulo to 75 by 1802 can be interpreted as a continuation of a pattern in which women remained in the city while men migrated into the new settlement areas of the captaincy to claim lands. In the latter case, however, women were no longer maintaining farms for men to return to after their efforts in more risky enterprises. Rather, the women were left behind by men gone to establish themselves in commercial agricultural enterprises in the interior after which, perhaps, they would return to fetch their womenfolk. In addition, adult female migration from rural areas into the urban center of São Paulo was clearly a factor. Urban attraction for single and widowed women has been, historically and geographically, a fairly universal phenomenon. Domestic manufacture provided an opportunity for income based on a common source of female labor in the prior domestic mode of production. In urban São Paulo by 1802 many women produced textiles, household implements, flour, candy, or quilts for sale.

By 1836 the sex ratio for the captaincy was 94.7 while that of the city of São Paulo had increased to 94, in aggregate demographic terms becoming an altogether normal population.

At the same time, the dependency ratio (see Tables IV:6 and IV:4) improved due to a substantial decline in the proportion of the population under nine for both sexes. This change reflected the change of economic orientation of men from rural activities (i.e., slaving expeditions, mining, the sertão, war), some of which took them outside the captaincy/province of São Paulo. It also showed the new attraction of the city of São Paulo as a redistributive and political center as well as the site for the new Law Faculty opened in 1828. Not only native paulistas, but also many immigrants to the region from Portugal and other parts of Brazil who had participated in the rush to the mines, found in late eighteenth-century São Paulo worthwhile investment possibilities for their new fortunes. These immigrants undoubtedly contributed to the increase in the proportion of population in productive ages. Female out-migration may have also occurred because of the 50 percent decline in textile employment from 1802 to 1836. By 1836 the category of "washerwomen," the lowest paid of all listed urban employments, more than doubled as a proportion of employed, apparently providing alternative employment for erstwhile textile producers.

Age and sex characteristics of the slave population demonstrated a fairly radical transformation over the period in the captaincy/province of São Paulo (see Table IV:6). The sex ratio increased from 117.27 male slaves per hundred females in 1798 to 154.05 males per hundred females in 1828. The ratio of adult slaves 11-59 to dependent slave population (0-9, 60+) also increased dramatically over the period from 167 in 1798 to 232 adult slaves per 100 dependent slaves in 1828.[6] These changes were due to the increased importation of slaves for use in the sugar and coffee plantations. Slave imports always favored young adult males. For the city of São Paulo, the increase in the dependency ratio reflected the exportation of able-bodied adult slaves from the urban to the rural areas in that period, leaving the weak, the old, and the small children behind.

The history of the racial composition of the city of São Paulo is difficult to define up until the beginning of the nineteenth century. It seems clear that most of the slave population was Indian until the opening of the mines at the beginning of the eighteenth century when large numbers of African slaves were brought into the southeast. By the end of the eighteenth century the Indian element was largely indistinguishable from the rest of the free population.[7] Although color was an important social characteristic, the

---

[6]Marcílio, "Crescimento demográfico," p. 185.

[7]Marcílio, "Crescimento demográfico," p. 12 and Roger Bastide and Florestan Fernandes, Brancos e negros en São Paulo (São Paulo, 1959), p. 12.

designation of "índio" or even "mameluco" seldom appeared in the late eighteenth-century censuses.

According to an estimate based on the 1767 slave census, approximately fifty percent of the population of the city of São Paulo was made up of slaves in 1765, decreasing to forty-five percent by 1777, according to the census made in that year.[8] By 1802 the proportion of slaves in the city's population had declined to 34.9 and, by 1836, to 30.4 undoubtedly through migration of slaves into the rural sugar and coffee-growing lands. Figures on the captaincy/provincial population in the period indicated that slaves constituted 23 percent of the population in 1818 and 27 percent in 1836.[9] The increased proportion of slaves in the city of São Paulo in the eighteenth century can be explained by the greater prosperity of that area compared with the rest of the captaincy. The relatively undeveloped urban and market services in the eighteenth century resulted in slaves being as necessary to the household economy in the urban as in the rural milieu, particularly since the latter was based on subsistence production.

The mixed racial composition of the free population of the city seems to have developed from the beginning of the eighteenth century. The 1765 census only lists 3.32 percent pardo (brown or mulatto) and only 1.1 percent preto or negrão (black). Unfortunately, the reliability of this data is doubtful because 95.45 percent of the 1765 population were not classified by race, only non-white members being specified in this way. However, the 1802 census listed 29.32 percent as free pardos and 6.04 percent as free pretos. From 1802 until 1836 the proportion of whites in the free population remained the same as in 1802 but 30.98 percent were pardos and 4.37 percent were pretos.

The development of economic specialization in São Paulo is well-documented in the three household censuses of 1765, 1802, and 1836.[10] In 1765 subsistence production activities, and especially subsistence agriculture were predominant for both the urban core and the rural districts of São Paulo.[11] Probably even those paulistanos who listed another occupation continued to cultivate the land for basic supplies of beans and corn. The urban area was differentiated from the rural bairros in 1765 by administrative activities,

---

[8]The 1765 census did not include slaves, but the 1767 census of the slave population of the captaincy of São Paulo by parish lists approximately one slave for every free member of the parish of the Sé in 1765. The 1767 slave census is found in DI, XIX, p. 285 ff. AESP, no. ordem 31, caixa 31, "Lista geral de todo o povo desta cidade e seus subúrbios, pertenecentes a comandancia do capitão de ordenança da mesma Antonio Francisco de Sá," 31 dezembro 1777.

[9]Marcílio, "Crescimento demográfico," p. 184.

[10]"Recenseamento de 1765: Listas da gente que compreende a cid. de S. Paulo e todo o seo termo de que he Cap. Mor Manoel de Oliveira Cardoso," DI, LXII, pp. 7-256; AESP, TC, no. ordem 32, caixa 32, Maços de população, capital 1802; AESP, TI, no. ordem 37A, caixa 37A, Maços de população, capital 1836. See Appendix IV:1 for a detailed listing of the documents included.

[11]Agriculture was not listed as an occupation in São Paulo for 1765 but later censuses including the incomplete listing for 1767: DI, LXII, pp. 257-363, do indicate the prevalence of agriculture even within the urban center at that time. Other documents such as the papers of the Morgado de Matheus--Captain-General of the captaincy from 1765 to 1775--and the records of the city council clearly indicate the subsistence character of the economy. See DI, XXIII, pp. 1-10, and Sérgio Buarque de Holanda, "Movimentos da população em São Paulo no século xviii," Revista do Instituto de Estudos Brasileiros, I (1966), pp. 58-60.

the density of residences, and an occupational structure including 27.5 percent of heads of households in income-producing activities of a non-primary category. In the rural bairros less than one percent of heads of households were engaged in non-primary occupations. This economy of self-sufficiency and subsistence developed in isolated circumstances in which means of transport and roads passable by animals were lacking, trade was very slow, and the population was somewhat unstable. Those responding to commercial opportunities in connection with the mining economy after 1695, and the development of the cattle trade in Rio Grande do Sul after 1730, prudently continued to pursue subsistence activities on the side as a hedge against hard times. Not only were commercial and artisan activities insecure in the sense that earnings were extremely variable in a highly uncertain market, but basic commodities were often difficult to purchase within the community. No permanent marketplace existed in São Paulo before 1774. Most local merchants were peddlers (mascates or quintandeiras) who sold their goods from door to door. Surplus agricultural goods were usually sold along the roads leading into town. Scarcities of flour, meat, salt, corn, and foodstuffs in general were repeatedly commented upon in the debates of the city council in the 1760s. The captains-major of the outlying districts were ordered to see that farmers plant as much as possible and bring surplus produce to the city to sell.[12]

The period from 1767 to 1802 has often been viewed as one of decadence in the center-south of Brazil, principally because of the decline in gold production.[13] Nevertheless, it was a time of considerable commercial development, which was facilitated by basic improvements in transport and communications. It was also a time of population growth for the urban center of São Paulo as indicated by its two percent per year growth rate from 1777-1802. The reconstruction of the road to Santos, begun in 1780, and finally paved as far as Cubatão in 1792, had dramatic implications for the cost and speed of transport of products to port. Likewise the use of mule team transport, which began to be important after 1750, became the dominant mode of transport in the center-south after 1780, greatly facilitating commerce in general. The trade in the mules themselves also contributed to the volume of trade in this period. Mules sold at the Sorocaba fair were frequently brought to São Paulo and redistributed to the North and East and to the coast, along with other produce.[14]

---

[12]ACMSP, XIV, 3 de janeiro de 1763. Similar references can be found in ACMSP, XV, 5 de marco de 1766, 27 de janeiro 1768, 30 de janeiro 1768, 17 de janeiro 1770.

[13]Alice Canabrava, "Uma economia de decadência: os níveis de riqueza na capitania de São Paulo 1765/67," Revista Brasileira de Economia, XXVI, no. 4:122-23. Richard M. Morse, From Community to Metropolis: A Biography of São Paulo, Brazil (Gainesville, 1958), pp. 16-17. Celso Furtado, The Economic Growth of Brazil, translated by Ricardo W. de Aguiar and Eric Charles Drysdale (Berkeley and Los Angeles, 1965), p. 98 says, "With the exception of the Maranhão nucleus, the colonial economy underwent a period of serious depression in the last decades of the eighteenth century. In the gold region, the depression was particularly serious and was to last for the next fifty years. This decline was also indirectly to affect the southern cattle-breeding region, which had to cope with a prolonged period of internal difficulties.

[14]On the importance of the Feira de Sorocaba see Aluísio de Almeida, O tropeirismo e a feira de Sorocaba (Sorocaba, 1968). Alfredo Ellis, Jr., A economia paulista no século xviii (Sao Paulo, 1950), pp. 195-97 discusses the influence of the mule in the eighteenth and nineteenth centuries and the central location of the city of São Paulo in this configuration. See also Caio Prado, Jr., "O fator geográfico na formação e no desenvolvimento da cidade de São Paulo," in Evolução política do Brazil e outros estudos (São Paulo, 1969).

Captains-general after 1765 developed policies intended to promote direct trade with Portugal through the port of Santos. These policies stimulated the expansion of commercial agriculture as well as the development of Santos as a port and São Paulo as an entrepôt.[15] By 1797 sugar exports from Santos had reached 114,550 arrobas.[16] In addition to sugar, other produce exported through Santos, or redistributed through São Paulo included coffee, rice, cotton, tobacco, and some wheat.

By 1802 the importance of agriculture within the urban core of São Paulo had declined dramatically. Only in the newly developed area of Santa Efigênia was agriculture reported as a major activity by over 10 percent of households, and most of those were producing for commercial purposes.[17] Agriculture and stock raising continued to be pursued as a second occupation by 14 percent of urban households, and undoubtedly garden plots of corn and beans were cultivated by many others.[18] Economic differentiation had proceeded to the point where nine out of ten urban households could depend upon the marketplace for a significant proportion of basic commodities and services, and could specialize in specific productive activities for exchange purposes.

Roads improved greatly by 1802, but much produce was still damaged in bad weather and the stretch of the São Paulo-Santos road between Cubatão and Santos continued to be traversed by canoe.[19] São Paulo had yet to develop exports, and Santos still lacked satisfactory port facilities. The emphasis on Rio de Janeiro as the port from which cloth importers most commonly bought their goods demonstrates the relative economic advantage of dealing through Rio de Janeiro at this time.

Between 1802 and 1836 important changes had taken place in São Paulo. The road from Cubatão to Santos was completed and another road, passable by carts, was in the planning stages. The export market for sugar was booming and production had increased dramatically throughout the plateau.[20] The residence of the Portuguese court in Rio de Janeiro (1808-1821) and the "opening of the ports" in 1808, the preferential trade treaties with England in 1810 and 1827, the final separation of Brazil from Portugal in 1822, and the elimination of the personal power of Dom Pedro I in 1831 were all important political events with sometimes contrary commercial repercussions for the period. However, the absolute change in trade between 1802 and 1836 was that of

---

[15]See Chapter II on trade policies of the captains-general from 1765 to 1808.

[16]Maria Theresa Schorer Petrone, A lavoura canavieira em São Paulo (São Paulo, 1968), p. 152.

[17]See Table V:9 on the use of agriculture by bairro in São Paulo in 1802.

[18]See Table V:5 for an occupational distribution for São Paulo in 1802. Gilberto Freyre, Sobrados e mucambos (Rio de Janeiro, 1961), I, pp. 165-67 discusses the continuation of some subsistence gardening and animal raising in urban areas well into the nineteenth century.

[19]Luis Lisanti Filho, "Comércio e capitalismo: o Brazil e a Europa entre o fim do século xviii e o ínicio do século xix," Tese de Doutoramento do Departamento de História da Universidade de São Paulo (São Paulo, 1962), pp. 10-14 points out the terrible expenses incurred by merchants just to traverse this three kilometer stretch from Cubatão to Santos. From January 1800 to January 1801 the merchants spent 3,591,710 reis or 16.9 percent of the total value of that year's exports on transport between these two points.

[20]See Lisanti Filho, "Comércio e capitalismo" for a detailed study of Itú, Campinas, and Porto Feliz in this period. Also see Maria Petrone, A lavoura, pp. 152-78.

growth and invigoration.[21] The opening of the Law Academy in São Paulo in 1827 also had given new importance and brought a different kind of population into the city. Although the rate of population growth of the urban center slowed in the 1765-1836 period to .75 percent per year, the growth rate of the province increased substantially reaching 2.75 percent per year between 1818 and 1836.

The 1836 census analysis clearly indicates the continuing process of the social and economic differentiation of the urban from the rural areas of São Paulo. The urban area was increasingly focused on administrative activities, local mercantile and artisan activities, and incipient cottage industry. The rural area, on the other hand, had substantially substituted commercial agriculture for the earlier subsistence mode of production. The emphasis was on exchange as opposed to self-sufficiency.

Analysis of household composition in 1802 and 1836 reveals a highly significant increase in the proportion of non-related dependents or agregados in the household, particularly in the urban area where agregados increased from 4.8 percent in 1765 to 20.7 percent of membership of households in 1802 and 26.9 percent in 1836. The major reasons for this change are explicable in terms of the availability of land, occupational structure, income distribution, and cost of living in the period. In part, the heightened presence of the agregado was probably also associated with the declining proportion of households with slaves. The percentage of slaves in the population remained fairly stable but ownership was gradually concentrated in the hands of the commercial agriculturalists.[22] The value of the slave rose with the expansion of export agriculture and lower-income people sold their few slaves or did not replace old slaves who died. The agregado, usually a single or widowed person, occasionally a woman with small children, was happy to acquire a place to live in return for labor and contributions to the household economy. Although less servile, the agregado could replace the slave without having to be bought, and could be dispensed with should he or she not be an asset.

The increase in complex households within the urban center is also evidence that residence inside the city was becoming more attractive. Whereas a new marriage in the eighteenth-century implied a new household and usually a new clearing for a house and farm, the relative scarcity of land and the growing urban labor market in the first half of

---

[21]On the British influence in Brazilian trade see Alan K. Manchester, British Preeminence in Brazil: Its Rise and Decline (Chapel Hill, 1933) and Richard Graham, Britain and the Onset of Modernization in Brazil 1850-1914 (Cambridge, 1968). For the effects of these events in São Paulo, see Morse, From Community to Metropolis, pp. 45-77.

[22]See Table IV:2 on the changing proportion of households owning slaves in 1778, 1802, and 1836. Marcílio, "Crescimento demográfico," pp. 87 and 188-89 gives evidence for growth in the proportion of households with over forty slaves in the captaincy/province of São Paulo, while the proportion of slaves in the population remained fairly constant at about 30 percent.

the nineteenth century had a centripetal effect on residential patterns.[23] The subsistence level household economy was both less feasible and less attractive in the economic circumstances of mid-nineteenth century São Paulo than was the case three quarters of a century earlier.

The social and economic transformation of São Paulo in this period was reflected in the history of popular housing construction. In the last half of the eighteenth and the early nineteenth century popular housing was based on the expectation that residence would be temporary. Ubiquitous materials, available without cost, were utilized in construction. Most popular houses (casas têrreas) were made of wattle and daub (pau-a-pique)--a kind of wicker frame plastered with mud--and covered with a grass thatch. The floor was beaten earth. The house usually consisted of three rooms, including a living room (sala), a kitchen (cozinha), and a bedroom (cuarto), all without windows. Fireplaces built on three round stones to hold an earthen pot occupied different parts of the kitchen. Green wood, the major fuel, filled the rooms with smoke and was vented through the doors.[24] It was assumed that place of residence was temporary because of the prevailing swidden method of agriculture. Land was cleared by burning, and crops were cultivated in the ashes.[25] When the soil was exhausted, a new house and farm were marked out on virgin land and the process began anew.[26]

---

[23]The dominance of the small (less than six) nuclear family household in eighteenth and nineteenth century Brazil has been agreed upon by several scholars in recent studies. See the discussion in Marcílio, "Crescimento demográfico," pp. 176-80. She found that children normally formed their own households at marriage. See also Donald Pierson, Cruz das Almas (Rio de Janeiro, 1966), p. 261; Oracy Nogueira, Família e comunidade: um estudo sociológico de Itapetininga, São Paulo (Rio de Janeiro, 1962), I, p. 236; Emilio Willems, Cunha: tradição e transição (São Paulo, 1947); Lia F.G. Fukuí, "Parentesco e família entre sitiantes tradicionais," Tese de doutoramento em ciencias sociais na Universidade de São Paulo (São Paulo, 1972), p. 390. Evidence and discussion on the development of land values can be found in Antonieta de Paula Sousa, "Expansão da propriedade rural paulista" Anais do Nono Congresso Brásileiro de Geografia, III (1940), pp. 711-17. See also the very fine section in Marcílio, "Crescimento demográfico," pp. 284-88.

[24]John Mawe, Travels in the Interior of Brazil (London, 1812), pp. 70-75.

[25]The Morgado de Matheus described this method of agriculture (slash and burn) in a letter to the Conde de Oeyras on 23 December 1766, DI, XXIII, pp. 1-10. "As rossas fazem-se com muita facilidade; não hé mais que picar nos morros ás arvores todas de uma parte, e derrubar de alto as primeiras; estas precipitadas levão diante de si ás vezinhas, e humas depois das outras, e fica tudo razo. Secas em poucos dias, ataca-se-lhe o fogo e nas cinzas planta-se e nunca mais se lhe bole até vir a colheita; isto hé muito suave, colhem para si o que lhe basta, mas nada sobeja, de tal sorte que sendo-me precizos duzentos alqueires para huma expedição ocupeí toda a Comarca de Parnaiba, e foi necesário sucessivas deligencias para se ajuntarem as migalhas, quando nesse Reyno qualquer vigário pobre vende duzentos alqueiros, e em qualquer parte se acha; isto hé o que lhes renden as rossas."

[26]Sainte-Hilaire described how these precariously built houses would literally disintegrate around the residents, the latter moving their belongings from one side to the other as the rains began to penetrate the walls, until the house was utterly in ruins. Auguste de Sainte-Hilaire, Viagem a província de São Paulo (São Paulo, 1972), pp. 250-52.

The houses of the affluent were generally made of limestone or more frequently of taipa de pilão--either of which was strong enough to stand for centuries.[27] Such houses often had tiled roofs, doors, and windows with locks and, less commonly, flooring laid down in the formal living room. The lay-out followed a common plan, with slight modifications. In the front of the house was a section intended to separate the family from the outside world, or to allow persons outside the household to be entertained without their penetrating the actual living space of the home. Here the porch (alpêndre), chapel (capela), and the guest room (hóspedes) were situated. Beyond this area came the formal living room (sala), followed by the sleeping compartments along a corridor. Sometimes a less formal living room or veranda was located behind the sleeping compartments. In the back, often annexed to the house, was the kitchen, primitive toilet facilities, and sometimes the slave quarters. The size of the house varied from a minimum of about seven rooms, with four sleeping compartments, to about twelve rooms, with eight sleeping compartments, though there are nineteenth-century examples of houses with sixteen to twenty-eight sleeping compartments.[28]

The single-story house with the beaten earth floor (casa têrrea) was fairly universal in São Paulo, regardless of income level, up until the end of the eighteenth century. By 1772, according to Sainte-Hilaire, there were only six houses in the city of São Paulo with more than one floor.[29] The house of more than one story (sobrado) became common among wealthy households in the early nineteenth century. More labor and better materials began to be utilized in the sobrado while the casa têrrea, and especially the beaten-earth floor as such, came gradually to be associated with the poor.[30]

The upper story of the sobrado, which retained the floor plan of the traditional casa têrrea, became the actual family residence. The lower section of the house, with its less valued beaten earth floor, was reserved for slaves, horses, carriages, or used as a store. The 1836 census lists indicate that these lower rooms were often rented out to artisans and shopkeepers, or even to poor families. Although the sobrado was more common in the urban area, wealthy fazendeiros of the rural bairros also adopted the sobrado as the preferred type of housing in the nineteenth century. Finally, towards the middle of the nineteenth century, the one- or two-story house with a raised floor (casa de porão alto) began to appear in the urban areas for purely residential use. This latter type of house had no rooms with beaten earth floors and could be devoted entirely to family use. The sobrado and the casa têrrea of taipa, as well as the thatched pau-a-pique huts, continued to be used and constructed alongside the new casa de porão alto in the nineteenth century. In essence the divergence of the rural economy from that of the city in the period of 1765 to 1836, as well as the greatly increased social and economic

---

[27]For taipa de pilão, parallel supports of wicker of wood were filled with moistened and tightly rammed earth, which, hardened by the sun, would stand for centuries.

[28]The size of the house was distinguished in property listings by number of lanços which really referred to groups of rooms on one or two sides of a corridor or, in a house of three lanços, rooms between and on both sides of two corridors. Oracy Nogueira suggests a median of 8.5 rooms for houses of property owners (as distinguished from agregados or tenants) in 1952. Other evidence is found in Luis Saia, "Notas sobre a arquitetura rural paulista do segundo século," Habitação 1958, #1, pp. 45-50, reprinted from Revista do Serviço do Patrimônio Histórico e Artístico Nacional 8 (1944), pp. 211-75; Alcântara Machado, Vida e morte do bandeirante (São Paulo, 1930), pp. 33-54; Nestor Goulart Reis Filho, Quadro da arquitetura no Brásil (São Paulo, 1970), pp. 21-42.

[29]Sainte-Hilaire, Viagem, p. 152.

[30]Reis Filho, Quadro da arquitetura, p. 28, pp. 37-38.

distance between the upper and middle income households and those of the poor, were concretely manifested in terms of a multiplication of types of construction, sizes, and values of houses. The pace of differentiation in terms of individual income and types of occupations as well as social overhead capital was paralleled in the residential landscape of the city and countryside of São Paulo over this period.

URBAN DIFFERENTIATION: 1765, 1802, AND 1836

The only existing map of the community of São Paulo before 1810 is that made by Affonso A. de Freitas, presumably developed from literary evidence, of São Paulo de Piratininga in 1560 (see Map IV:1).[31] The urban space of São Paulo in 1560 was entirely contained between the small rivers known as the Anhangabaú and the Tamanduatié.[32] There were then about one hundred households and a free population of around 450 people. The famous triangle of streets connecting the largo of São Bento (then the residence of Tebirica), the Igreja do Colégio, the Igreja Matriz (the Sé), and the largo de São Francisco (then the Casa do Senado) had already been laid out as the primary vertices of the city. These streets were the internal continuations of the major roads leading to São Paulo. Present-day rua São Bento was the caminho pra volta grande to the North, and to the South it became the legendary caminho de sertão. What was to become Rua Rosário ran from the caminho pra volta grande in the North to the Igreja do Colégio in the West. The street continuing from the Igreja do Colégio, now known as the rua do Carmo, passed the old village of Tebirica, and merged with the caminho velho do mar in the Southeast. The rua Direita was at that time a path which ran west from the Igreja do Colégio and the Sé, past the Casa do Sénado, dividing in the Southwest into the caminho do sertão and the caminho novo do mar.

In !765 the local census made by the urban militia companies or ordenanças at the orders of Captain-General Luis Antonio de Sousa, the Morgado de Matheus, listed households by street and number and mentioned landmarks as special indicators.[33] On

[31]Reproduced in Aroldo de Azevedo, A cidade de São Paulo (São Paulo, 1956), II.

[32]See Map IV:1 for 1560.

[33]"Recenseamento de 1765." The urban militia was organized by territorial unit and was therefore particularly suited to making a census. The orders to take the census were given by the captain-general to the captains-major of each locality. The actual censuses were done by the sargentos de milícias or the cabos de esquadra who usually were given between fifteen and sixty households to census. Two methods were used. One--clearly dominant at least after 1798--was that in which the census-taker went from house to house in the given neighborhood on a given day in which everyone was instructed to be at home for that purpose. This method is described in DI, LXIV, p. 20. The other method involved setting a day or a period of days in which all heads of household had to appear at the seat of the city council to give the relevant information. DI, LVIII, p. 13. The church vicars were also frequently asked to assist with the census, DI, XLIII, p. 66. The purposes of the census were both military and economic. São Paulo was the captaincy closest to the territory disputed between Portugal and Spain after 1740 and the captain-general was expected to enlist soldiers to assist in this effort. The census provided information for conscription purposes. The male population between 18 and 65 was undoubtedly underenumerated to some degree because of efforts to avoid the draft. It was not, however, all that easy to hide when the census-taker was a neighbor. The census data on occupations and production was related to the official effort to promote agriculture and commerce, in order indirectly to increase revenues from export taxes.

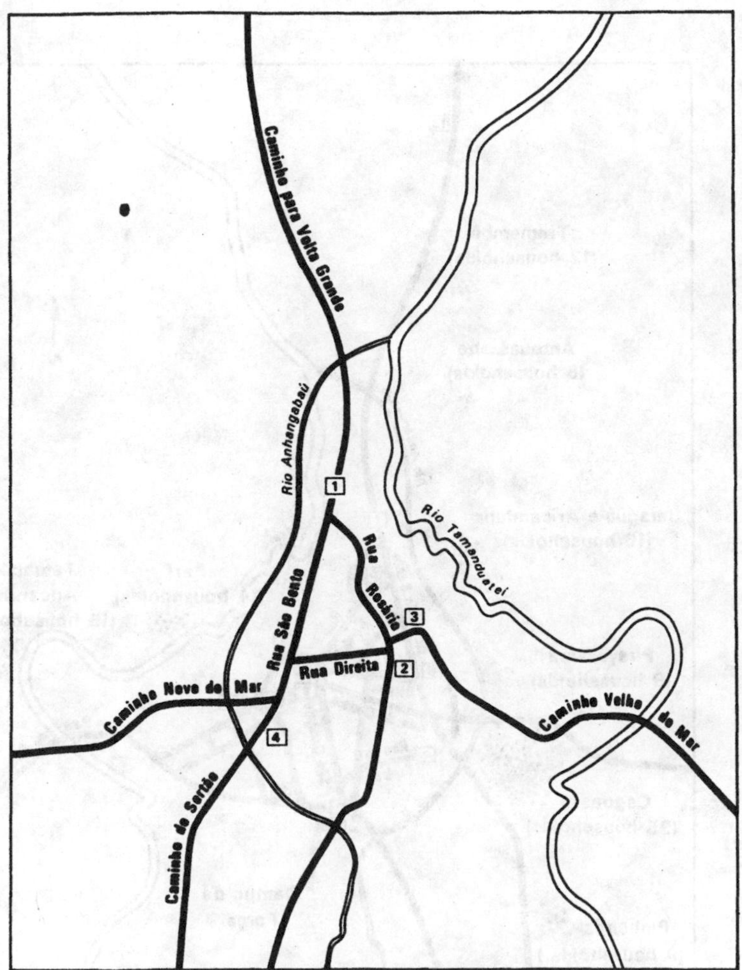

Map IV:1 São Paulo de Piratininga in 1560
Source: Based on a map presented by Affonso A. de Freitas, reproduced in Aroldo de Azevedo, A cidade de São Paulo (São Paulo, 1956)

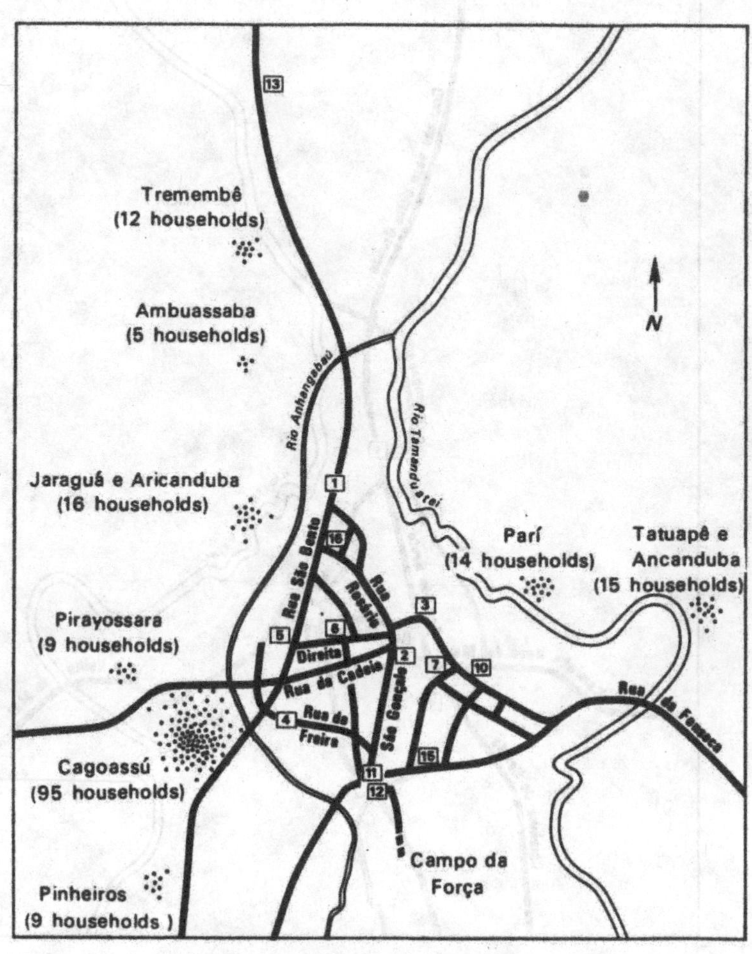

Map IV:2 São Paulo in 1765
Source: Reconstructed from the manuscript census of 1765, with assistance from historical discussions of street names and landmarks

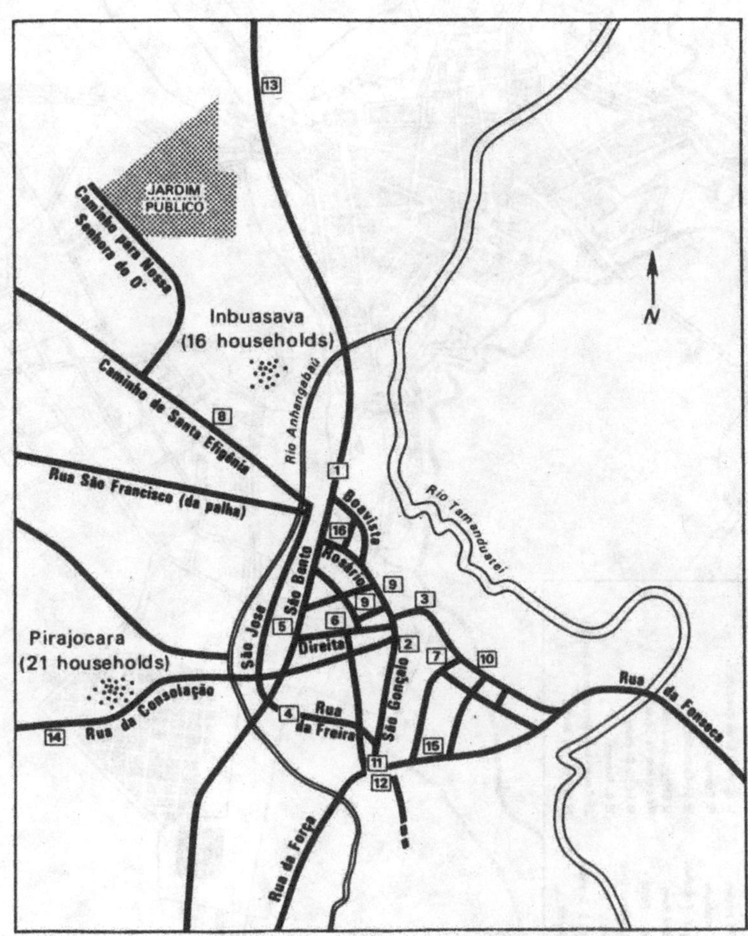

Map IV:3 São Paulo in 1802
Source: Reconstructed from the manuscript census of 1802, with assistance from historical discussions of street names and landmarks

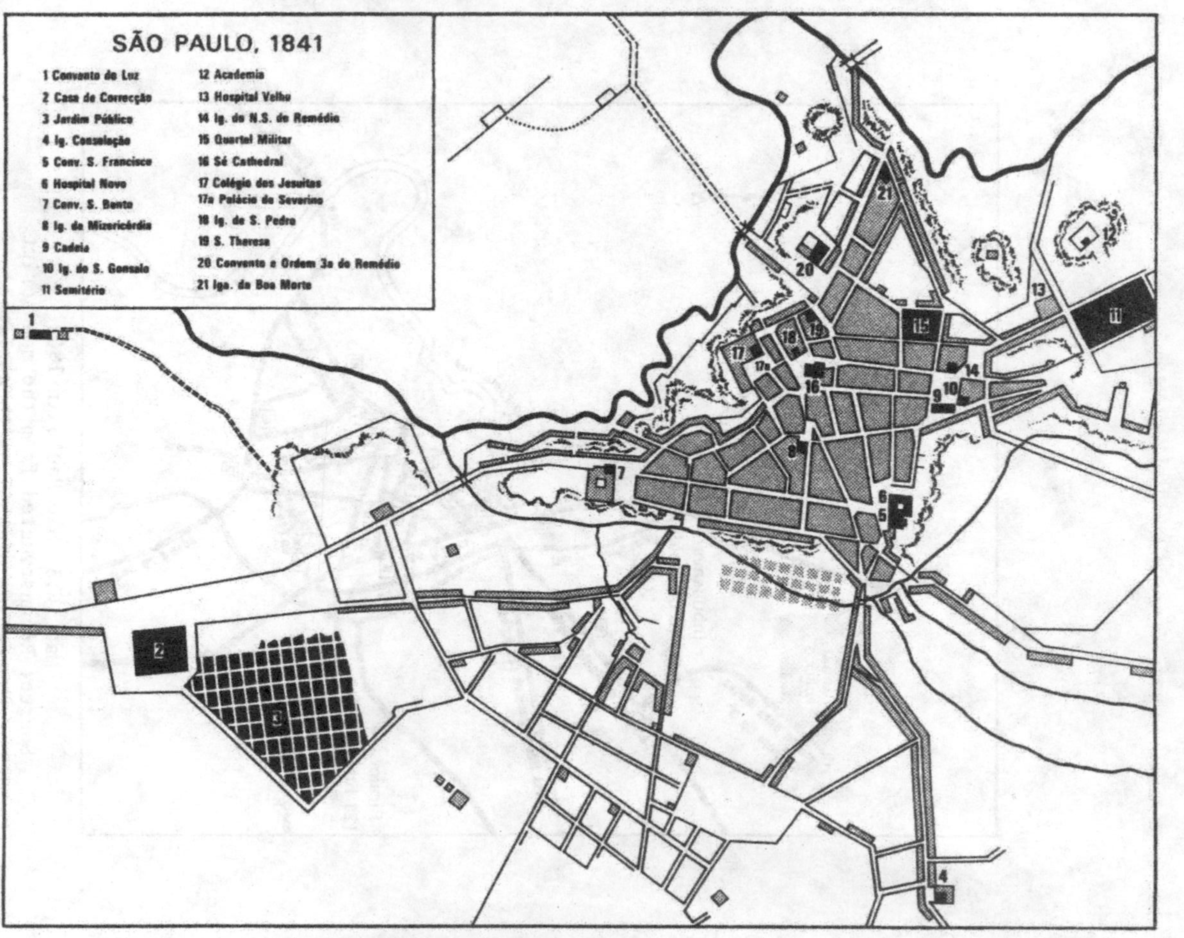
SÃO PAULO, 1841
1 Convento da Luz
2 Casa de Correcção
3 Jardim Público
4 Ig. Consolação
5 Conv. S. Francisco
6 Hospital Novo
7 Conv. S. Bento
8 Ig. da Mizericórdia
9 Cadeia
10 Ig. de S. Gonsalo
11 Semitério
12 Academia
13 Hospital Velho
14 Ig. de N.S. do Remédio
15 Quartel Militar
16 Sé Cathedral
17 Colégio dos Jesuitas
17a Palácio do Severino
18 Ig. de S. Pedro
19 S. Theresa
20 Convento e Ordem 3a do Remédio
21 Iga. da Boa Morte

Map IV:4 São Paulo in 1841

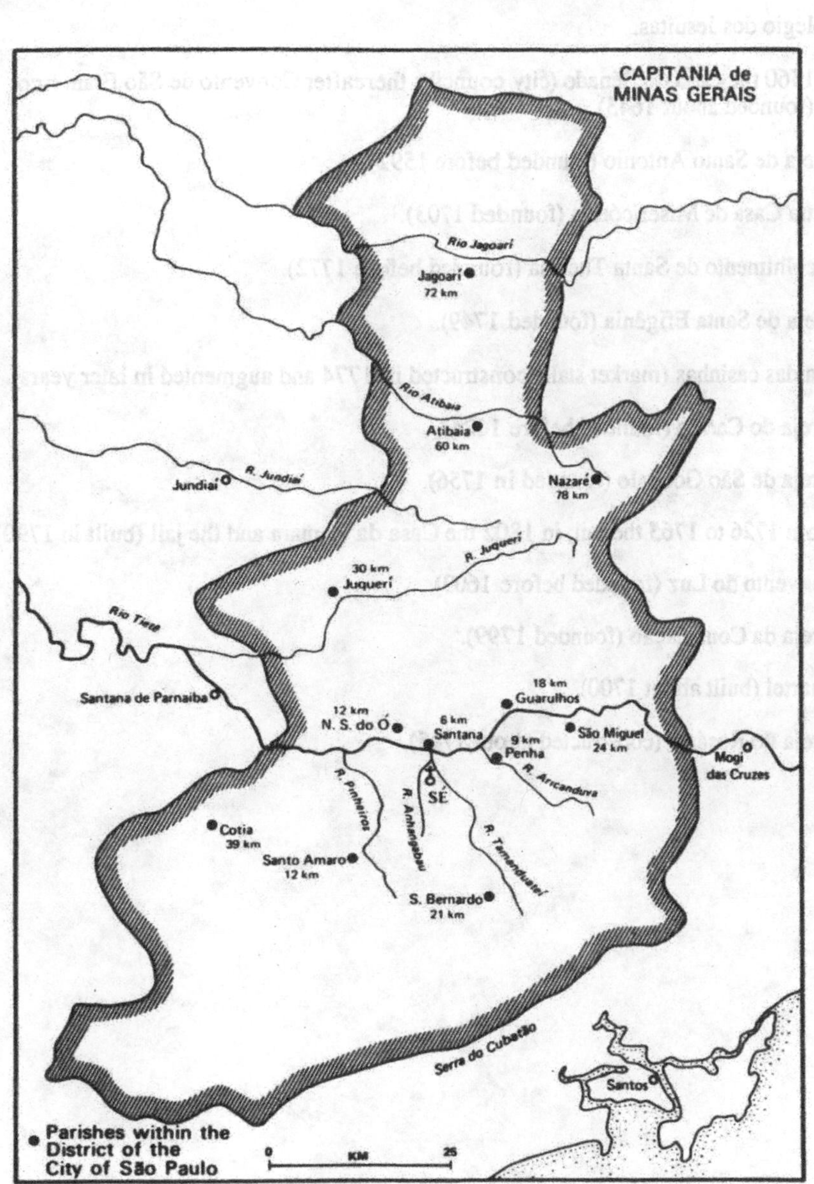

Map IV:5 District of the City of São Paulo, 1750-1796

Key to Maps IV:1-4

1. In 1560 Casa da Tebirica; thereafter Convento de São Bento (founded 1598).
2. Cathedral of the Sé (reconstructed in 1745).
3. Colégio dos Jesuitas.
4. In 1560 the Casa do Sénado (city council); thereafter Convento de São Francisco (founded about 1643).
5. Igreja de Santo Antonio (founded before 1592).
6. Santa Casa de Misericórdia (founded 1703).
7. Recolhimento de Santa Theresa (founded before 1772).
8. Igreja de Santa Efigênia (founded 1749).
9. Rua das casinhas (market stalls constructed in 1774 and augmented in later years).
10. Igreja do Carmo (founded before 1624).
11. Igreja de São Goncalo (founded in 1756).
12. From 1726 to 1765 the jail; in 1802 the Casa da Camara and the jail (built in 1790).
13. Convento do Luz (founded before 1603).
14. Igreja da Consolação (founded 1799).
15. Quartel (built about 1700).
16. Igreja do Rosário (constructed about 1745).

TABLE IV:7

The Numbers of Households in the Urban and Rural Districts of São Paulo, 1765, 1802, and 1836

Urban Districts	1765	1802	1836
1. First Company (Sé)	299	504	1,081
2. Second Company (Santa Efigênia)	147	323	620
3. Third Company (Brás)	122	242	162
Total Urban Households	568	1,069	1,863
Rural Districts			
1. Nossa Senhora do O	57	157	259
2. Santana[1]	83	134	--
3. Nossa Senhora da Penha e França, e São Miguel	100	168	214
Total Rural Households	240	459	473
Total Urban and Rural	808	1,528	2,336

[1]The 1836 listing for Santana was missing from the document collection. From other sources it seems that Santana may have been included in the district of Santa Efigênia in 1836, but the Santa Efigênia listings did not include Santana. Santana may have been one of the two missing "quarteirõens" from the Santa Efigênia collection. I included an estimate for each of these which was a simple average of the numbers of households in other "quarteirõens" within Santa Efigênia. If Santana was one of those, the number of households was greatly underestimated.

SOURCE: See Appendix IV:1 which provides a detailed accounting of the census listings for each district for each year. The 1765 census was divided into districts according to the geographical area mentioned in the census. This is also shown in Appendix IV:1.

the basis of this census, I developed a street map (Map IV:2) which will serve to compare residential density and geographic area in São Paulo in 1765, with that of 1560. The street plan of 1765 expanded the triangle nucleus north to south, and to the Northeast from the 1560 plan, moving the east-west leg from the Largo de São Francisco-Praça da Sé line to one more southerly along a level with the Igreja de São Gonçalo. Otherwise the population living within the old nucleus became more dense and streets were marked out dissecting the triangle.[34]

Ten streets were specifically mentioned in the 1765 census, including all of the five named in the Freitas map for 1560. Cross-streets or "travessas" were sometimes included in the listing of a major street. In one instance the rua do canto do Cirurgião Fonseca até o berço de Sta Thereza e Travessas headed a list of ninety-three households, over ten percent of total households in the census, implying that some of these "cross-streets" must have been fairly significant.[35] Beyond what were probably about fifteen streets, the 1765 census includes the bairros of Ambuassuaba, Piryossara, and Jaraguá, which lay just to the west side of the Anhangabaú, the bairro of Caguassú to the Southwest (later to be Consolação), and the bairros of Parí, Ancanduba, and Tatuapé on the northeastern side of the Tamanduateí.[36] The whole of the area discussed above can be considered roughly equivalent in area to that included in the three urban militia companies pertaining to the city in the 1802 census. In 1765 the urban nucleus of São Paulo was composed of 568 households, or about 2,400 free residents. Table IV:7 compares the districts and household listings for 1765, 1802, and 1836.

In addition to the community proper, the 1765 census included household lists of more distant bairros, later to be made vilas in their own right. (See Map IV:5) In 1765, however, the boundaries of São Paulo still included a large area in a radius of about fifty kilometers around the triangular urban nucleus. The ancient bairros of Nossa Senhora do O (about 10.5 kilometers North-Northwest of the main nucleus), Nossa Senhora da Penha de França (10.5 kilometers to the Northwest), São Miguel (also to the Northwest, usually

---

[34]Landmarks appearing in the 1765 census, not listed in 1560, included the Igreja de Santo Antonio (founded before 1592), the Convento de São Bento (1598), the Convento do Lux (before 1603), the Igreja do Carmo (before 1624), the Convento de São Francisco (about 1643), the Santa Casa de Misericórdia (1703), the hospital of the Santa Casa de Misericórdia (1715), the re-constructed Catedral da Sé (1745), the Igreja do Rosário (1746), the Igreja de São Gonçalo (1756), and the Recolhimento de Santa Theresa (before 1722). Founding dates of churches were mostly extracted from Leonardo Arroyo, Igrejas de São Paulo (São Paulo, 1966), passim.

[35]The street listing in the 1767 census includes the "Rua do pelourinho até o largo da Sé" (nine households), and the "Rua que principia de Pascoal Alves do Araujo ate o largo da Sé" (ten households) which may have been included in the cross-streets of the 1765 listing. Another two streets not specifically mentioned in the 1765 census were the "Rua da boa vista" (which I have assumed to have been included under "Rua Rosário") and the "Rua da quitanda," both present in the 1767 census.

[36]Identification of these bairros was arrived at with the help of Maria-Luiza Marcílio, La ville de São Paulo: peuplement et population 1750-1850 (Rouen, 1970), pp. 23-24; and A.N. Ab'Saber, "O sítio urbana de São Paulo," in Aroldo de Azevedo, ed., A cidade de São Paulo, I, p. 174 ff.

included with Penha in census lists), and Santana (directly to the North of the triangle) were all jurisdictionally within the city.[37]

Each of these bairros was initially developed through the erection of a chapel. The decision by a fazendeiro to build a chapel meant that land near the church must be provided for the homes and farms of the future worshippers.[38] The Igreja de Nossa Senhora de O was founded in 1610 on the fazenda of the bandeirante Manuel Prêto who was reported to own over one thousand Indian slaves. In 1615 Manuel Prêto petitioned the church fathers to allow the celebration of masses, baptisms, marriages, and burials in his chapel, claiming that the city was too far away for him or his people to go to the main church.[39] The small chapel of São Miguel was probably founded about 1562, believed to be the date of origin of the community. Apparently this chapel was rebuilt in 1622, financed by Fernão Munhoz, another bandeirante. The original chapel of Nossa Senhora da Penha de França was founded by Mateus Nunes de Siqueira some time before 1667. In 1668 and again in 1673 Mateus Nunes de Siqueira made requests to the city council for the grant of additional lands (sesmarias) in order to "enlarge the chapel."[40] These lands were not needed for the actual church site but rather to provide room for the houses and farms of the new devotees of the chapel.[41] In fact, while building a chapel and attracting members to form the parish, the fazendeiro was physically creating a personal power base around himself. It was no accident that the first captains-major of each of these bairros was generally either the initiator of the chapel or else his son.

In 1765 the bairro of Nossa Senhora do O was made up of 57 households with a free population of 257 persons.[42] The highest property value mentioned was 700 mil reis and only one head of household in O in 1765 served on the city council at any time.[43] Very few professions were listed, undoubtedly because agriculture was the universal occupation, an assumption which is borne out in later censuses of the bairro. By 1778 the number of households had increased to 99, 55.5 percent of which owned one or more slaves. This was the highest percentage of households owning slaves of any bairro in São Paulo. During the late eighteenth century, the bairro of Nossa Senhora do O was in a pre-eminent position relative to other agricultural districts within the jurisdictional boundaries

---

[37]Marcílio, La ville, pp. 51-70 discusses the evolution of the territorial dimensions of the parish of the Sé (which initially included the entire area covered by the 1765 census) and also the history of the administrative boundaries of the city itself.

[38]See Rubens Borba de Moräes, "Contribuições para a história do povoamento de São Paulo até fins do século XVIII," Geográfia, ano I, no. 1 (1935):69-87.

[39]Arroyo, Igrejas, pp. 122-23.

[40]Ibid, p. 146.

[41]Ibid, p. 150.

[42]Marcílio, La ville, p. 123 states that O had eighty-eight households in 1765--thirty-one more than listed in the census. The reason for the difference in her figures is not clear.

[43]The city council member was Estevão Franco da Rocha, aged 27, property value 400 mil reis, later to become a senhor de engenho. He was three times member of the city council between 1775 and 1788, and had already served as a fiscal official (almotacel) in 1763.

of the city because of the greater emphasis on commercial agriculture, and especially sugar production.[44]

The bairro of Santana evolved from a Jesuit fazenda known as the Fazenda do Tieté or Santana on the site ceded to the Jesuits in 1673.[45] The Fazenda do Tieté became an important cattle ranch by the mid-eighteenth century, and the chapel's parishioners likewise began cattle ranches around it.

The bairro of Santana included 94 households in 1765 and a free population of 416. Like Nossa Senhora do O, few occupations were mentioned. Property values listed included one for 1,659 mil reis and two households with wealth of 800 mil reis each, making Santana a more prosperous bairro than Nossa Senhora do O at this time. In 1778 there were 120 households, 47.5 percent of which held one or more slaves. The following year's census listed 124 households, fifteen of which claimed ten or more slaves. Women headed seven of these fifteen households, including the largest slaveholder of the bairro, Escolástica Barbosa de Lima, who had twenty-two slaves and was widowed.[46] Only two of these fifteen were on the city council at any time between 1760 and 1820.

The bairro of Nossa Senhora da Penha de França included only thirty-six households, a total of 164 free inhabitants in 1765.[47] Later censuses tended to lump the bairros of Penha and São Miguel together, making comparisons over time difficult. In 1765 São Miguel had 85 households or 396 free inhabitants, making a total of 121 households for the two bairros. The 1778 census lists 153 households for Penha and São Miguel combined, a reasonable increase from the combined 1765 figure. The highest property value given for either bairro was 500 mil reis, making these two the poorest bairros in terms of assessed wealth within São Paulo boundaries. Consistent with these findings, the slaveholding census of 1778 indicated that only 43.1 percent of households owned one or more slaves in that year.

Most houses in the rural bairros of São Paulo in 1765 were of the simple thatched pau-a-pique variety with three windowless rooms. A few wealthier families--particularly those with large fazendas--lived in houses of durable taipa de pilão with a tiled roof and from seven to twelve rooms. Housing construction in the urban center of São Paulo in 1765 varied little from the rural scene. Since subsistence agriculture predominated even in the urban area, the latter continued to demonstrate the characteristics of the countryside. The tendency of the wealthier commercial class to reside in the city did, however, mean that the better houses of taipa de pilão were more common in the city.[48]

The census of 1802 for the three militia companies comprising the urban core of São Paulo demonstrates that the basic outline of the city had not altered since 1765,

---

[44]By 1802 the bairro of O was producing 74.6 percent of the rum (945 canadas) within the area studied, 51.73 percent of the corn (1,879 alquieres), and 41.77 percent of the beans (921 alqueires). Over forty-eight percent of households were engaged in agriculture and/or cattle raising for sale--the highest percentage of the bairros studied.

[45]Maria Celestina Teixeira Mendes Torres, O bairro de Santana (São Paulo, 1970), p. 17.

[46]Escolástica Barbosa de Lima was the widow of Marcellino Pereira de Oliveira, who came from a long paulista line (titulo Prados, according to Silva Leme). Her fortune was made in the mines of Cuiabá.

[47]Marcílio, La ville, p. 123 stated that Penha included one hundred households with a free population of 450 persons in 1765. Again, the reason for the difference from the census listing is not self-evident.

[48]Reis Filho, Quadro da arquitetura, pp. 37-38.

though the density of households was considerably increased.[49] See Table IV:7 and Map IV:3. In spite of there being no new streets listed in that area since 1765, the first company, which included the triangle area proper, had grown by 119 percent in households. The second company, the area of the West and Northwest of the Anhanguabaú, had increased in numbers of households by 101 by 1802. Geographical expansion was evident particularly in the section around the Igreja de Santa Efigênia (founded in 1794), along the road to the bairro of Nossa Senhora do O, as well as the neighborhood peripheral to the Igreja da Consolação, founded in 1799 in the Southwest of the city. East of the largo do colégio and east of the Tieté to the North was the section belonging to the third company, including such landmarks as the convent of Santa Theresa, the Palace of the Bishop, and the Convent of Carmo. Although no streets were listed, my best estimate is that the third company had 97 percent more households in 1802 than in 1765. By 1836 these three companies were known as 1) the Sé, 2) Santa Efigênia, and 3) Brás. The free population of the three urban companies comprising the city of São Paulo in 1802 was 4,482, with a slave population of 2,703 and 46.93 percent of households owning slaves, as shown in Table IV:2.

In 1791 the first building ever especially constructed for the municipal council and the jail was erected near the Igreja São Gonçalo in what is today the Praça João Mendes. Previously the council had always met in rented buildings or in the private homes of members.[50] The fund to finance the new meeting house was begun in 1783 and, like most public improvements, was based on private contributions.[51] In his visit to São Paulo in 1816 Auguste de Sainte-Hilaire described the casa da camara in the following way:

> The municipal town hall forms one of the angles of a square plaza. It is a beautiful building, two story, decorated with a false front, measuring about 77 feet in length by twenty feet in width, with nine windows in the front. The jail is located on the ground floor on the right and upstairs on the same side. In São Paulo, as in other places in Brazil, the prisoners can stand in the windows of the jail, conversing with passersby.[52]

Two important innovations during this period emphasized the increasingly redistributive character of the city of São Paulo. One was the mule team shelters or pousos which were built at several points peripheral to the city to provide permanent resting and re-loading areas for teams coming and going from Santos and the interior. The development of these shelters was a specific concern of Captain-General Manoel Mendonça de Mello e Castro (1797-1802), who considered that the lack of pousos for the mule teams had been an important hindrance to commerce.[53]

---

[49]AESP, TC, no ordem 32, caixa 32, Maços de população, capital, 1802. See Map III:3.

[50]Luis Saia, Fontes primárias para o estudo das habilitações, das vias de comunicação e dos aglomerados humanos em São Paulo, no século, xvi (São Paulo, 1948), p. 4; Hermes Vieira, História da polícia civil de São Paulo (São Paulo, 1955), pp. 108-09.

[51]Vieira, Ibid, pp. 108-09.

[52]Auguste de Sainte-Hilaire, Viagem, p. 157.

[53]"Memória sobre a communicação da ville de Santos com a cidade de São Paulo," DI, XXIX, pp. 112-13.

The other important innovation was the establishment of the most fundamental of urban institutions--a fixed and municipally regulated marketplace. In 1773 the wealthy merchant Jerônymo de Castro Guimarães proposed that the city council build a series of stalls (casinhas) to centralize and control the sale of non-perishables. He pointed out that the dispersal of sellers in the street made it difficult for both fiscal officials controlling licensing, weights and measures, as well as tax collectors, to locate the sellers. Furthermore, Castro Guimarães offered personally to loan the necessary capital to the city council, taking the profits of the market as security.[54] In early 1774 six stalls were ready; by the end of 1774 there were fifteen; in 1794 larger stalls replaced the early ones and more were built, making a total of twenty-two by 1798.[55] The records of the city council indicate that during the first decade after the establishment of the marketplace there were constant food scarcities and complaints that farmers did not grow surpluses nor bring them to the marketplace.[56] By 1795, however, municipal income from the rent of the marketplace stalls was second only to that derived from the municipal meat market.[57] The fact that the urban population of São Paulo was relying on the marketplace for most of their daily comestibles is clearly demonstrated by the practical disappearance of agricultural production from the urban household economy during this period.

The rural districts had also been growing and changing in the thirty-seven years since 1765, though increase in free population was only 24.6 percent over the period, with the slave population remaining stationary. See Table IV:8. Both the percentage of slaves in the population and the percentage of households with slaves had declined over the period 1778 to 1802. It is notable, too, that these percentages were lower in the urban areas. In a general way it is plain that the free urban population was more prosperous than the free rural population in 1802, as was also true in 1778 and in 1765.

By 1802 the residential landscape of both rural and urban bairros had altered considerably. Although the thatched pau-a-pique construction continued to prevail in the rural area, the number of the better built houses of tile limestone and taipa de pilão had noticeably increased. The incipient development of the export market and commercial farming were visibly manifested in extensive rural properties with engenhos and multiple dwellings which began to appear in the richer property inventories in this period. One of the most impressive was the country residence of Captain Major José Antonio da Silva who died in Santana in 1797:

---

[54]ACMSP, XVI, 24 dezembro 1773, 13 dezembro 1774. Affonso de E. Taunay, História da cidade de São Paulo no século xviii (São Paulo, 1949), II, no. 1:133.

[55]Taunay, Ibid.

[56]RGCMSP, XI, 26 agosto 1780, 23 janeiro 1783, 13 outubro 1783.

[57]RGCMSP, XII, janeiro 1796, pp. 21-23.

TABLE IV:8

The Free and Slave Populations of São Paulo by Bairro (1802)

Bairro	Free	Slave	%SL[1]	%HH SL[2]
First Company	1949	1317	40.3	49.4
Second Company	1436	740	34.01	41.8
Third Company	1092	646	37.2	49.4
Total Urban	4477	2703	37.6	46.93
N.S. do O	909	469	34.03	49.7
Santana	732	315	30.09	36.6
Penha/S. Miguel	910	284	23.79	37.5
Total Rural	2551	1068	29.51	41.40

[1] %SL indicates the percentage of slaves in the population of the given bairro.

[2] %HH SL indicates the percent of households in the given bairro which own slaves.

SOURCE: Maços de população, capital, 1802.

> Included in the country estate in the suburbs of this city in the area called the bairro of Santa Ana at the residence of the deceased there is a house of two lanços, walls made of taipa de pilão, tiled roof, and a small damaged upper room with chapel windows, in addition to another casa têrrea of three lanços, walls of taipa de pilão, and a tiled roof, and a room with an altar and oratory all completely painted with the following images: Nossa Senhora do Rosário with her silver crown, São Francisco das Chagas, Santo Antonio dos Senhores Crucificado and a small altar with two images of the baby Jesus and other preparations of the same oratory all done with much gold, in addition to two other buildings of taipa de pilão behind the first two, also tiled, each with a cane crusher, one in very good condition and the other slightly damaged, with a cask in which to make rum, and the needed utensils all in good condition of wood and leather, and other small tools concerned with the making of rum. There are utility areas for the house, slave quarters and planted farm lands including banana groves, manioc, sugar cane, cotton, and the usual subsistence crops. There is a sheep pen made of woven bullrushes covered with tiles. All this aforementioned estate and lands are marked off with a trench which surrounds all the lands in the title, all of which is valued at four hundred mil reis.[58]

The appearance of the urban streets was more homogeneous than that of the countryside by 1802. Urban residence had become markedly more attractive by the development of the urban marketplace, and the increased availability of artisan and other services, together with the new commercial importance of the city. Not only were the richer households constructing sobrados of stone and tile, but due to the general valorization of the urban area, poor owners of property were beginning to sell. New houses of taipa were constructed to replace the pau-a-pique huts. Abundant indications that urban properties were relatively more valuable than those in the countryside are found in references to urban house rentals as well as the evident price differential of urban and rural properties in this period.[59]

Considerable demographic growth as well as urban improvements accompanied the economic and political developments in the city of São Paulo from 1802 to 1836. The number of households in the urban area grew by 74.28 percent over the period as indicated by the São Paulo census of 1836. Proportional growth in households was most important in the area of Santa Efigênia (91.95 percent) and, secondly, in the southern area

---

[58]AESP, Inventários não publicados, Inventário of Jose Antonio da Silva, 1797, caixa 92.

[59]Compare the large estate owned by José Antonio da Silva in Santana in 1797 described above and valued at four hundred reis with the following valuations of urban properties for the same year: A casa têrrea made of taipa de pilão of two lanços and a tiled roof on the Rua do Rosário valued at three hundred mil reis (Inventário of José Antonio da Silva, 1797, Ibid.), a tile-roofed sobrado of taipa de pilão, also on the Rua do Rosário, together with a small casa têrrea of one lanço, made of taipa, with a small backyard assessed at six hundred mil reis (Inventário of Jose Pacheco Missel, 1797, caixa 92). Also in 1797 a tiled casa têrrea of two lanços, made of taipa de pilão, was evaluated at nearly forty-five mil reis but actually sold for two hundred. (Inventário of José Pacheco Missel, 1797, caixa 92).

of the Sé (66.6 percent).[60] Viewed in another way, the Sé and Brás averaged a combined growth of 8.78 households per year from 1765 to 1802, and 14.62 households per year from 1802 to 1836; Santa Efigênia averaged 4.76 households per year in the first period and 8.74 households per year in the second period. While the Santa Efigênia area, which included elite suburban agricultural estates by 1836, was growing at a faster rate, the largest proportion of new households were still being established in the triangular heart of the city. The increasing desirability of residence in urban São Paulo had an upward effect on land values in property inventories.[61] This tendency was also revealed by the architectural changes of the period, and the increased use of more valuable building materials.

The valorization of urban properties in the early nineteenth century. is clear from changes made in the construction of houses.[62] According to Alcântara Machado, there were a few two- and three-story houses in the seventeenth and eighteenth centuries in São Paulo.[63] Nevertheless, the one-story residence with a beaten earth floor predominated until about the 1820s. In 1836 Daniel Kidder reported that most of the houses in São Paulo had two stories.[64] Although houses continued to be constructed predominantly of earth (taipa), bricks, both sun-baked and cooked, and stone were becoming common.[65] In the mid-nineteenth century the house with the raised floor (casa de porão alto) both one-story and several-story, introduced the fashion of the house as a purely residential environment, in contrast to the earlier sobrado, in which the lower floor was used as a store or to keep slaves or a carriage.[66] The valorization of the residence in terms of structure, material, and general complexity is an indication of the increased value of urban property as well as the increased importance of the urban dwelling to the individual owner. As Daniel Kidder pointed out, "The city (São Paulo) is the central convergence

---

[60]The administrative redefinition of the parishes of the city in the early nineteenth century makes comparison with the 1802 period a little difficult. If, however, Brás and the Sé are combined, a procedure justified by the fact that much of what was the third company in 1802 was included in the southern district of the Sé in 1836, it appears that number of households had grown in that area by 66.6 percent.

[61]Property inventories for São Paulo in the eighteenth and nineteenth centuries are stored in the historical section of AESP in caixas 50 through 94 (1740-1820) of the "Inventários não publicados." The assertion that property values increased in São Paulo over the period is based on examination of these documents.

[62]Analysis of urban developments and land use on the basis of architecture can be found especially in Reis Filho, Evolução urbana, pp. 112-81 and Quadro da arquitetura, the latter focusing on the eighteenth through the twentieth centuries. Additional material, though less historically oriented, is found in Luis Saia, Notas sobre a evolução da morada paulista (São Paulo, 1957) and "Notas sobre a arquitetura rural paulista do segunda século," Revista do Servico Patrimonio Histórico e Artistico Nacional, No. 8 (São Paulo, 1944), pp. 211-75.

[63]Alcântara Machado, Vida e morte do bandeirante, pp. 33-36; João Capistrano de Abreu, Capítulos de história colonial: 1500-1800 (Brásilia, 1963), pp. 128-29.

[64]Daniel P. Kidder, Reminiscências de viagens e permanências no Brásil: provincias do sul, translated by Moacir N. Vasconcelos (São Paulo, 1972), I, p. 189.

[65]Marcílio, "Crescimento demográfico," p. 175.

[66]Reis Filho, Quadro da arquitetura, pp. 33-42.

point of all of the province. Many of the most wealthy agriculturalists have houses in the city and spend very little time on their estates because they can better orient the sale of their crops from São Paulo."[67]

Although there was much to complain about in terms of city services in 1836, at least part of the new attraction of São Paulo was derived from the development of educational facilities in the urban area. In 1799, for the entire district of the city of São Paulo there was one professor of rational and moral philosophy, one rhetoric professor, one Latin grammar teacher, and one primary school teacher.[68] By 1836 São Paulo boasted nine primary schools (seven for boys, two for girls), and one state-supported orphans' boarding school for each sex.[69] The development of higher education was spurred by the separation from Portugal which made necessary the establishment of local institutions to train potential state employees in law, government, and other disciplines. São Paulo, selected as one of the two cities in which law academies were to be located, opened the academy's doors in 1828 and by 1836 had graduated 253 bachelors in law and awarded nineteen doctorates. The academy gave a five-year course, and employed nine professors.[70] Specialized educational institutions for the study of botany (founded in 1799, and expanded in 1825), agriculture (founded 1836), and topography completed the educational offerings of the city.[71]

Medical facilities in the city were also showing some improvement. A military hospital had been established in Santa Efigênia in 1810, but the hospital of the Santa Casa de Misericórdia was abandoned at about the same time, the patients of the Santa Casa being sent to the Military Hospital.[72] According to a hospital document of 1820, there were 132 available beds in the hospital, twelve without mattresses and seventy-two lacking even one blanket, though there was an average of more than one sheet per bed.[73] In spite of its shortcomings, the hospital was sizable for the time and it included, in addition to the facilities for patients, a pharmacy which was open to the public and sold a large selection of medicines.[74]

Smallpox vaccine was introduced to São Paulo in 1802 --an important innovation since the populace had been regularly visited by the pox

---

[67]Kidder, Reminiscências, p. 191.

[68]At that time only the districts of the cities of São Paulo, Santos, Curitiba, and Paranágua within the captaincy had any schools at all. "Memória economico-política de capitania de São Paulo," Anaes do Museu Paulista, IV (São Paulo, 1961), pp. 160-63.

[69]Daniel Pedro Muller, São Paulo em 1836: ensaio d'um quadro estatístico da provincia de S. Paulo (São Paulo, 1920), p. 264.

[70]In addition, there were preparatory courses for the formal law course in Latin, English, French, rhetoric, rational and moral philosophy, geometry, history, geography, and general philosophy.

[71]Muller, São Paulo em 1836.

[72]There was also a lepers home, which could only comfortably admit four patients at a time.

[73]AESP, TC, "Orçamento das roupas necessárias para as camas dos doentes do hospital real desta cidade, 1820," no. ordem 36, caixa 36.

[74]Auguste de Sainte-Hilaire, Viagem, p. 159.

(bexigas) in every decade since 1765.[75] Measures taken against the disease in the eighteenth century demonstrated equal measures of common sense and witchcraft. From 1769 the contagious quality of the disease was known. Ideas such as those of attracting the disease to herds of animals made to roam the streets (on the theory that there was some specific quantity of disease-bearing particles), or attempting to weaken the pestilence with perfume, illustrate the levels of desperation and ignorance of the time. By the late eighteenth century more scientific measures were being tried. In 1798 an edict was passed that smallpox victims should be buried some distance from the city, and in 1800 two houses outside the urban center were arranged in which to care for those afflicted with the pox.[76] Cases of smallpox were still being reported in 1806 and some citizens apparently doubted that the vaccine had any effect.[77]

The prevalence of disease was not unrelated to the rudimentary level of city services, frequently executed on a personal rather than an official basis in the early nineteenth century. Public fountains had been erected in 1792 on the Largo da Misericórdia and in 1814 on the Largo do Piques. Projects for piping of water were proposed in 1842, 1852, and 1857 but none of these proposals were followed through.[78] Slaves were the usual porters of water as well as the carriers of the huge sewage barrels or "tigers" which were emptied into open sewers. There was no fire department and the townsmen cooperated in a bucket brigade to fight any blaze at the signal of church bells rung out in a code to specify the location.[79] Street cleaning and paving were the responsibility of the residents, and both were executed rather unevenly, the pavement frequently being completed only in front of buildings.[80] The procurator of the city council was in charge of seeing that the streets, public fountains, and bridges were in order and that stray pigs and cattle were not allowed to run loose through the streets. By 1836 São Paulo already had most of the common problems of the modern urban city, and had begun to develop some solutions, but the majority of "community needs" continued to be provided for by family, friends, and slaves, rather than through community services.

Table IV:9 shows the distribution of slaves by household in the urban districts for 1778, 1802, and 1836. Households owning slaves declined about six percent from 1778 to 1802 and two percent from 1802 to 1836. Slaves in the urban population increased by one percent from 1778 to 1802, but the distribution of slaves among slave-holding households did not alter perceptibly. It appears that some new households did not acquire slaves while some of those with from one to four slaves sold those slaves they had. The

---

[75]Affonso de E. Taunay, História da cidade de São Paulo no século xviii (São Paulo, 1951), II, no. 2:235-45. The minutes of the city council meetings frequently referred to this problem throughout the period.

[76]Ibid., pp. 240-42.

[77]There was much resistance to the vaccine on the grounds that being innoculated demonstrated a lack of faith in the powers of our blessed lady of Penha who was regularly carried to the center of the city when disease threatened. Captain-General Mello Castro e Mendonça wrote to the crown that it was "morally impractical" to innoculate all the adult population of São Paulo, RIHGB, TE, Document 4711, 1806.

[78]Taunay, História, II, no. 1, pp. 187-95; Affonso A. de Freitas, Diccionário histórico, topográfico, ethnográfico, ilustrado do município de São Paulo (São Paulo, 1929), I, p. 53 ff.

[79]Morse, From Community to Metropolis, p. 156.

[80]Sainte-Hilaire, Viagem, p. 156.

TABLE IV:9

The Distribution of Slaves by Household in the Urban Bairros of São Paulo, 1778, 1802, and 1836

	1778 NHH = 303		1802 NHH = 1068		1836 NHH = 961	
Slaves	I	II	I	II	I	II
1	53.4	100.00	47.1	100.00	43.56	100.00
2- 4	42.27	96.67	35.6	95.5	29.97	91.84
5- 7	21.67	78.59	16.7	74.3	11.74	62.22
8-10	14.09	65.18	9.7	58.4	4.74	37.36
11-14	9.5	52.73	6.3	46.5	2.17	23.26
15+	5.44	37.49	3.6	32.8	1.14	14.48

I. Percentage of households in district with given number or more of slaves.

II. Percentage of slaves in households with given number or more of slaves. For example, 23.26 percent of the slaves in the Sé were owned by households with eleven or more slaves in 1836.

SOURCE: Maços de população, capital, 1778, 1802, and 1836. The 1836 figure includes only the central urban district of the Sé.

proportion of slaveowners with from two to seven slaves increased most significantly in the urban bairros in this period at the same time that those with fifteen or more slaves declined.

The increased percentage of slaves in the urban population in 1802 can be interpreted as an indication of greater wealth and prosperity for the free urbanites in the late eighteenth century. The declining proportion of households owning slaves suggests further that the increase in prosperity included some proportion of the population at the partial expense of the rest. Finally, the limitations in number of slaves acquired in a household in the urban districts can be interpreted as a function of the differentiation of town from countryside. Slave labor in the urban setting was used almost entirely for domestic purposes and to hire out in the trades. The function of the slave in terms of household food production was rapidly disappearing as the commercial production of foodstuffs for the market increased in the suburban areas. Large numbers of slaves were neither useful nor desirable in the urban setting by 1802. In fact slaves were frequently sent out on their own during the day with no order other than that they pay some given sum to their master every day or every week. The slave could hire himself out as he pleased and save any surplus he managed to earn for the eventual purchase of his freedom.[81]

The rural districts of Nossa Senhora do O and Penha and São Miguel had also grown over the period 1802 to 1836, though at a slower rate, both proportionately and absolutely than the urban districts. Households in Nossa Senhora do O increased 65.61 percent, an average rate of three new households per year. In Penha and São Miguel, on the other hand, households increased by only 27.38 percent, an average of 1.35 houses per year. The difference in growth rate reflects the difference in prosperity of the two districts. Significantly, the low rate of increase in households in the rural area in this period was associated with a substantial increase in commercial agricultural production. It seems likely that land ownership was being concentrated into progressively larger and more commercialized estates in this period.[82] In addition, migration from these bairros toward the new coffee and sugar lands as well as to the urban areas contributed to the low population increase.

The growing inequities in the rural bairros between 1802 and 1836 were clearly reflected in changes in popular housing. While the poorer households (often living in a house on someone else's land) continued to reside in thatched pau-a-pique huts, the rich elaborated ever-larger, more luxurious and complex residential and productive establishments on their rural estates. The sobrado began to appear in the countryside, while the casa têrrea of taipa, built in an earlier time, was used as a second house for dependent kindred or agregados.

---

[81] João Maurício Rugendas, Viagem pitoresco através do Brasil, translated by Rubens Borba de Morães (São Paulo, 1972), p. 147 ff discusses the situation of the urban slave in Rio de Janeiro about the year 1825.

[82] Although I have no concrete empirical proof of concentration of land ownership specifically within the district of the city of São Paulo, the evidence for the province of São Paulo in this period is good and has been commented on by several authors. See Alice Piffer Canabrava, "A repartição da terra," pp. 104-10; Marcílio, "Crescimento demográfico," pp. 285-87; Alberto Passos Guimarães, Quatro séculos de latifundio (Rio de Janeiro, 1968), pp. 80-98; Maria Sylvia de Carvalho Franco, Homens livres na ordem escravocrata (São Paulo, 1969), pp. 95-110; Lucila Herrmann, "Evolução da estrutura social de Guaratinguetá num período do trezentos anos," Revista de Administração, II (March-June, 1948), pp. 108-12.

CONCLUSION

The population growth of the free population of the city of São Paulo included a period of rapid growth at the rate of two and a half percent per year from 1777 to 1802, declining to 1.01 percent per year from 1802 to 1836. In the latter period the captaincy/province of São Paulo grew at the rate of 2.75 percent per year between 1818 and 1836. These data support Richard Morse's theory of the "ruralization" of Latin American populations in the early nineteenth century. According to Morse the decline in the proportion of the Latin American population living in cities in this period may have resulted from a transformation in the character and functions of cities paralleling changes in the economic structure.[83] In terms of São Paulo--a primarily administrative center before 1765--the dissolution of the domestic mode of production led initially to an increase in the rate of population growth and an expansion in urban industry from 1765 to 1802. In the period from 1802 to 1836 decreased opportunities in urban domestic industry combined with the expansion in increasingly capitalized commercial agriculture on the plateau to result in many "urban" functions being incorporated into the structures of the sugar and coffee plantations--for example those of banking, transport, and some artisan activities. This "ruralization" trend was only reversed with the development of factories for the production of textiles, bricks, pasta, glass, beer, and other general items of consumption at the end of the nineteenth century.

The process of urban change included demographic alterations in the composition of the São Paulo population as well as increased residential density, changes in types of housing and construction materials, the development of urban institutions such as the marketplace, the hospital and the orphanage, and an improvement (somewhat) in basic services. The evolution of an older population with a "normal" sex ratio is a potent indicator that São Paulo had developed beyond its traditional ceremonial and administrative roles. The attraction of adult males was related to the important political and commercial developments within São Paulo in this period. At the same time the differentiation in types of housing along with a greater concentration in slave ownership implies that the new development of São Paulo may have also exacerbated socio-economic differences among households within the community. That this was the case will be argued in the next chapters.

[83]Richard Morse, "The Development of Urban Systems in the Americas in the Nineteenth Century," Journal of Interamerican Studies & World Affairs 17, no. 1 (February 1975):4-26. Maria-Luiza Marcílio, La ville de São Paulo (Rouen, 1968), p. 171.

V

From Bandeirantes to Coffee Barons: Occupational Differentiation and Crop Specialization in São Paulo: 1765, 1802, and 1836

The transformation of the São Paulo economy from one of subsistence in 1765 to one of exchange oriented toward exports by 1836 is most dramatically revealed in the analyses of occupational structure and of agricultural production. Since production in the subsistence economy was located within the household, and since the development of production for exchange also initially occurred predominantly within a household context, the fact that the censuses are household based allows the process of transformation to be minutely and vividly displayed through these censuses. It is not so much the fact that this change took place--that is hardly surprising and of course has been repeatedly replicated in many parts of the world. What is important is the process whereby it took place--in social, economic, and political terms. For the transformation--while it is measurable in purely economic terms--was by no means purely economic in process or in consequences. The close look afforded by the manuscript censuses will allow an unraveling of the process which so altered the lives of São Paulo residents in the nineteenth century.

In fact the course of economic and demographic differentiation of the community of São Paulo from its immediate hinterland from 1765 to 1836 proceeded very much as expected in terms of other studies of urbanization. The urban area, which in 1765 was distinguished from the rural bairros only by a few artisans and traders and lacked even the basic Weberian characteristics of a marketplace, was increasingly populated by businessmen, retailers, administrators, textile, and service workers in both the periods between 1765 and 1802, and from 1802 and 1836. Most important, the subsistence household economy of 1765 was replaced by a general dependence upon the urban marketplace and a household economy based on exchange within the urban bairros by 1802. In the same period the rural household economy evolved from a subsistence mode of production to one in which about 50 percent of households in the rural bairros were combining subsistence cultivation with production intended for the urban market. See Table V:1. By 1836 production for individual subsistence purposes was much reduced, replaced by a fundamental dependence upon the marketplace for basic foodstuffs, not only in the specifically "urban" areas, but also in nearby rural bairros which became more and more specialized in terms of crops produced. By 1836 it was not only adjacent parishes within the district of the city of São Paulo which produced primarily for the urban market of São Paulo, but also more distant parishes in the area of Atibaia, Jundiaí, and Novo Braganca whose own urban markets were less developed.

Transport and roads played an important role in these changes. The opening of roads on the plateau and between communities as well as the expansion of easy transport in the form of mule teams were essential to the practicability of the differentiation of space utilization for economic purposes. The costs of transport were an important barrier to the development of markets in the late eighteenth century, not only between the plateau

TABLE V:1

São Paulo Households Engaged in Agriculture for Subsistence and/or Sale, 1765, 1802, and 1836

(percent)

	1765	1802	1836
URBAN			
Subsistence only	100	4.4	
Subsistence and sale	--	5.5	9.2*
Agriculturalist, but no crops this year	--	--	--
Non-agricultural	--	90.0	90.8*
RURAL			
Subsistence only	100	38.8	17.0*
Subsistence and sale	--	29.8	40.8*
Agriculturalist, but no crops this year	--	7.8	--
Non-agricultural	--	23.5	42.2I*

SOURCE: These figures were calculated by the author, based on the original household-level census manuscripts, Maços de população, capital, 1765, 1802, 1836, AESP.

*The census manuscripts for the bairros of Santana were missing from the archives, so that figures for the rural area are based on the manuscripts for Nossa Senhora do O and Nossa Senhora da Penha and São Miguel. The agricultural households noted in the urban area were almost entirely in Santa Efigênia where fruit and tea were grown for the urban market.

and Santos, critical for export purposes, but also between different settlements on the plateau. The development of communications networks in the effort to reduce transport costs and compete with coastal producers in sugar production also facilitated the development of local markets for products with much lower margins of profit. The involvement with and profitability of the export market occupied an ever-larger proportion of the population, making the latter progressively less willing to engage in subsistence activities. As a result, both the prices of basic foodstuffs and the market for same increased.

During the early period of development, which in this study is represented by the 1802 cross-sectional analysis, the benefits of economic expansion tended to be generalized to a large proportion of households. Small producers of rum, households selling small surpluses of basic foodstuffs, rice or cotton, or a few livestock were common in the rural parishes at that time. The proportion of reasonably well-off households and even some who participated on the city council grew significantly in the rural bairros over the period 1765 to 1802 in response to the incipient market developments and improvements in transport. Growth in the number of households in the rural bairros was considerable during these years.

From 1802 to 1836 the focus of production for the export market and even for local commercial production became general. Concern over the availability of lands for more export crops and large-scale production was shown in litigation and statements by provincial leaders. The concentration in land ownership and production by 1836 was observable in the census lists from which the small producers of rum and even subsistence crops had largely disappeared between 1802 and 1836, leaving only a few slave-holding fazendeiros and their agricultural dependents where four times as many commercial producers had been thirty-four years earlier. By 1836 the bulk of rural commercial production was concentrated on a few large agricultural estates. Growth in numbers of households in the rural area from 1802 to 1836 was less than that which normally would have been provided by natural increase, but levels of production were substantially increased.[1] The transformation was complete.

OCCUPATIONAL DISTRIBUTION 1765, 1802, 1836

The occupational distribution by head of household in 1765 (see Table V:2) indicates that there were a few individuals practicing the basic professions needed for the existence of minimal urban services in São Paulo. The stores for dry and wet goods, the doctors and lawyers, the artisans, barbers, carpenters and brick-layers--all in very small numbers--served the urban population of São Paulo itself and a small area in the hinterland. The presence of workers in these occupations was a reflection of the size of the resident population and had no relationship to the external economy. Only the relatively large number of businessmen/merchants (twenty-nine) gives any indication of São Paulo's future as entrepôt or her special geographic advantages. The large proportion of households not listing occupation (72.5 percent in the urban area) is indicative of households engaged solely in subsistence agriculture. The domestic mode of production and consumption was so pervasive in 1765 that the census-taker did not consider it worth mentioning. As suggested earlier, those households listing other occupations were probably also engaged in subsistence agriculture.

Between 1765 and 1802 a basic spatial and social differentiation had taken place between the rural and the urban areas, as demonstrated by the occupational listing for

[1] Alice Canabrava, "Uma economia de decadência: os nivels de riqueza na capitania de São Paulo, 1765/67," Revista Brazileira de Economia, 26, no. 4 (out/dez 1972):83 suggests that this area was experiencing a negative annual rate of growth in the period 1805 to 1818.

1802 (see Table V:3). The appearance of so many households whose major productive activity was sewing or making cloth is evidence that a very significant entrance of low-income workers into the exchange economy had taken place. In spite of the large labor force, the production was small. These were home-based workers spinning from small garden patches of cotton, making clothes and cloth suitable only for slaves or the poor. Most of these households were headed by women, a sex whose employment alternatives were, in any case, severely limited. Other possible means of urban livelihood for women were the service occupations (especially noticeable were the laundresses) and, for those lucky enough to own property, income from renting out the labor of slaves or from the lease of a house.

Professions in the area of business and commerce had doubled since 1765 in the urban area of São Paulo with 16.23 percent of households gaining their principal livelihood in this area by 1802. Fifty-five of these were in the business of importing dry-goods into São Paulo for sale. Those who specified stated that they brought their goods from Rio de Janeiro, or, in one case, from Lisbon. In terms of imported goods, if not for exports, the port of Rio de Janeiro was still more important for São Paulo merchants than was Santos.

The incipient transition of the local economy to a system of exchange was strongly apparent in the appearance of importers for food from nearby towns (20 households), the small grocers (39 households), and the taverners (4 households). Sainte-Hilaire noted in 1819 that fazendeiros of the communities near São Paulo sent food surpluses to the city of São Paulo, instead of to their own less-developed markets.[2]

Reliable and regular transport service was critical to the development of a market economy in São Paulo and especially to the expansion of exports from the interior provinces. The very significant increase in São Paulo from one mule team driver-owner in 1765 to twenty driver-owners in the urban area and three in the rural area by 1802 is one of the clearest indicators of the movement from a subsistence to an exchange economy. The importance of the mule team driver (tropeiro) to the businessman and the fazendeiro alike was widely recognized as being critical in the early nineteenth century, almost amounting to a question of dependency.[3] Households engaged in artisan

---

[2]Auguste de Sainte-Hilaire, Viagem a província de São Paulo e resumo das viagems aõ Brasil, translated by Rubens Borba de Morães (São Paulo, 1972), p. 136.

[3]João Maurício Rugendas, Viagem pitoresca através do Brasil (São Paulo, 1972), pp. 21-22 wrote in the 1820s that for a traveler the most important consideration was "to find an honest and experienced tropeiro, capable of taking care of and guiding the animals during the trip. Any economy in this respect would be counter-productive and would lead to disagreeable consequences. It would be craziness to imagine that any slave could be employed as a tropeiro. (...) Here, even more than in Europe, the principal personnages are the four-legged ones; you are completely dependent on them and consequently on the tropeiro. It is enormously important from every point of view that he be honest, experienced, and decisive." Maria Sylvia de Carvalho Franco, although intending to show the dependence of the tropeiro upon the fazendeiro, often managed to do the opposite. She states, "in the phase in which commercial fazendas were developing, the fazendeiro was literally tied down to the tropeiro depending on his willingness to furnish him with animals, within reasonable periods of time and at reasonable prices. Homens livres na ordem escravocrata (São Paulo, 1969), p. 64. The profession of tropeiro was one with considerable economic potential and social mobility. See Sainte-Hilaire, Viagem, pp. 136-37 and Carvalho Franco, Homens livres, p. 68.

TABLE V:2

Occupations Listed by Household for Urban and Rural Areas, São Paulo, 1765

	Urban	Rural
I. Extractive Occupations		
Farmers (not given)	--	--
Fishermen	1	2
Miners	2	
Driver of Pack Animals	1	
Total	4	2
Percentage Total Households		(.8)
II. Artisan Occupations		
Cobblers	15	
Tailors	17	1
Cutlers	1	
Cabinetmakers	1	
Saddlers	2	
Goldsmiths	2	
Blacksmiths	4	
Tinsmiths	2	
Coppersmiths	1	
Total	45	1
Percentage Total Households	(7.92)	(.4)
III. Construction Activities		
Bricklayers and Masons	2	3
Carpenters	11	
Stone and Mosaic Workers	1	
Total	14	3
Percentage Total Households	(2.46)	(1.25)
IV. Textiles		
Silkmakers	1	
Total	1	0
Percentage Total Households	(.18)	
V. Service Occupations		
Hairdressers, Barbers	7	
Total	7	0
Percentage Total Households	(1.23)	(0.0)

	Urban	Rural
VI. Business and Commerce		
Small grocers	19	
Salesclerks	2	
Businessmen	29	
Total	50	0
Percentage Total Households	(8.80)	
VII. Professions		
Notary Publics	1	
Lawyers	3	
Medical Doctors	2	
Pharmacists	3	
Surgeon-Major	1	
Treasurer General for Absent Persons	1	
Total	11	0
Percentage Total Households	(1.94)	
XI. Artistic Occupations		
Painters	3	
Musicians	1	
Total	4	0
Percentage Total Households		
XII. Religious Orders[1]		
Nuns (Beata)	3	
Religious Orders (male)	2	
Total	5	0
Percentage Total Households		
XIII. Military Income		
Total	12	1
Percentage Total Households	(2.1)	(.9)
XIV. Non-Productive Occupations		
Students	3	
Total	3	0
Percentage Total Households		
XV. No Occupations Listed[2]		
Total	412	233
Percentage Total Households	(72.5)	(97.0)
Total Households	568	240

[1]Religious residing in institutions were not listed in this census.

[2]Agricultural activities were not listed as an occupation in this census, although it is known that subsistence agriculture was the predominant occupation.

TABLE V:3

Occupations Listed by Household for Urban and Rural Areas, São Paulo, 1802

	Urban	Rural
I. Extractive Occupations		
Farmers	77	251
Ranchers	3	1
Fishermen	7	4
Absentee Farmers	1	0
Total	88	256
Percentage Total Households	(8.55)	(56.26)
II. Artisan Occupations		
Cobblers	21	6
Tailors	30	
Cutlers	1	
Cabinetmakers	3	
Saddlers	9	
Goldsmiths	5	
Horse-shoers	2	
Blacksmiths	14	
Tinsmiths	2	
Coppersmiths	1	
Total	88	6
Percentage Total Households	(8.55)	(1.32)
III. Construction Activities		
Bricklayers and Masons	4	
Carpenters	28	5
Mosaic workers	2	
Total	34	5
Percentage Total Households	(3.30)	(1.10)
IV. Textiles		
Seamstresses	190	
Spinners and Weavers	56	50
Quilt-makers	5	3
Silkmakers	3	0
Cotton Carders	5	
Total	259	53
Percentage Total Households	(25.17)	(11.6)
V. Service Occupations		
Hairdressers, Barbers	8	
Cooks	1	
Door keepers	1	
Laundresses	19	
Total	29	—
Percentage Total Households	(2.82)	0

	Urban	Rural
VI. Industry		
Comb and Whistle Manuf.	2	10
Sugar and Rum Mfg.	1*	51
Flour Miller	1	
Total	4	61
Percentage Total Households	(.38)	(13.40)
VII. Business and Commerce		
Small grocers	39	7
Salesclerks	3	
Businessmen	24	3
Dry-Goods Wholesalers	55	1
Beverage Importers and Wholesalers	14	
Taverners	4	
Exporters of food products	1	
Importers of food from nearby towns	20	
Sugar venders (retail)	2	
Slave dealers	3	
Slave assistants	2	
Total	167	11
Percentage Total Households	(16.07)	(2.42)
VIII. Rentier		
Landlords	9	
Slave dealers (rentals)	42	
Total	51	0
Percentage Total Households	(4.91)	
IX. Transportation		
Pack Animal Driver/Owner	20	3
Total	20	3
Percentage Total Households	(1.92)	(0.66)
X. Professions		
Scribes	11	
Notary Publics	1	
Latin Grammar Teachers	4	
Teachers Primary School	3	
Lawyers	7	
Doctors	3	
Royal Public Service Employees	19	3
Total	48	3
Percentage Total Households	(4.62)	(0.66)

*The Sugar Mill was actually located in São Carlos, but the owner lived in urban São Paulo.

	Urban	Rural
XI. Artistic Occupations		
Painters	5	
Musicians	3	
Writers	3	
Actors	3	
Total	14	0
Percentage Total Households	(1.35)	
XII. Religious[1]		
Secular	39	4
Total	39	4
Percentage Total Households	(3.75)	(0.88)
XIII. Paid Military	98	1
Percentage Total Households	(9.43)	
XIV. Other		
Laborers	9	21
Living off capital or "goods"	18	
Widows on "goods" of late husband	4	
Assistance of son	21	
Assistance of parents	17	
Beggars	19	26
Student	1	
Total	89	47
Percentage Total Households	(8.57)	(10.3)
XV. No Occupation Listed	11	6
Percentage Total Households	(1.06)	(1.32)
Total Households	1,039	456
	(100.00)	(100.00)

[1]Religious residing in institutions were not included in this table, nor in the census generally.

SOURCES: Maços de população, capital, 1802. This table includes only what has been coded as first-listed or principal occupation of household. There were as many as five occupations coded per household. See text for discussion of multiple occupations. Also see Appendix IV:1 for a discussion of the methodology involved in the development of the occupational distributions.

occupations related to livestock--saddlers, horseshoers, and blacksmiths--increased more than fourfold since 1765, providing additional proof of the growth in the transport sector.

Another notable aspect of the occupational distribution was the large number of carpenters--twenty-eight in the urban area alone. Carpenters were in considerable demand for the construction of sugar engenhos. The high price of sugar on the international market during the Napoleonic Wars was a great stimulation to production. Complaints against carpenters behind in construction of sugar mills were common in the first quarter of the nineteenth century. If the mills were not finished in time, the planters suffered losses as they could not process the cane.[4]

In the rural bairros the major occupation for 56.02 percent of the combined heads of households was agricultural. The fifty-one sugar producers in the district of Nossa Senhora do O have been classified under industry, but undoubtedly the presence of these sugar mills encouraged a specialization in cane on neighboring farms.[5] Crop specialization was evidence of the development of exchange characteristics in the rural economy.

The cottage textile industry occupied fifty-three or 11.6 percent of rural households. This was the occupational category next in importance to agriculture and industry in the rural area, though textiles were still more prominent in urban São Paulo.

Significant modifications in the strategies of particular household economies also seem to have occurred between 1765 and 1802. Whereas in 1765 27 percent of urban heads of households listed an occupation to supplement subsistence production, in 1802 heads of households frequently listed several occupations. Some heads listed as many as five occupations with 42 percent listing more than one occupation other than subsistence agriculture. There were importers who doubled as retail salesmen; some cloth traders were also involved in cattle dealing or headed mule trains (tropeiros). Many acquired additional income by renting out slaves as day laborers; the latin grammar teacher worked part time as a scribe. Only 6 percent of household listings, however, indicated that another member of the household besides the head contributed income to the household economy. The prevalence of multiple occupations in 1802 functioned, like the universal involvement in subsistence activities of 1765, as a kind of safeguard against the failure of any particular undertaking. While the economic situation in São Paulo had altered substantially in the thirty-seven years between the censuses, commerce continued to be a difficult and risky business. Prices varied widely depending upon how recently a ship had come into Santos. Prices rose proportionately as local stocks diminished and fell when arrivals of new merchandise entered (and sometimes flooded) the market.

The occupational structure for the urban districts of the Sé and Santa Efigênia in 1836 is presented in Table V:4. Compared to 1802, the proportions of heads of households in extractive and artisan occupations were similar, but there were a few notable differences. The most striking change took place in the area of textiles. The

---

[4]In 1818 Antônio da Silva Prado had this difficulty and the next year he threatened to sue the carpenter if he did not finish the mill in time for the next crop. Further evidence of the importance of the carpenter in this period is found in the petition of a captain-major of Porto Feliz, in 1821, asking that a carpenter be exempted from military service because of the need for his services in building engenhos. Maria Thereza Schorer Petrone, A lavoura canavieira em São Paulo (São Paulo, 1968), pp. 100-01.

[5]The senhores de engênho themselves were more interested in the actual manufacture of sugar than in the growing of cane. It was in his interest to have as many agriculturalists dependent on his mill as possible, since the mill normally kept half of the sugar produced as payment. The engênho do Sergipe do Conde operated without having cane fields of its own, relying on the cane from neighboring farmers throughout the period from 1622 to 1653. História geral da civilicação brasileira, I, Tomo 2, sob a direção de Sérgio Buarque do Holanda (São Paulo, 1973), p. 209.

number of tailors fell and persons working as seamstresses and weavers declined to about 50 percent of their numbers in 1802, probably reflecting the consequences of competition with English products. Services, especially meat-cutters and laundresses, increased substantially, possibly as a result of the greater dependence on the market for basic supplies and, in the case of laundresses, the growing necessity to procure help for services formerly performed by slaves. The large number of laundresses--who earned only twenty to thirty mil reis per year--may also suggest that many former seamstresses had become laundresses. New industrial occupations in 1836 included pottery, brick-making, soap-making, hat-making, cigarette-making, and the manufacture of gunpowder, though these industries offered little employment since slaves were commonly utilized. The substantial proportional increases in heads of households with commercial or professional occupations were predictable consequences of the increasingly redistributive and administrative character of urban São Paulo by 1836.

More interesting insights to the changes in social life in São Paulo by 1836 can be derived from an analysis of the mapa geral--a listing of workers by parish in the district of São Paulo in 1836. (See Table V:5). In this document an average 2.2 occupations per household were listed for the urban parishes of the Sé, Santa Efigênia, and Brás. It is obvious from the census manuscripts that most multiple-worker households were surviving on a low-income base. Entrance of several household members into the labor market was apparently a means of increasing total household income. Compared to the census-based occupational distribution, the mapa geral lists unusual numbers of small grocers and female day laborers in all bairros. The difference between the two distributions may have been a result of "hidden" employment of women in lower-income households.[6] Women selling homemade sweets, handiwork of some kind, or garden produce may not have reported this kind of economic activity for the census, but the

---

[6]Two examples of many possible are the following:

I. Census of Sul do Sé, 1836, Quarteirão 17, Fogo 13

Head: Benedito Jozé de Carvalho, 29, pardo, livre, born São Paulo, single, carpenter, 144 mil reis annual income.

Francisco de Almeida, 20, pardo, liberto, born São Paulo, married, tailor, 120 mil reis annual income.

Sidusina, 19, parda, livre, born São Paulo, married, washes clothes.

Anna Candida de Jezus, 22, preta, liberta, born São Paulo, single, lives by washing clothes.

II. Ibid., Quarteirão 9, Fogo 19

Head: Luzia Maria, 30, branca, São Paulo, single, seamstress.

Gertrudes Maria da Conceição, 48, parda, livre, Cidade, single, laundress.

Filho Marcelino Jozé, 18, single, soldier, musician, salaried.

Manoela Maria, 32, parda, livre, single, laundress.

Luis Joaquim, 31, branco, single, tailor, 72 mil reis annual salary.

Brasileira Joaquim, 29, parda, liberta, single, seamstress.

required license to do so led to the listing in the mapa geral.[7] The female day laborers--more than three times the number of male day laborers--similarly must have come from low income families which acquired extra income through the household member's work as laundress, wet nurse, or servant. Since the census-based table lists the occupations for the heads of households for the same bairros, it is clear that these categories of small grocers and female day laborers were not frequently principal household occupations, but rather sources of supplementary income.

The occupational distribution by head of household for the rural bairros of Nossa Senhora do O and Penha and São Miguel in 1836 (see Table V:6) indicates no significant differences from the 1802 distribution, apart from an increase in number of businessmen. On the other hand, according to the total occupational distribution in the mapa geral (Table V:5), it is evident that the number of small vendors listed for the rural bairros was extremely large, making up 38.4 percent of total rural occupations. In fact, the number of vendors was more than equal to the number of households in the two bairros, probably meaning that the proportion of households involved in agriculture for commercial purposes had grown to include practically the entire population in these bairros. As noted in the section on urban occupations, the "vendors" could easily have been women from poor households either involved in roadside businesses or house-to-house sales.

RISE IN VALUE OF LABOR AND LAND AND DISTRIBUTION OF SLAVES

The development of spatial and social differentiation of land and labor use between 1765 and 1836 as demonstrated in the occupational data was intimately associated with the development of a road and port system and the concurrent rise in land values after 1780.

Late eighteenth and early nineteenth century property inventories provide evidence that mean values of both improved and unimproved properties increased substantially in the first two decades of the nineteenth century. Before 1800, the assessed worth of improved properties was generally low relative to that of slaves, animals, or furniture. For example, the property inventory of Maria de Araujo (1756) lists the sítio de Pirapôra (a small fazenda) which included a house with four corridors (lanços, probably about sixteen bedrooms) made of taipa, with wooden doors, windows, and locks, with other smaller buildings, and the surrounding land with its fruit trees and planted areas, all valued at 50 mil reis.[8] This value should be compared with a cotton sheet at 1,600 reis, a quilt for 3,840 reis, a horse for 20 mil reis, a ten-year-old slave girl for 70 mil reis, and a twenty-five-year-old male slave for 150 mil reis. Often the houses included in the property inventories were sold to facilitate the division of the estate.[9] It was only when land became relatively scarce and began to acquire value at the beginning of the

[7]All street and shop vendors were required to obtain a license from the procurador of the city council. The difficulty in enforcing this regulation is obvious from the frequent statements in the minutes of the city council that vendors must report to the procurador. See, for example, ACMSP XV, 12 dezembro 1770, p. 627.

[8]AESP, Inventários não publicados, Inventário do Maria de Araujo, 1765; caixa 56.

[9]AESP, Inventários não publicados, Inventário do Salvador de Oliveira, 1663; caixa 7. Every one of six improved properties listed in the inventory were sold for an average of about five mil reis, equivalent at that time to the value of a mattress or four towels.

TABLE V:4

Occupational Structure of the Urban Parishes of the Sé and Santa Efigênia by Head of Household and Total Population, According to the 1836 Census of São Paulo

OCCUPATION	HEAD	PERCENT	TOTAL	PERCENT
I. EXTRACTIVE				
Agriculturalists	101		115	
Income from Fazenda	7		9	
Cattle ranchers	5		16	
Chácara owners (orchards, etc.)	6		9	
Woodcutters	4		5	
Fishermen	7		8	
Administrators Fazenda	0		2	
Total Extractive	130	9.17	164	10.03
II. ARTISAN				
Cobblers	26		50	
Tailors	19		37	
Coppersmiths	2		3	
Blacksmiths	27		35	
Horseshoers	2		6	
Saddlers	5		8	
Goldsmiths	14		18	
Watchmakers	1		1	
Spoonmakers	1		1	
Tanners	1		1	
Cabinetmakers	6		18	
Guitarmakers	4		4	
Apprentices	0		1	
Total Artisan	108	7.62	183	11.19
III. CONSTRUCTION				
Bricklayers/Masons	3		6	
Carpenters	20		35	
Total Construction	23	1.62	41	2.51
IV. TEXTILES				
Seamstresses	118		156	
Weavers/Spinners	18		21	
Silkmakers	1		2	
Total Textiles	137	9.66	179	10.95

OCCUPATION	HEAD	PERCENT	TOTAL	PERCENT
V. SERVICES				
Barbers	4		4	
Butchers and Meatcutters	10		10	
Bakers	3		3	
Cooks	3		4	
Laundresses	45		60	
Starch/Iron clothes	3		8	
Gardeners	1		1	
Messengers	2		4	
Servants	0		1	
Doormen	0		1	
Total Services	71	5.01	96	5.87
VI. INDUSTRIAL				
Potters	12		28	
Brickmakers	4		4	
Soapmakers	0		1	
Hat makers	2		2	
Cigarette makers	1		1	
Gunpowder mfgs.	2		2	
Total Industrial	21	1.48	38	2.32
VII. PROFESSIONAL				
Public Employees	42		53	
Lawyers	8		10	
Professor Law Faculty	7		7	
Bailiffs	3		3	
Doctors	1		0	
Surgeons	4		4	
Pharmacists	5		5	
Scribes	3		3	
Accountants	3		3	
Engineers	2		2	
Elementary Teachers	2		2	
Men of Letters	2		2	
Total Professional	82	5.78	94	5.75
VIII. BUSINESS/COMMERCE				
Businessmen	186		206	
Small grocers	37		50	
Greengrocers/ street venders	25		36	
Large grocers	31		33	
Salesclerks	10		29	
Taverners	4		7	
Drygoods store-keepers	1		1	

OCCUPATION	HEAD	PERCENT	TOTAL	PERCENT
Moneylenders	1		1	
Collectors Tithes	1		1	
Total Business/ Commerce	296	20.87	364	22.26
IX. TRANSPORTATION				
Owner/Drivers mule teams	14		14	
Assistants to Driver	4		6	
Oxcart Drivers	19		20	
Total Transportation	37	2.61	40	2.45
X. RELIGIOUS				
Priests	19		24	
Chaplains	2		3	
Sacristans	4		5	
Bishop	1		1	
Total Religious	26	1.83	33	2.02
XI. PAID MILITARY				
First and Second Line and Pensioned Off.	51		54	
Municipal Guard	46		80	
Total Military	97	6.84	134	8.20
XII. ARTISTIC				
Painters	5		5	
Musicians	8		11	
Buglers	2		4	
Adorners	1		1	
Actors	2		3	
Total Artistic	18	1.27	24	1.47
XIII. NON-PRODUCTIVE				
Students	54		74	
Assistance Parents	2		6	
Assistance Sons	2		2	
Beggars	6		7	
Pensioners	3		5	
Total Non-Productive	67	4.72	94	5.75
XIV. OTHERS				
Day Laborers	28		45	
Capital ("Bems")	24		24	
Landlords	5		8	
Slave dealers (renters)	4		4	

OCCUPATIONS	HEAD	PERCENT	TOTAL	PERCENT
Various undefined occupations ("agencias")	53		58	
Arrangements ("arranjos")	3		5	
Income or salary	1		2	
Not Legible	2		5	
Total Others	120	8.46	151	9.24
XV. NOT GIVEN	185	13.05	---	----
TOTALS	1,418	100.00	1,635	100.00

HEAD: Numbers of heads of households in given occupations.

PERCENT: Percent of total heads of households in given occupations.

TOTAL: Total occupations listed in households for all members.

PERCENT: Percent of total occupations listed in particular occupations.

NOTE: This table is based on the available census manuscripts for the urban area of São Paulo in 1836,lacking the parish of Brás, and six Quarteiroens whose census lists were missing from the archives. Maços de população, capital, 1836.

TABLE V:5
General Occupational Structure of the Urban and Rural Areas of the City of São Paulo, According to the Mapa Geral of 1836

OCCUPATION	URBAN	PERCENT	RURAL	PERCENT
I. EXTRACTIVE				
Agriculturalists	253		282	
Fishermen	11		3	
Farm Laborers	13		297	
Woodcutters	3			
Laborers in Tea	23			
Total Extractive	303	8.92	582	49.70
II. ARTISAN				
Cobblers	61		6	
Tailors	57		0	
Cabinetmakers	27		0	
Saddlers	13		0	
Goldsmiths	28		0	
Blacksmiths	47		3	
Horseshoers	7		0	
Tinsmiths	4		3	
Coppersmiths	2		0	
Coopers	2		0	
Watchmakers	3		0	
Tanners	1		0	
Total Artisan	252	7.42	12	1.02
III. CONSTRUCTION				
Bricklayers	6		0	
Carpenters	58		9	
Total Construction	64	1.89	9	.77
IV. TEXTILES				
Seamstresses	144		27	
Weavers	1		1	
Silkmakers	3		0	
Total Textiles	148	4.36	28	2.39
V. SERVICES				
Barbers	6		0	
Meat cutters	14		0	
Doormen	5		0	
Gardener	1		0	
Servants	5		0	
Total Services	31	.91	0	.00

OCCUPATION	URBAN	PERCENT	RURAL	PERCENT
VI. INDUSTRIAL				
Potters	24		13	
Gunpowder mfgs.	2		0	
Brickmakers	1		0	
Guitarmakers	5		1	
Screenmakers	0		4	
Hat makers	1		0	
Cigarette mfgs.	11		0	
Total Industrial	44	1.30	18	1.54
VII. PROFESSIONAL				
Notary Publics	1		0	
Lawyers	8		0	
Medical Doctors	5		0	
Pharmacists	7		0	
Surgeons	4		0	
Secondary Teachers	2		0	
Substitute Professors	5		0	
Professors Law Academy	9		0	
Men of Letters	8		0	
Scribes	10		2	
Public Employees	80		0	
Judges	8		4	
Primary Teachers	5		1	
Bailiffs	3		0	
Total Professional	155	4.57	7	.60
VIII. BUSINESS/COMMERCE				
Businessmen	327		8	
Small grocers	1,413		447	
Collectors public funds	3		0	
Total Business/ Commerce	1,743	51.34	455	38.86
IX. TRANSPORTATION				
Owners mule team	34		5	
Assistants	54		8	
Oxcart Drivers	18		0	
Total Transportation	106	3.12	13	1.11
X. RELIGIOUS				
Secular Clergy	37		3	
Nuns	58		0	
Seminary Students	19		0	
Novitiates	35		0	
Monks	5		0	

Priests	22		4	
Sacristans	11		2	
Total Religious	187	4.76	9	.70
XI. MILITARY				
Troops	11	.32	5	
XII. ARTISTIC				
Painters	9		0	
Musicians	14		0	
Buglers	2		0	
Sculptors	0		3	
Total Artistic	25	.74	3	.26
XIII. DAY LABORERS				
Male	122		4	
Female	391		40	
Total Laborers	513	15.11	44	3.76
TOTAL OCCUPATIONS (excluding institutions and non-productive occupations)	3,395	100.00	1,171	100.00
NON-PRODUCTIVE				
Students	175		0	
Beggars	12		5	
Lepers	19		0	
"Agregados"	140		101	
Total Non-Productive	346	8.81*	1068.24*	

*Percentage of total occupations (including non-productive) in these categories. The category "agregado" appears on the mapa geral as an occupation next to the category "day laborer" but the meaning of it in terms of occupation was unspecified.

SOURCE: Maços de população, capital, 1779-94, but clearly identifiable as the mapa geral for 1836 in spite of being undated. Details corresponding to figures cited by Daniel Muller, São Paulo em 1836, pp. 49-51 included the names of bairros listed within the district, the total numbers of priests, tax collectors, doctors, surgeons, pharmacists, businessmen, property owners, literate persons, judges of various types, and lawyers for the entire district. There were no figures which, if listed on the mapa, disagreed with Muller's data.

TABLE V:6

Occupational Structure of the Rural Parishes of Nossa Senhora do O, Penha, and São Miguel, by Head of Household, According to the 1836 Census

OCCUPATION	N.S. O	P./S.M.	TOTAL	PERCENT
I. EXTRACTIVE				
Agriculturalists	112	119	231	
Cattle Ranchers	2	2	4	
Fishermen	1	0	1	
Total Extractive	115	121	236	57.70
II. ARTISAN				
Cobblers	2	2	4	
Blacksmiths	1	2	3	
Tinsmiths	1	0	1	
Total Artisan	4	4	8	1.96
III. CONSTRUCTION				
Bricklayers	0	0	0	
Carpenters	2	5	7	
Total Construction	2	5	7	1.71
IV. TEXTILES				
Seamstresses	0	8	8	
Weavers/Spinners	8	26	34	
Quilt-makers	0	3	3	
Total Textiles	8	37	45	11.00
V. INDUSTRIAL				
Potters	1	11	12	
Screen-makers	0	3	3	
Brick-makers	1	0	1	
Total Industrial	2	14	16	
Rum mfg.	1	0	1	
Total Industrial	3	14	17	4.16
VI. PROFESSIONAL				
Public Employess	0	1	1	.24
VII. BUSINESS/COMMERCE				
Businessmen	14	1	5	
Small grocers	0	8	8	
Total Business/Commerce	14	9	23	5.62

OCCUPATION	N.S.O	P./S.M.	TOTAL	PERCENT
VIII. TRANSPORTATION				
Mule Team owners	5	2	7	1.71
IX. RELIGION				
Priests	0	1	1	.24
X. MILITARY				
First-line	2	0	2	.49
XI. ARTISTIC				
Sculptors	0	3	3	
Musicians	0	1	1	
Painters	0	1	1	
Total Artistic	0	5	5	1.22
TOTAL LISTED OCCUPATIONS	153	199	352	
OCCUPATION NOT LISTED	42	15	57	13.94
TOTAL HOUSEHOLDS	195	214	409	100.00

SOURCE: Maços de populaçāo, capital, 1836.

nineteenth century that the question of land ownership became relevant.[10] The 1818 compilation of land titles for the captaincy of São Paulo by owner and amount of land was the first concrete official recognition of the increasing value of land in the captaincy.[11] The official termination of the free land grants or sesmarias in 1822 and the leí das terras of 1850 specifying that land could only be acquired by purchase are proof that land acquired commercial value throughout Brazil in general in the early nineteenth century. It was in this period that unimproved lands began to be included in property inventories along with other improved and movable property.

The rise in land values was to a large extent a function of the expansion of the sugar trade from the plateau and bears direct testimony to the increased exchange value of products from the land. Finally, the effect of the increased exchange value for commercial agricultural production on free subsistence agriculturalist households was 1) an increased incentive to produce for sale because of the availability of new products which could be purchased only for cash; 2) pressure from commercially oriented producers to sell property (if owned) or displace squatters on well-located land; and 3) the appearance of a market for free labor on commercial farms. The general effects of this can be seen in Table V:1.

The increased value of labor--a necessary complement to the rise in land values--provided an indirect stimulus for rural crop specialization. High profits in the specialized commercial production of crops led fazendeiros to seek to concentrate labor in the production of these commodities rather than to utilize some of their labor force for the day-to-day needs of the fazenda. The result was the development of a market for subsistence crops and necessary utensils as well as for other articles such as shoes, clothes, and flour. Finally, the increase in cash available to the general population from the sale of services to the large landowners provided an improved market for the products of artisans. The rural occupational distributions of 1802 indicate that crafts and commercial occupations had arisen among subsistence producers as a supplement to their farming activities. In 1802 agricultural production for commercial purposes was most pervasive in Nossa Senhora do O including 48.4 percent of households, followed by Santana with 31.3 percent of households, and Penha/São Miguel with only 11.3 percent of households engaged in agriculture for sale. See Table V:7.

Tables V:8, V:9, and V:10 define more specifically the kind and value of the commodities produced in the rural bairros. Table V:8 indicates the proportion of households in each bairro engaged in agriculture which listed each product. In Nossa Senhora do O about 85 percent of agricultural households grew some basic food crops and half produced brandy and raised livestock. Eighty-seven percent of farm households in Santana cultivated basic crops, but only 25.3 percent produced brandy and about 30 percent raised cattle for sale. The agricultural households of the districts of Penha/São Miguel were almost entirely involved in production of basic food crops with only 6.93 percent of households producing brandy and 9.9 percent raising livestock.

Table V:9 shows the proportion of each bairro's income deriving from agriculture, rum, and livestock. Table V:10 indicates the proportion of the value of each product coming from each bairro. It is clear that Nossa Senhora do O was the most prosperous of the three districts, dominating the production of rum, and raising a significant proportion of colts and calves. Santana's productions valued less, but her cattle ranches boasted larger herds and Santana was also the district most important in the production of rice and

---

[10]José de Souza Martins, A imigração e a crise do Brasil agrária (São Paulo, 1973), p. 88 discusses the valorization of land as reflected in rent of property in São Bernardo in the first half of the nineteenth century. For the city of São Paulo see the pages later in this chapter.

[11]AESP, Bems rústicos, 1818.

manioc meal. The districts of Penha and São Miguel, with the largest number of households for the rural area, only realized 9.13 percent of the total value of rural produce. Over 70 percent of the value of Penha/São Miguel's outputs came from basic foodcrops, emphasizing the subsistence orientation of the area. The few ranchers of Penha/São Miguel were easily the wealthiest residents of the two bairros, bringing in almost 26 percent of income from 10 percent of farm households.

By 1836, this tendency in the rural bairros toward production for exchange as opposed to subsistence was manifested in terms of specialization in crops and other types of agricultural products.

Tables V:11 and V:12 show the volume productions of major crops, livestock, and industries in O, Penha, and São Miguel in 1836, as well as the relative importance of these products in the total output of the district of São Paulo. The tables indicate that in Nossa Senhora de O both the cultivation of all basic foodstuffs and cattle ranching declined while production was concentrated in rum and a beginning was made in coffee. Brick manufacture had also developed some importance in this district. In Penha and São Miguel--the most subsistence-oriented of the bairros studied in 1802--a tendency to de-emphasize such crops as beans and corn was evident, while manioc flour, rice, and cotton production was greatly expanded. The most startling change in Penha, however, was the development of livestock from almost nothing in 1802 to that of being one of the two most important cattle-raising parishes in the district, along with that of Cutia.[12]

Crop specialization was accompanied by a major increase in production as compared with 1802 and, in an apparent paradox, by a low or even negative rate of population increase in the rural bairros in this period. The contrast between the general prosperity and the numbers of small producers of products for market in 1802 and the concentration of production on a few estates by 1836 was marked. Both subsistence and small producers were being progressively eliminated from the land. The unusual number of land litigations and complaints of illegal land appropriations in the first decades of the nineteenth century was evidence that this process was well in progress.[13] A general rush to register ownership of unclaimed lands occurred. Squatters and their heirs were often deprived of lands which they had long occupied but had never registered: these

[12]Crops whose cultivation within the district were clearly concentrated in certain bairros in 1836 included rice (Guarulhos, 61.07 percent of districts production), coffee (São Bernardo, 91.01 percent), peanuts (Juquery, 90.56 percent), tobacco (Cutia, 100 percent), manioc flour (Guarulhos, 48.67 percent; São Bernardo, 32.42 percent). These figures are based on the mapa geral of 1836, found in AESP, TC, No. ordem 31, caixa 31.

[13]Comments by provincial president Almeida Torres in 1820 on land litigation problems are found in Revista do Instituto Histórico e Geográfico Brasileiro, XXXVI, p. 256. See Marcílio, "Crescimento demográfico," pp. 285-88 on the captaincy of São Paulo; and AESP, Cartas de datas de terras, VI, for the city of São Paulo from 1800 to 1820. Further cases of harassment, bullying, threats, and even kidnapping as a means of forcing cession of lands are found in AESP, TC, "Requerimentos sobre dívidas, heranças, queixas, relaxação de prisões, annos 1800-1819," no. ordem 34, caixa 93.

TABLE V:7

São Paulo Households Engaged in Agriculture Subsistence and/or Sale in 1802, by Bairro

(percent)[1]

BAIRRO	I	II	II	IV	Total
First Company	10	25	0	469	504
	(2.0)	(5.0)		(93.1)	(100.0)
Second Company	27	29	1	266	323
	(8.4)	(9.0)		(82.4)	(100.0)
Third Company	10	5	0	226	241
	(4.1)	(2.1)		(93.8)	(100.0)
Total Urban	47	59	1	960	1068
	(4.4)	(5.5)		(89.9)	(100.0)
N.S. do O	55	76	20	6	157
	(35.0)	(48.4)	(12.7)	(3.8)	(100.0)
Santana	41	42	16	35	134
	(30.6)	(31.3)	(11.9)	(26.1)	(100.0)
Penha/S. Miguel	82	19	0	67	168
	(48.8)	(11.3)		(39.9)	(100.0)
Total Rural	178	137	36	108	459
	(38.8)	(29.8)	(7.8)	(23.5)	(100.0)

I. Subsistence Agriculture

II. Households engaged in agriculture for both subsistence and sale.

III. Agriculturalists who did not have significant crops or planted little this year, so that no crops were listed.

IV. Agricultural activity was either not mentioned or else there was reported to be no agricultural activity in the household.

[1]Figures in brackets indicate the percentage of households in each bairro engaged in the listed mode of agricultural production.

SOURCE: Maços de população, capital, 1802.

TABLE V:8

The Proportion of Agricultural Households Engaged in the Production of Each Crop in Rural Districts of São Paulo, 1802

PRODUCT	N.S.O	SANTANA	P./S.M.
Beans	84.7	86.7	89.0
Corn	82.4	74.7	78.2
Manioc Meal	29.0	36.1	26.7
Rice	17.6	21.7	11.9
Rum	48.1	25.3	6.9
Colts	38.9	12.0	.0
Calves	48.9	4.8	.0
Oxen, Steers	11.5	30.1	9.9

SOURCE: Maços de populaçāo, capital, 1802.

NOTE: The base number used for each district was that of households actually engaged in some kind of agriculture. For Nossa Senhora do O, N Households was 131, for Santana, 83; for Penha and São Miguel, 101.

TABLE V:9

Proportions of Income Earned in Foodcrops, Rum, and Livestock in Rural Districts of São Paulo, 1802

SOURCE OF INCOME	N.S.O.	SANTANA	P./S.M.
Food Crops	50.1	52.4	72.3
Rum	28.5	11.2	1.8
Livestock	21.4	36.4	26.0
	100.0	100.0	100.0

SOURCE: Based on the data presented in Table V:10.

TABLE V:10

Value of Agricultural and Livestock Productions in the Districts of São Paulo in 1802

PRODUCT	VALUE	PERCENT OF PRODUCT PRODUCED IN EACH DISTRICT			
		N.S.O.	S.A.	P./S.M.	2nd CO.
Beans	1,411,200	41.8	27.3	23.7	7.2
Corn	3,111,480	51.7	21.7	19.2	7.3
Manioc Meal	2,203,300	21.7	34.1	27.6	16.6
Rice	149,600	23.6	37.0	30.9	8.4
Rum	2,025,600	74.6	19.8	2.0	3.6
Calves	192,240	83.1	8.2	.0	8.6
Colts[1]	969,600	77.2	15.8	.0	2.5
Oxen Steer[1]	2,368,400	9.4	47.9	24.9	12.6
Total	12,449,820	42.5	28.8	18.2	9.1

1. The first company produced 4.46 percent of the total value in colts and 6.24 percent of the total value in beasts of burden, giving it 1.34 percent of the total value of total production.

SOURCE: Productions were a total of all those given by household in Maços de população, capital, 1802. The values were taken from the median prices given in the "Mapa dos preços correntes na paroquia da cidade de S. Paulo no anno de 1802." All values are in reis.

TABLE V:11

Volume Production of Major Crops, Livestock, and Industries in Nossa Senhora do O in 1802 and 1836

PRODUCT	1802	1836	PERC. PROD. 1836
Manioc Flour (alqueires)	455	121	1.18%
Beans (alqueires)	921	70	1.61%
Corn (alqueires)	4,471	1,438	3.15%
Rice (alqueires)	65	0	--
Cotton (alqueires)	--	6	1.11%
Rum (canadas)	945	1,613	73.42%
Coffee (arrobas)	3	30	3.41%
Horses	156	18	1.11%
Pack Animals	5	--	--
Steers	31	7	.78%
Bricks (thousands)	0	80	100.00%

PERC. PROD.: Percent of the total production of given product in the district of São Paulo which derives from the parish of Nossa Senhora do O in 1836.

ALQUEIRE: A dry measure of 13.8 liters.

ARROBA: 14,685 kilograms

CANADA: 2.77 liters (wet)

SOURCES: 1802 figures calculated from sum of household production figures taken from AESP, TC, No. ordem 32, caixa 32, Maços de população, capital, 1802. 1836 figures taken from the mapa geral for 1836, found in AESP, TC, No. ordem 31, caixa 31, Maços de população, capital, 1779-94, undated document.

TABLE V:12

Volume Production of Major Crops and Livestock in Nossa Senhora da Penha e França and São Miguel in 1802 and 1836

PRODUCT	1802	1836	PERC. PROD. 1836
Manioc Four (alqueires)	579	1,145	11.13%
Beans (alqueires)	523	200	4.59%
Corn (alqueires)	1,662	887	1.95%
Rice (alqueires)	85	336	16.03%
Cotton (arrobas)	0	35	6.48%
Rum (canadas)	25	49	2.23%
Sheep	0	93	18.83%
Horses	0	872	53.93%
Pack Animals	95	0	3.41%
Steers	0	259	29.05%

PERC. PROD.: Percent of the total production of given product in the district of São Paulo which derives from the parishes of Penha and São Miguel.

ALQUEIRE: A dry measure of 13.8 liters.

ARROBA: 14,685 kilograms

CANADA: A liquid measure of 2.77 liters.

SOURCES: 1802 figures calculated from sum of household production figures taken from AESP, TC, No. ordem 32, caixa 32, Maços de população, capital, 1802. 1836 figures taken from the mapa geral for 1836, found in AESP, TC, No. ordem 31, caixa 31, Maços de população, capital, 1779-94, undated document.

families sometimes found these lands registered away from them. Other modes of concentration of property included sale and legal dispossession.[14]

Land scarcity was not the problem. Rather the interest of politically active commercial entrepreneurs lay in artificially limiting land supply in order to control export production and transform subsistence farmers and small producers into workers dependent upon the more capitalized establishments for their livelihood.[15] Thus the 1836 census records indicate a decline in households and in total population and a relative increase in persons, even families, living in various dependent arrangements as agregados or tenant farmers on the larger estates.[16]

CONCENTRATION OF PROPERTY

The increased specialization and commercialization of local crops by 1836 suggests the possibility that land holdings may have also become increasingly concentrated in the rural bairros in the nineteenth century. Although these lands were relatively infertile and their productions marginal compared to the paulista west, the unwillingness of sugar and coffee planters to use lands for subsistence crops coupled with the high prices of foodstuffs had made commercial specialization in subsistence crops a reasonably profitable business.[17] Concrete proof that some degree of concentration of land ownership did take place over the period 1802 to 1836 in other areas of the captaincy is demonstrated through analysis of the census of landowners and the size of their holdings taken in 1818. Unfortunately, the section of the landowners census (bems rústicos) pertaining to the district of the city of São Paulo is not in the archives.

[14]It was possible to secretly petition concession to lands occupied by others, but whose title was in doubt, and acquire the land that way. When the concessions of sesmarias were made, there was a month in which complaints and counter-claims could be made, but if the new claimant waited for the month to lapse before taking over the lands, no one could dispute him. AESP, TC, "Requerimentos sobre dívidas, heranças, queixas, relaxação de prisões, annos 1800-1819," no. ordem 34, caixa 93 includes several petitions by small holders complaining of harassment, bullying, threats, and even kidnapping as a means of forcing them to cede lands (or sell them) to powerful local landholders.

[15]By 1820 most of the land of the province of São Paulo had been officially granted or sold, although much of it had not been cultivated. See James Henderson, A History of Brazil (London, 1821), pp. 86-87. This fact should not be seen as indication of a land "shortage." The official "use" of the titles was to produce laborers, and that was also what happened in practice. See J.F. de Almeida Prado, D. João VI e o início da classe dirigente do Brasil, 1815-1889 (São Paulo, 1968), pp. 31-46 on the great land grants to friends of the government in the early nineteenth century and the efforts to force small farmers into social and economic dependency.

[16]Although perpetually dependent and imprisoned by not being privileged to hold title to land, the landless agriculturalist was not tied to any particular estate, except through ritual kinship and patronage. The instability of the rural worker was well known; the poverty and marginality of the agregado was so great that any apparent advantage could draw him to another fazenda. See Caio Prado, Jr., Evolução politica do Brazil e outros estudos (São Paulo, 1969), pp. 227-28.

[17]Buarque do Holanda, História geral, Part II, I, p. 102 discusses the problems of high food prices and cost of living in the first half of the nineteenth century, as well as the problem of inflation.

Nevertheless, the available data provides a clear picture of land use and ownership in the captaincy of São Paulo in 1818 which can also be utilized to interpret the case of the district of the city of São Paulo.

Alice Canabrava's analysis of the distribution of property ownership for the captaincy indicates a high concentration of land in the hands of a few proprietors (49.14 percent of the registered properties were owned by 1 percent of the total number of landholders).[18] There was considerable variation in level of concentration depending upon type of land use. The area peripheral to the district of São Paulo (Atibaia, Nova Braganca, Jundaiaf) which mainly produced basic foodcrops for the urban market had the lowest degree of concentration of ownership (42.72 percent of the registered area was owned by 5 percent of landowners), while the areas of sugar and coffee production and the centers of livestock were much more highly concentrated.[19]

The concentration of slave ownership in the rural bairros of São Paulo after 1800 provides further support for both the valorization of property and a concentration of land ownership. (See Tables V:13, V:14, and V:15.) Whereas in 1778, 68.3 percent of the slaves in the rural districts of São Paulo were owned by 16.1 percent of total households, each of which had eight or more slaves, by 1836, 66.2 percent of the slaves were concentrated in 6.7 percent of the households, each of which owned eight or more slaves. Households with fifteen or more slaves changed even more dramatically. In 1778 the 3.2 percent of households with fifteen or more slaves controlled 20.1 percent of all the slaves. By 1836 such households declined to 2.7 percent, while the proportion of the total slave population owned by those households more than doubled to 44.2 percent. The picture is thus one of an increasing concentration of available capital and labor within a declining number of agricultural establishments.

The result of a concentration of land ownership for the landless peasant was usually to put him in a position of even greater dependence on the large landowner. The fazendeiro frequently allowed the peasant to use a portion of land for a fee, or in return for services or a certain portion of his crops.[20] Often, it was the control of the free peasants' labor, which was the real goal of the fazendeiro rather than the land itself. The small agriculturalist could be controlled through his need for land.

INCOME DISTRIBUTION 1836

The emerging picture of São Paulo in 1836 is a mixed one of economic growth and expansion of trade and production on the one hand, and on the other, evidence of concentration of slave and land ownership and strong indications that lower-income families were developing joint residence patterns and were forced to acquire several household incomes in order to live reasonably. It would seem that a deterioration in the distribution of real income and thus in the mean standard of living had taken place between 1802 and 1836, precisely at the time when the transformation from a domestic to an exchange household economy was relatively complete.

---

[18]"Uma economia," p. 98. The "inventário dos bens rústicos," a list of properties, their extension and owners was taken in 1818 for the captaincy of São Paulo. It is archived in the AESP but is not generally available for research.

[19]Ibid., pp. 89-91, 106-07. Canabrava noted the correlation of subsistence crops (which included basic foodstuffs grown for the local market) and a "less unequal" or less concentrated land distribution pattern. Also see data on Itú showing a change in ownership patterns with the development of more profitable crops.

[20]Faoro, Os donos do poder, I, pp. 246-47.

Other evidence of a probable deterioration in income distribution in São Paulo in this period include high food prices, price inflation and the rise in cost of living.[21] Inflation, coupled with the fixed wages and rates established by the city council for independent laborers and artisans, almost guaranteed a "price-wage lag" which in turn would lead to a more unequal distribution of wealth.[22]

In order to substantiate a theory of deterioration in income distribution in this period, an income distribution for both 1802 and 1836 would be needed--unfortunately an impossible task for 1802. The 1836 census does list income for a large percentage of households and an estimate of income distribution by head of household has been constructed from that base. Although the comparative perspective is lacking, such an estimate provides some sense of the relative well-being of the different occupational sectors in society, and the extraordinary range of concentration in incomes which existed.

Yearly income distributions for the urban parishes of the Sé and Santa Efigênia for 1836 were estimated both by sector (Table V:16) and in the aggregate (Table V:17). The basic assumption involved in the estimate was that, within any given occupational sector, the distribution of listed incomes was equivalent to the distribution of all incomes. In other words, the choice of the particular persons whose incomes were listed in the census was one optimistic to a more rather than less equal distribution of income. It is probably true that the incomes of the less affluent heads of households were less likely to be listed, and the inspectors of some "quarteiroens" did, in fact, state at the end of their lists that the incomes of the residents were not listed because they were insignificant.

Relevant to both the social and political significance of income in Brazil at this time is the fact that the Constitution of 1824 made income a major voting criteria. Thus, a male Brazilian citizen had the right to take part in the parochial assemblies if he had an annual income of at least 100 mil reis and if he were not a manual laborer. The purpose of the parochial assemblies was to choose the provincial electors who were required to have an annual income of at least 200 mil reis. The electors chose the deputies and senators who had to have annual incomes of 400 and 800 mil reis respectively.[23] An

---

[21]See note 17.

[22]Earl J. Hamilton, "American Treasure and the Rise of Capitalism," Economica, IX, no. 27 (Nov. 1929):355-56. Hamilton's article started a long historiographical debate concerning the connection between the "price revolution" and the process of capital accumulation. See Immanuel Wallerstein, The Modern World Systems: Capitalist Agriculture and the Origins of the European World Economy in the Sixteenth Century (New York, 1974), pp. 67-87 for a review of the debate. Recent evidence (1968), based on better data than that which Hamilton originally used, tends to confirm the general hypothesis that there was a decline in real wages in sixteenth-century western Europe. E.H. Phelps-Brown and Sheila V. Hopkins, "Builders Wage-rates, Prices and Population: Some Further Evidence," Economica, XXVI, no. 101 (Feb. 1959):21 present evidence for real wage-shrinkage in the sixteenth century for southern England, France, Alsace, Munster, Augsburg, Valencia, and Vienna in Table II. Jean Fourastie and Rene Grandamy, "Remarques sur les prix salariaux des céréales et la productivité du travailleur agricole en Europe du XVe et XVIe siècles," Third International Conference of Economic History, Munich 1965 (Paris, 1968), p. 650 provide data indicating that the real price of wheat in Europe quadrupled between the fifteenth and the seventeenth and eighteenth centuries. The point about the unequal distribution of wealth is made by John Maynard Keynes, A Treatise on Money (London, 1950), II, p. 162.

[23]Imperial Constitution of Brazil, 1824 (Articles 5, 45 and 95). See also Joaquim Pires Machado Portella, Constituicão política do imperio do Brasil (Rio de Janeiro, 1876), pp. 40, 70, and 72.

TABLE V:13

The Distribution of Slaves by Household in Rural Bairros of São Paulo, 1778

	NH = 99		NH = 124		NH = 159	
	N.S. do O.		Santana		P./S.M.	
Slaves	I	II	I	II	I	II
1	55.5	100.0	43.55	100.0	40.2	100.0
2- 4	52.5	99.1	37.1	97.7	35.2	98.2
5- 7	31.3	80.5	21.8	81.6	20.7	80.2
8-10	18.1	61.0	16.1	68.3	11.9	62.0
11-14	6.0	32.2	9.7	47.9	5.0	36.3
15+	5.0	28.4	3.2	20.1	1.9	20.2

I. Percentage of households in bairro with given number or more of slaves.

II. Percentage of slaves in households with given number or more of slaves. For example, in N.S. do O 32.23 percent of the total slaves in the bairro were in households owning eleven or more slaves.

SOURCE: Maços de populaçåo, capital, 1778.

N SLAVES: N Senhora do O = 344; Santana = 353; Penha/S. Miguel = 373.

TABLE V:14

The Distribution of Slaves by Household in Rural Bairros of São Paulo, 1802

	N.S. do O NHH = 157		Santana NHH = 134		Penha/S.Miguel NHH = 168	
Slaves	I	II	I	II	I	II
1	49.7	100.0	36.6	100.0	37.5	100.0
2- 4	40.1	96.8	26.9	95.9	25.0	92.6
5- 7	23.5	81.9	15.7	80.3	13.7	73.2
8-10	13.3	62.7	9.7	64.7	7.1	50.0
11-14	7.6	45.8	5.3	48.2	4.2	34.1
15+	2.6	25.8	3.7	39.7	1.8	17.3

I. Percentage of households in bairro with given number or more of slaves.

II. Percentage of slaves in households with given number or more of slaves. For example, 45.8 percent of the slaves owned by the households of Nossa Senhora do O were owned by households with eleven or more slaves.

SOURCE: Maços de população, capital, 1802.

N SLAVES: N.S. do O = 469; Santana = 315; Penha/S. Miguel = 284.

TABLE V:15

The Distribution of Slaves by Household
in Rural Districts of São Paulo, 1836

	N.S. do O NHH = 195		Penha/S.Miguel NHH = 208		Total Rural NHH = 403	
Slaves	I	II	I	II	I	II
1	34.4	100.0	21.6	100.0	27.8	100.0
2- 4	25.6	96.1	15.9	95.4	20.6	95.9
5- 7	14.9	81.8	7.2	77.6	10.9	80.2
8-10	8.7	65.9	4.8	66.7	6.7	66.2
11-14	5.6	53.9	1.9	47.7	3.7	51.6
15+	3.6	42.0	1.9	47.7	2.7	44.2

I. Percentage of households in district with given number or more of slaves.

II. Percentage of slaves in households with given number or more of slaves. For example, 53.86 percent of the slaves owned by the households of Nossa Senhora do O were owned by households with eleven or more slaves.

N SLAVES: N.S. do O = 440; Penha/S. Miguel = 264; Total = 704.

SOURCE: AESP, caixa 37A, no. ordem 37A, Maços de população, capital, 1836.

TABLE V:16

Income Distribution for the Urban Parishes of the Sé and Santa Efigenia, by Occupational Sector, São Paulo 1836

INCOME (milreis)		EXTRACT.		ARTISAN		CONSTRUCT.		TEXTILES
0 - 49	a)	38	a)	3	a)	1	a)	110
	b)	1,207.49	b)	63.2	b)	40.00	b)	2,907.78
50 - 99	a)	45	a)	13	a)	4	a)	10
	b)	2,484.51	b)	931.00	b)	215.00	b)	536.35
100 - 199	a)	19	a)	57	a)	14	a)	11
	b)	1,948.85	b)	7,147.81	b)	1,824.70	b)	1,179.96
200 - 399	a)	8	a)	32	a)	4	a)	5
	b)	2,162.72	b)	7,757.11	b)	886.07	b)	1,072.69
400 - 799	a)	10	a)	3	a)	0	a)	1
	b)	5,802.72	b)	1,200.00	b)	--	b)	400.00
800+	a)	10	a)	0	a)	0	a)	0
	b)	20,512.33	b)	--	b)	--	b)	--
TOTALS	a)	130	a)	108	a)	23	a)	137
	b)	34,118.10	b)	17,099.12	b)	2,965.77	b)	6,096.78

a) Number of heads of households in occupational sector with income in given bracket.

b) Total income listed by households in a) in given income bracket.

EXTRACTIVE: Agriculturalists, cattle ranchers, fishermen, administrators of fazendas, those receiving income from fazendas, those with chacaras (normally fruits or tea), woodsmen.

ARTISAN: Cobblers, tailors, coppersmiths, blacksmiths, horseshoers, saddlers, goldsmiths, watchmakers, spoonmakers, tanners, cabinetmakers, guitar-makers, apprentices.

CONSTRUCTION: Bricklayers, masons, carpenters.

TEXTILES: Seamstresses, spinners and weavers, silkmakers.

SOURCE: Maços de população, Capital, 1836. See Appendix V:2 for the methodology involved in these tables.

TABLE V:16 (continued)

INCOME (milreis)		SERVICES		TRANSP.		RELIGIOUS		BUSINESS
0 - 49	a)	26	a)	0	a)	0	a)	8
	b)	794.99	b)	--	b)	--	b)	325.82
50 - 99	a)	4	a)	13	a)	0	a)	39
	b)	240.00	b)	802.08	b)	--	b)	2,138.97
100 - 199	a)	22	a)	14	a)	11	a)	90
	b)	3,149.99	b)	1,457.69	b)	1,514.26	b)	10,259.33
200 - 399	a)	3	a)	10	a)	5	a)	57
	b)	600.00	b)	2,400.00	b)	1,343.70	b)	15,190.31
400 - 799	a)	0	a)	0	a)	0	a)	84
	b)	--	b)	--	b)	--	b)	41,427.71
800+	a)	0	a)	0	a)	10	a)	18
	b)	--	b)	--	b)	9,763.47	b)	29,943.84
TOTALS	a)	55	a)	37	a)	26	a)	296
	b)	4,784.98	b)	4,659.77	b)	12,621.43	b)	99,285.98

a) Number of heads of households in occupational sector with income in given bracket.

b) Total income listed by households in a) in given income bracket.

SERVICES: Barbers, bakers, laundresses, starchers and ironers of clothes. Incomes for butchers, meatcutters, a gardener and two messengers could not be found, for a total of sixteen unknown incomes in this sector.

TRANSPORTATION: Drivers of mule teams (<u>tropeiros</u>), assistant drivers (<u>camaradas</u>), oxcart drivers. The type of <u>tropeiro</u> who buys and sells cattle was classifified as a businessman.

RELIGIOUS: Priests, chaplains, sachristans, and the bishop.

BUSINESS: Businessmen, money lender, collector of tithes, drygoods retail store owners, lareg grocerty store owners (<u>armazen</u>), small grocery store owners (<u>vendas</u>), greengrocers and streetvendors, taverners, salesclerks.

SOURCE: Maços de população, Capital 1836. See Appendix V:2, for the methodology involved in these tables.

TABLE V:16 (continued)

INCOME (milreis)	PROFESSIONS	MILITARY	ARTISTS	LABORERS
0 - 49	a) 2 b) 61.85	a) 0 b) --	a) 0 b) --	a) 13 b) 401.97
50 - 99	a) 0 b) --	a) 0 b) --	a) 2 b) 100.00	a) 15 b) 757.37
100 - 199	a) 6 b) 646.72	a) 54 b) 7,725.91	a) 0 b) --	a) 0 b) --
200 - 399	a) 16 b) 3,772.14	a) 13 b) 3,804.14	a) 3 b) 1,000.00	a) 0 b) --
400 - 799	a) 36 b) 17,178.30	a) 26 b) 11,976.08	a) 0 b) --	a) 0 b) --
800+	a) 22 b) 36,582.45	a) 4 b) 5,099.45	a) 0 b) --	a) 0 b) --
TOTALS	a) 82 b) 58,241.46	a) 97 b) 28,605.58	a) 5 b) 1,100	a) 28 b) 1,159.33

a) Number of heads of households in occupational sector with income in given bracket.

b) Total income listed by households in a) in given income bracket.

PROFESSIONS: Public employees, lawyers, professors of the law academy, bailiffs, doctors, surgeons, pharmacists, scribes, accountants, engineers, elementary teachers, men of letters.

MILITARY: Pensioned military of previous militia units, first-line military, municipal guard.

ARTISTS: Only painters' incomes were included since musicians', buglers', adorners' and actors' incomes were lacking and there was no secure basis for an estimate.

LABORERS: Includes only "journaleiros" or day laborers. This category is undoubtedly highly undernumerated, as based on figures from Muller and from the <u>mapa geral</u> for 1836.

OCCUPATIONAL CATEGORIES NOT INCLUDED: Lives on capital ("bems"), rent of houses, salary of slaves, on "agencias" or "arranjos," assistance of parents or son, beggars, pension, and students.

SOURCE: Maços de população, 1836. See Appendix V:2, for the methodology involved in these tables.

TABLE V:17

General Income Distribution for the Household Heads of the Urban Parishes of the Sé and Santa Efigênia, São Paulo, 1836

INCOME (mil reis)	PERCENT NO. H.H.	PERCENT TOTAL INC.	HH (cum)	INC. (cum)
0 - 49	201	5,803.10	19.63 (41.96)	2.14
50 - 99	145	8,205.28	14.16 (52.19)	3.03 (5.17)
100 - 199	298	36,855.22	29.10 (73.21)	13.61 (18.78)
200 - 399	156	39,988.88	15.23 (84.21)	14.77 (33.55)
400 - 799	160	77,984.81	15.63 (95.49)	28.80 (62.35)
800+	64	101,901.54	6.25 (100.00)	37.64 (100.00)
TOTALS	1,024	270,738.83		
N.G.	394			
TOTAL H.H.	1,418			

N.G.: Income not given in the census lists.

NOTE: This tabulation was based on the available census manuscripts for 1836, the actual number of households for the Sé and Santa Efigênia at this point being 1,655, according to the mapa geral. These totals are based on the occupational income distribution in the preceding Table V:16 as estimated according to the method described in Appendix V:2. The cumulative percentage figures for households in this table included the households in which incomes and occupations were not given in the income bracket 0-49. The rationale for this procedure is that in most cases the absence of an income or occupation implies that the figure was very insignificant. For example, the inspector of Quarteirão 11 of Santa Efigenia noted at the close of his list that, "Incomes and the quantities and types of productions were not listed in this Quarteirão because the harvests were only sufficient for household consumption and some insignificant sales."

income of 100 mil reis per year qualified a head of household as a responsible citizen worthy of some political choice, as long as he did not work at a manual occupation. Nevertheless, only those earning 400 mil reis or more could personally participate in actual legislation, or even have that chance.

An independent measure of the estimate of aggregate income distribution is provided by the voting lists of 1842 for the Sé which indicate that 35.26 percent of male heads of household had incomes of 100 mil reis or above (could take part in the parochial assemblies), while 7.56 percent had incomes of 200 mil reis or above (were eligible to be provincial electors).[24] Compared with the estimated aggregate distribution, given above, which includes the additional assumption that households for which neither income nor occupation were listed had an income of less than forty-nine mil reis per year, 48 percent of heads of households were estimated to earn 100 mil reis or more and 27 percent were estimated to earn 200 mil reis or more.

Obviously the estimated distribution is optimistic compared with the figures from the voting lists. To make them similar the proportions of households in the income groups under 100 mil reis should include at least 10 percent more of the total heads of households. The proportion in the income bracket 100 to 199 mil reis should be increased substantially, and the income brackets above 200 mil reis should have about two-thirds less heads of households included. In spite of the apparently high bias in the direction of equality, the estimated distribution suggests that 37.64 percent of income was controlled by 6.25 percent of the heads of households, while 52.19 percent of heads of households earned a combined 5.17 percent of total income. Any change in the estimate would only tend to increase the proportion of income controlled by an even smaller percentage of households.

The income distribution by occupational sector (Table V:7) undoubtedly also suffers, and perhaps even more in some areas, from the bias of the aggregate distribution. To a large degree this is a result of the under-enumeration of certain occupations and incomes in the census. Comparing the occupational structure derived from the census lists with that of the mapa geral, the number of workers in textiles in the urban area from the census compares well with that of the mapa geral, meaning that the distribution given was probably correct. The sectors which, according to the same criteria, appear to have been most under-enumerated were the agriculturalists, cobblers, carpenters, potters, cigarette-makers, public employees, small grocers, businessmen, assistants to mule team drivers, military personnel, and day laborers. With the exception of businessmen and some military personnel, these are occupations of relatively low-income levels, indicating that any correction factor should be heavily weighted in the lower brackets.[25]

The occupational sectors with the largest proportion of workers with annual incomes under 49 mil reis were the extractive (29.23 percent), textiles (80.29 percent), services (47.27 percent), and day laborers (46.23 percent). Middle-income occupations with large proportions of workers earning from 100 to 199 mil reis included the artisans (52.78 percent), construction workers (60.87 percent), services (40 percent), transportation (37.84 percent), religion (42.31 percent), business and commerce (30.41 percent), and the military (55.67 percent). Those sectors with a substantial proportion

---

[24]AESP, TI, "Lista dos cidadoes activas, que podem votar nas eleiçoes primarias e ser votados para Eleitores da Provincia, formado pela Junta de Parochia em conformedade do capitulo um do regulamento numero 157 de 4 de maio deste anno e portaria do governo da provincia de 19 de agosto que marca o dia 16 de outubro para as eleicoes primarias, 1842" no. ordem 37A, caixa 37A. 19 quarteiroens do sul do Se, 10 quarteiroens do norte do Se; 1191 total households, 420 voters; 90 eligible.

[25]Of course many of these occupations would have been held by persons who were not heads of households, but providing supplementary income, or living as an "agregado."

earning 400 mil reis or more included extractive (15.38 percent), religion (38.46 percent), business (34.46 percent), professional workers (70.73 percent), and military officers (30.93 percent). These latter groups were those privileged to be eligible for the positions of deputies and senators.

This picture agrees with general impressions of the elite, as well as those middle-range occupations with some possibility of mobility such as merchants, mule team drivers, cattle ranchers, and possibly agriculturalists. The analysis also reinforces previous discussion of the type of lower class household poor enough to need to include non-related members as lodgers and to require that women work as laundresses and seamstresses.

CONCLUSION

In 1765 virtually every household in the urban and rural districts of São Paulo was involved principally in subsistence agriculture; for most households it was the sole occupation (see Table V:1). We have seen that households produced for their own internal needs and for informal exchange with kinfolk and neighbors without the use of cash. They also produced for more formal contributions like the food offered for neighborhood church festivals and the traditional payments in kind given to the city council members. The heads of a small number of households possessed a significant amount of property based on slaves or the mining economy, but they too cultivated subsistence crops in addition to their other activities. The fact is that very few households were involved in the exchange economy in 1765 beyond the occasional purchase of iron utensils, firearms, and salt. By 1802 urban households engaged in agriculture had declined radically to 9.9 percent. In the rural bairros in 1802, 67.6 percent of households were engaged in agriculture: 38.8 percent were pursuing subsistence agriculture, and 29.8 percent were producing crops for sale as well.

The census reports clearly show that the rural bairros of the district of the city of São Paulo were experiencing a period of relative prosperity in 1802 as compared with 1765. Population growth, larger households, and an increase in agricultural livestock production, as well as new types of crops, were evident. Textile and sugar production (both for sale) was particularly striking. Notably, this relative prosperity was seen in small, less socially important households and households with few slaves in 1802 as well as in elite households. In this period the division of labor and the use of money as exchange value became common, but control over the means of production--land, tools, and access to commerce--was relatively unrestricted. This situation contrasted markedly with that of 1836, when the concentration of property and production and the impoverishment of the majority of households is clear.

From 1802 to 1836 the percentage of households in the urban area engaging in agricultural production showed little change (down from 9.9 to 9.2 percent). In the rural area those households producing for both subsistence and sale increased from 29.8 to 40.8 percent in the same period, while those producing only for subsistence purposes declined from 38.8 to 17 percent. Most striking in 1836, as compared with 1802, was the regional specialization of crops. The bairro of Nossa Senhora do O concentrated its production on sugar, that of São Bernardo on coffee and manioc flour, that of Cutia on tobacco.[26] This crop specialization was a concrete demonstration that by 1836 production for sale had effectively taken the place of the domestic mode of production within the city of São Paulo, even in the rural bairros.

The differentiation of the urban from the rural areas of São Paulo can be viewed in terms of the desire of a small dominant group to control labor, and the utilization of land

---

[26]See note 12.

policy as a means of realizing that end. In the period from 1765 to 1802 land had no commercial value and those who were not ceded lands had little difficulty in settling without title. To the contrary, it was highly desirable for both the crown and the local government that families settle permanently in some accessible location. The complaints of the period were of desertion and vagrants, not of squatters. Settled families were available for military drafts, and they were automatically made part of the urban militia groups responsible for road and bridge building, as well as police and certain administrative activities. The road-building function was of extreme importance in the latter half of the eighteenth century when roads were being built and improved between the new areas of agricultural development in the West Paulista, and the very critical road from São Paulo to Santos was being constructed. The urban militia also built the shelters for the mule teams on the edges of São Paulo and along the roads from the "sugar cities" as well as on the road to Santos. In this period the responsibility for a particular road or bridge was tied, whenever possible, to the militia group resident in the area where the work needed doing. In that way the workers had a personal interest in the project. At the same time the captain-major being the most influential landholder in the area of the worker's residence made the workers easier to control.[27] In this period it was plainly in the interests of the dominant class to allow small proprietors and subsistence farmers to co-exist with the large landowners.

As the value of land rose with the expansion of markets for agricultural produce and the cost-reducing improvements in infra-structure, the population grew and the situation changed. It was no longer possible for the subsistence farmer to easily find areas in São Paulo to squat without meeting resistance. Land disputes were common and even squatters of earlier periods were pushed off their lands. These poor agriculturalists had nowhere to go unless they accepted a position of shareholder (parceiro) or agregado on the estate of a powerful neighbor. In such circumstances the control of the large agriculturalist over the poor landless peasant was at a maximum. The peasant became entirely dependent upon the sale of his labor for income, and on the "generosity" of the landowner for a place to live. Whereas in the earlier period the peasant was retained within a district and controlled through his relation to lands which seemed to be his own, in the later period the restricted alternatives of the peasant meant that he could be better utilized by depriving him of his lands. Whether he accepted a dependency relationship with a large landowner, or went to the city in search of day labor or to learn a trade, he continued to be available for enrollment in the military and to increase the free labor force.

---

[27]The "company" militia leaders also had a personal interest in population increase within the particular bairro, in terms of their own political power and support as well as "favors" which could be exacted from less powerful neighbors.

VI
Household Economy and Composition in an Urbanizing Frontier Community

The development of the market economy and related changes in mode of production in São Paulo between 1765 and 1836 had a rapid, direct, and profound influence on the organization of households and on family formation. The dramatic changes in household organization and family formation in this period can in part be understood in terms of the fact that the household was predominantly the locus of production as well as labor in São Paulo until the end of the nineteenth century. The small, predominantly nuclear family units of the 1765 subsistence economy were replaced by 1802 in urban São Paulo with larger, more complex households with a substantially differentiated pattern of headship. This period was notable for the dramatic increase both in households headed by women and in persons living within the urban household yet unrelated to its head. The 1836 census analysis reveals a bimodal household organization in both the urban and the rural bairros. Elite households continued to expand while nonelite households decreased in size. Members unrelated to the head of household increased to 26 percent of household members.

On the household level, the change from a subsistence to a market economy implied a dramatic, even violent, reorientation of social existence as well as of productive activities. The household in the subsistence economy was an interdependent unit of production and consumption, locked into wider systems of kinship and neighborhood through which mutual aid flowed and communal action was organized. The advent of an economy based upon market exchange ultimately meant the total disruption of society, both in terms of the structure and functions of the household unit itself and in terms of the political and economic relationships among households in the community.

THE HOUSEHOLD AS A UNIT OF STUDY

Any household economy is a function of household composition, the specific economic base of the household, exchange relationships with other households, and the over-all economic conditions of the time and place. Household composition, in turn, depends upon demographic variables, availability of land and housing, inheritance considerations, and the degree to which day-to-day needs have to be met from within the household. Alterations in what kinds of needs actually have to be met by the household may result in a change of membership needs, just as changes in what a household may be able to offer to potential members may affect membership.

The members of the household have been elsewhere defined as follows: "they slept habitually under the same roof (a locational criterion); they shared a number of activities (a functional criterion); they were related to each other by blood or by marriage (a kinship criterion)."[1] The first two characteristics are taken to be universal, while the third, in most cases, will be true for at least part of the members of a household. All common residing members listed under one head of household who can be viewed as having shared production and/or consumption activities are defined as members in this study. Slaves of a household are defined as part of the household, though a distinction will generally be made between the free household (all members except slaves) and the household (including slaves).

The distinction between the "houseful," all of those living in a particular building, and the "household," as suggested by Laslett, only becomes relevant in this study for the 1836 census. For both the 1765 and 1802 census lists, "houseful" and "household" are coterminous and identical. There are no cases in which domestic units outside of the household, that is with an independent household economy, lived in "rooms or units" within the same house. For the 1836 census, in the urban setting, the designations "in the same house" (na mesma casa), and "downstairs" (baixos) are common. Sometimes these additional units were listed within the "houseful" as entirely separate without comment, sometimes they were listed separately but as within the same household. In some districts the observation that the head of household "rents rooms" is followed by a listing which includes numerous agregados (usually unrelated dependents), lodgers among them. These considerations are further confused when those living "downstairs" appear to be related to those in the main house. In this study I have followed the lead of the census-taker; a unit is analyzed as a separate household if the first member of that unit is designated a "chefe" or head of household. Such a designation would seem to imply a separate household economy.

HOUSEHOLD ECONOMY AND HOUSEHOLD ORGANIZATION IN SAO PAULO 1765 TO 1836

Tables VI:1 and VI:2 show household size and composition for the urban and rural bairros of São Paulo, respectively, for the census years of 1765, 1802, and 1836. It is clear that mean household size in São Paulo was always fairly small, and that the nuclear family unit always predominated. Although cases of more or less extended and complex households certainly existed in São Paulo during the eighteenth and nineteenth centuries, the stereotype of the large extended traditional family in Brazil has obviously been grossly over-generalized.[2]

The broadening of the kin group within the free rural household from 1765 to 1802 consisted principally of increased numbers of households in which spouse and children of (usually) a daughter of the head of household remained within the household, as well as an increased number of resident unmarried or widowed siblings of the head. The presence of an aged parent was fairly common in both rural and urban households even in the 1765 census--for those households which included non-nuclear kin. In households headed by a married pair, relatives of the head were more frequently encountered than those of the wife. Female heads of households were, however, just as,

[1]Peter Laslett (ed.), Household and Family in Past Time (Cambridge, 1972), p. 25 suggests this definition.

[2]Other studies agreeing with these observations include Maria-Luiza Marcílio, "Crescimento demográfico e evolução agrária paulista 1700-1836," Tese de livre docencia no historia no Universidad São Paulo (São Paulo, 1974); Lia Freitas Fukuí, "Parentesco e família entre sitiantes tradicionais," Ph.D. dissertation U.S.P. (São Paulo, 1972); Donald Pierson, Cruz das almas (Rio de Janeiro, 1966); Antônio Candido, Os parceiros do Rio Bonito (Rio de Janeiro, 1964).

TABLE VI:1

Mean Household Size and Household Composition in Rural São Paulo in 1765, 1802, and 1836

	1765	1802	1836
Mean household size	4.32	5.56	4.46
Mean children of head	2.39	2.90	2.19
(Percent total members)	55.23	52.19	49.1
Mean nuclear members	3.99	4.48	3.76
(Percent total members)	92.5	80.6	84.3
Mean kin-related members	.0996	.235	.107
(Percent total members)	3.27	7.68	6.1
Mean non-related members	.183	.65	.43
(Percent total members)	4.23	11.71	9.69

NOTE: The figures for 1765 and 1802 pertain to the <u>bairros</u> of Nossa Senhora da Penha e França, São Miguel, Santana, and Nossa Senhora do O. The 1836 data does not include Santana since the census manuscripts were missing from the archive.

TABLE VI:2

Mean Household Size and Household Composition in Urban São Paulo in 1765, 1802, and 1836

	1765	1802	1836
Mean household size	4.05	4.20	3.76
Mean children of head	2.06	1.72	1.23
(Percent total members)	50.86	40.95	32.70
Mean nuclear members	3.6	3.11	2.59
(Percent total members)	88.89	74.0	68.89
Mean kin-related members	.257	.221	.164
(Percent total members)	6.35	5.26	4.36
Mean non-related members	.189	.871	1.01
(Percent total members)	4.67	20.7	26.86

NOTE: Urban São Paulo is defined as specified in the discussion in Chapter IV and Appendix IV:1 which makes spatial approximations between the censuses. The 1836 data is based on the census lists for the parishes of the Sé and Santa Efigênia.

or even more likely to include female kin in the household as were male heads. From 1765 to 1802 the percentage of spouses and children of children of the head of household within the São Paulo free household (both urban and rural bairros) increased from .96 percent to 3.45 percent (.002 level of significance), while the proportion of other related kin increased from 2.31 percent in 1765 to 4.23 percent in 1802. The extended family element within the free household in São Paulo was, then, quite limited throughout the period 1765 to 1836.

Next to the nuclear family members, the most important element in the free household throughout the period both for the rural and the urban bairros were the free non-related members or agregados. In the rural bairros the increase in proportion of agregados in the free household from 1765 to 1802 (from .18 to .65) was highly significant (.002 level). For the urban area the proportion of agregado members in the free household jumped from 4.67 percent in 1765 to a striking 20.7 percent by 1802, and an even more extraordinary 26.86 percent of total household members by 1836.[3]

Types of agregado included orphans who were accepted to be raised in the household, teenagers brought in to help with domestic tasks, apprentices of artisans, other employees and their families living in, distant less-well-off relatives who have not been

[3]Difference in proportions for rural area significance test, $z = 6.93$; .002 level = 3.08 on the two-tailed test. Difference in proportions for urban area highly significant at the .002 level.

identified in the lists as relatives, lodgers, and miscellaneous persons. According to Ení de Mesquita the main defining characteristic was that of having no land or house of their own.[4] Along with the increase in the proportional importance of the agregado within the household there also occurred a strong decline in the contribution of orphans to the category of agregado over this period, from 39.92 percent of agregados in 1765 to only 5.53 percent by 1802. In the 1836 listing the category of orphan was only encountered twice.[5]

The significance of this change is to be found in the age composition of this group. In 1765, 78.2 percent of the orphan group was under fourteen years of age, and 60.4 percent were under the age of ten, indicating that a significant majority of the orphans would not have acted as productive members of the household. By comparison, 70 percent of the non-orphan agregados were between the ages of ten and forty-four--in the most productive period of their lives. The decline in the contribution of orphans to the agregado group probably implies an even more important increase in the proportion of agregados in productive ages over this period. This evidence suggests that the presence of agregados in both rural and urban households in the late eighteenth century (many of whom fell into dependent ages) was frequently motivated by kinship and ritual kinship obligations, inheritance considerations and other social factors. The dramatic increase in the presence of agregados of productive ages in the urban bairros by 1802 would seem to have been associated with more immediate pragmatic needs of the urban household economy (such as child care, labor within a domestic industry, or income for rent and consumption needs) by the early nineteenth century. In the urban area by 1802 agregados were often encountered as workers in a domestic cottage industry or retail business.[6]

Tables VI:3 and VI:4 indicate the composition of heads of households in the urban and rural bairros of São Paulo in 1765, 1802, and 1836, according to age and type of head. Households headed by a married pair declined markedly in both the rural and urban bairros from 1765 to 1836--from 64.32 to 55.03 percent of households in the rural area, and from 53.8 percent of urban households in 1765 to only 29.16 percent by 1836. The remaining households were all headed by never-married, widowed or separated males or females.

Proportions of households headed by a married pair in São Paulo over this period were comparatively low for a pre-industrial community. Laslett's figures on pre-industrial English communities suggest an average of 70.4 percent of households as being headed by a married pair while Armstrong gave 73 percent as the equivalent statistic for York households in 1851. Compared to contemporary communities in Brazil, Guaratinguetá (São Paulo) in 1775 included 76.4 percent of married heads of households.[7] On the other extreme is the case of Vila Rica (Minas Gerais), in 1804,

---

[4]Ení de Mesquita, "O Papel do Agregado na Região de Itú 1773-1830," Coleção Museu Paulista, Serie de História, VI (São Paulo, 1977), p. 42. This study discusses the use of the agregado as household labor particularly in the urban population in eighteenth and nineteenth century Itú.

[5]Perhaps this was in part a result of the establishment of the Santa Casa orphanage in 1824. See Laima Mesgravis, A Santa Casa de Misericórdia de São Paulo, 1599?-1884 (São Paulo, 1974), pp. 178 ff.

[6]See Lenina Menezes Martinho, "Organização do trabalho e relações sociais nas firmas comerciais do Rio de Janeiro: primeira metade século XIX," Revista do Instituto de Estudos Brasileiros, 18 (1976), pp. 41-62 for a similar phenomenon.

[7]These proportions were all significantly different on the .002 level.

TABLE VI:3

Composition of Households by Type of Head in Rural São Paulo in 1765, 1802 and 1836

	1765			1802			1836		
AGE	1	2	3	1	2	3	1	2	3
15-29	29	5	2	37	4	7	37	5	12
30-44	54	5	9	128	22	35	76	8	32
45-59	36	6	20	69	11	37	66	16	41
60+	29	5	30	46	12	39	40	20	40
	148	21	61	280	49	118	219	49	125
N.G.	7	1	3						1
Total	155	22	64 *	281	49	118 *	219	49	126
Percent	64.32	9.12	26.55	62.64	10.96	26.4	55.03	12.31	31.41

NOTE: The rural households include the bairros of Nossa Senhora da Penha e França, São Miguel, Santa Anna and Nossa Senhora do Ó. The 1836 data does not include Santa Anna.

KEY: 1 = married male heads of households with wife present.
2 = single male heads of households including never-married males, widowed males and married males separated from their wives.
3 = single female heads of households including never-married females, widowed females and married females whose husbands are absent.

Percent = percent of total heads of household in each census year in each category of head.

NG = Age of head of household not given in the census manuscript.

TABLE VI:4

Composition of Households by Type of Head in Urban São Paulo in 1765, 1802 and 1836

	1765			1802			1836		
AGE	1	2	3	1	2	3	1	2	3
15-29	25	28	26	54	33	87	38	80	69
30-44	151	29	58	169	44	168	101	86	136
45-59	111	31	55	112	49	110	66	50	61
60+	56	27	52	56	32	74	28	37	47
	343	115	191	391	158	439	233	253	313
N.G.	13		1			5		4	1
Total	356	115	192	391	158	444	233	257	314
Percent	53.8	17.37	28.85	39.38	15.9	44.71	29.2	32.2	39.3

NOTE: The urban bairros are those defined in Appendix I as urban, including the three companies of the "cidade" in 1802 and the parishes of the Sé and Santa Efigenia in 1836.

KEY: 1 = married heads of households with wife present.
2 = single male heads of households including never-married males, widowed males and married males whose wives are absent.
3 = single females heads of households including never-married females, widowed females and married females whose husbands were absent.

Percent = percent of total heads of household in each census year in each type of head.

N.G. = Age of head of household not given in the census manuscripts.

where only 23.6 percent of the heads of household were married males living with their wives.[8]

Social and economic factors conducive to a situation in which a preponderant majority of households were headed by single (unaccompanied) males and females are associated with a diversified economic structure, and a wide range of employment possibilities. Vila Rica in 1804 was the case of a mining town in economic recession, but which still exhibited pronounced characteristics of a transient, migrant population and an active commercial sector. The transience of the male population would probably explain the high frequency (45 percent in 1804) of never-married female heads of household, often with children. The greater employment opportunities of an urbanized, commercialized and monetarized community would likewise have attracted single population--both male and female. São Paulo's location at the top of the break in the Serra between the port of Santos and the plateau all but destined the capital for commercial importance. The relative wealth and occupational diversification of São Paulo even in 1765 compared to other communities in the captaincy probably also explains the attraction of single population to São Paulo. Guaratinguetá, on the other hand, was much less diversified economically by 1775 than was São Paulo in 1765, and also had a much lower proportion of households headed by unaccompanied males or females.[9]

The decline in married heads of households in rural São Paulo from 1765 to 1836 was accompanied by a corresponding rise in the proportion of single male heads of households, and, even more significantly, by an increase in proportion of single female heads of households. Within the category of single male heads were included never-married males, widowed males, and married males whose wives were absent. From 1765 to 1836 the contribution of never-married males in the rural area declined while that of both widowed males and married males whose wives were absent rose.[10] Most significant was the category of widowers which increased as a proportion of total household heads from .83 in 1765, to 5.28 in 1836. At the same time the average age of the single male head of household increased significantly from 1765 to 1836.[11]

---

[8]Laslett, ed., Household, p. 208; Lucila Herrmann, "Evolução da estrutura social de Guaratinguetá n'um período de trezentos anos," Revista de Administração II (marco/junho 1948), p. 32. Donald Ramos, "Marriage and the Family in Colonial Vila Rica," HAHR, 55, no. 2 (May 1975):220.

[9]Alice Canabrava, "Uma economica de decadência: os níveis de requeza na capitania de São Paulo 1765/67," Revista Brazileira de Economia, XXVI, no. 4, p. 122.

[10]Within the category of single male heads of households, the changes in proportions never-married and widowed were significantly different from 1765 to 1836 at the .002 level.

[11]In the rural bairros in 1765 47.6 percent of single male heads were under 44 years of age, while in 1836 only 26.53 percent of single male heads fell into that age group. Similarly, in 1765 only 23.8 percent of single male heads in the rural area were aged 60 or over while in 1836 the percentage was 40.8. This increase in average age of single male head actually occurred between the 1802 and the 1836 census years, the average age of single male head of household being on the whole slightly lower in 1802 than in 1765.

Single female heads of household in the rural bairros also increased by 1836 to 31.41 percent, from a base of 26.55 percent in 1765.[12] In exact opposition to the trend for single male heads in the rural area, the tendency over time was for the contribution of never-married female heads to increase as a proportion of total heads in the rural bairros, while the proportion of widows to total heads declined. Never-married single female heads of household in the rural bairros increased from 2.49 percent in 1765, to 6.32 percent in 1802, to 14.32 percent in 1836. Widowed single female heads of households, on the other hand, declined as a proportion of total heads of households in the rural areas from 20.33 percent of total heads in 1765, to 16.78 percent in 1802, to 15.83 percent in 1836. Nevertheless, by 1836 the proportional importance of widows as heads of households was still greater in the rural bairros than any other type of head except for the married pair. Consistent with the increase in never-married female heads of household was the radical decline in the average age of single female heads in the rural area over the same period, from 18.03 percent under age 44 in 1765, to a surprising 35.59 percent under age 44 by 1802.[13]

The temporal correlation of the increase in kin-related and agregado members within the household along with the rise in the proportional importance of female heads of household is suggestive of the hypothesis that female heads of households found the presence of relatives and extra persons more useful or desirable than did male heads. Analysis of the household composition of households in Penha in 1836 headed by widows and never-married women lends support to this hypothesis. Households headed by either widows or never-married women in Penha in 1836 included 37.37 percent of total Penha households. Agregados associated with these households included 47.13 percent of total related non-nuclear members of Penha households. These figures demonstrate that the likelihood of both agregados and kin being included in the household was significantly greater for households headed by never-married or widowed females, than for all other types of heads of households taken as a group.

The occupational breakdown of these households further reveals the general poverty of female-headed households, particularly those headed by never-married women. Sewing, spinning, and quiltmaking were listed as the major occupations for over 53 percent of female-headed households in Penha in 1836 and for 60.5 percent of those headed by never-married women. These aforementioned occupations were precisely those which, as was shown in Chapter V, were the least remunerative of any listed in the 1836 census. Of the remainder of female-headed households, 55 percent, mostly widows, were subsistence farmers or else sold vegetables, homemade articles, or sweets. The correlation between female heads and poverty is given further support through the analysis of income and type of head of household for Nossa Senhora do O in 1836. Incomes over 100 mil reis annually were claimed by 17.19 percent of total households, but only by 9.3 percent of female-headed households.[14] Thus there appears to have been a relationship between female-headed households, poverty, and the presence of kinfolk

---

[12]Proportions of single female heads of households were significantly different between 1802 and 1836 at the .05 level for the one-tailed test. See Ann Hagerman Johnson, "The Impact of Market Agriculture on Family and Household Structure in 19th Century Chile," HAHR 58, no. 4 (1978): 625-48 for a discussion of female-headed households in rural areas of out-migration.

[13]Female heads of households aged 60 or over declined from 46.88 percent of rural female heads in 1765, to 33.05 percent in 1802, to 32 percent in 1836.

[14]This compares with 27.6 percent of male-headed households in Nossa Senhora do O with income above 100 mil reis per year, and 18.6 percent of households headed by a married pair.

and especially of agregados in the household.[15] The increase in proportion of female-headed households probably also implied, then, an increase in the proportion of low-income households in 1836. Furthermore, the increased percentage of agregados in the poor household may have been a means of accommodation to the changing reality of São Paulo in this period. We will return to this point again with respect to the urban situation.

Within the urban bairros of São Paulo, the importance of households headed by single males or females was much greater throughout the period 1765 to 1836 than in the rural area. The proportion of households headed by single males included 17.37 percent of households in 1765, 15.9 percent in 1802, and 32.17 percent in 1836. Contrary to the rural situation, the contribution of never-married males within this category increased dramatically between the censuses of 1802 and 1836. In terms of average age, the proportion of single male heads under 44 years of age increased from 49.57 percent in 1765 and 48.73 percent in 1802 to 65.61 percent in 1836. Undoubtedly the attraction of the law academy as well as the political activity of the city had much to do with this change.

The proportion of households headed by single females in the urban area included 28.85 percent in 1765, 44.71 percent in 1802, and 39.3 percent in 1836. It must be emphasized that these are extremely high rates of female headship for a western society at any known time. It is interesting to note that whereas the proportion of households headed by single females in the rural bairros (which was very similar to that of the urban bairros in 1765) did not increase by 1802, a very significant increase in single female heads of household occurred in the urban area. On the other hand, the rural bairros experienced a significant increase in female heads of household between 1802 and 1836, the same period in which a slight but significant proportional decline in female heads of household took place in the urban area. The trend in both rural and urban areas was for an increased contribution of never-married females among heads of households, the difference being that never-married female heads of households predominated in the urban bairros over the period, while widowed female heads of household remained the majority though declining in importance, in the rural area.

The proportion of female heads of household under age 44 in the urban bairros increased from 43.98 percent in 1765 to 65.5 percent in 1863.[16] Many of the never-married female heads of households (frequently with children) were probably women who had entered consensual unions and subsequently found themselves abandoned and unmarriageable. These figures suggest that consensual unions may have been formed at earlier ages and formed more frequently in the late eighteenth century as compared to 1765 because of the economic improvements of the time. The further decline in mean

---

[15]Ramos, "Marriage and the Family," p. 220 associated the large percent of female-headed households (45 percent in 1804) with the incidence of poverty, in connection with the decline in gold production. On the other hand, Silvia M. Arrom, "Marriage Patterns in Mexico City, 1811," Journal of Family History 3, no. 4 (Winter 1978):376-91 finds that of the 32.6 percent of households headed by women, the largest number were headed by widowed Spanish (rather than Indian or casta) women. She therefore found no relationship of economic level with the female-headed household. Kathleen Waldron, "A Social History of a Primate City: the Case of Caracas 1756-1810" (Ann Arbor, 1977) also found female headed households in significant proportions in the late eighteenth century.

[16]The difference in age structure of widowed as opposed to never-married (unaccompanied) female heads of households is striking. In 1802 never-married female heads of households included 53.2 percent under age 39 while only 16 percent of the widowed heads of households were in that age bracket. The mean age of the never-married female heads of households was 34.1 as compared to 53.1 for the average widowed head of household.

age of urban never-married female heads of households by 1836 suggests that the consensual union was becoming increasingly unstable. The increase in unmarried (unaccompanied, never-married) mothers as a proportion of total mothers from 6.02 in 1765 to 34.3 in 1836 provides strong support for the hypothesis that consensual unions were both more common and less stable in the early nineteenth century than was the case in 1765.

In general the composition of the heads of households in the urban bairros of São Paulo between 1765 and 1863 changed in the sense of becoming younger and more characterized by households headed by non-married persons. Widows and widowers seemed to prefer the rural environment to the urban, while never-married householders clearly found the urban center more attractive. The age composition of married male heads of households also became slightly younger in the urban area over the period, while the same group in the rural bairros of São Paulo was somewhat older by 1836.

Among the elite urban households of São Paulo, modifications in the composition of types of heads of households from 1765 to 1836 reflected some of the same changes which are discussed above for the city as a whole. Data on the elite households of urban São Paulo in 1765, 1802, and 1836 are presented in Tables VI:5 and VI:6. The proportion of elite households headed by a married pair, always the most important category for elite households, declined from 66.67 percent of urban households for 1765 to 46.54 percent by 1836. Over the same period the contribution of single male elite heads of households to total elite households increased from 19.05 percent to 43.4 percent. Never-married male household heads alone increased from 7 percent in 1765 to 28.3 percent in 1836, accounting for the most difference. It is notable that elite households headed by single and especially young never-married males were substantially more significant than such households in the urban population generally. Single female heads of households, with widows predominating in all three years, declined from 14.28 percen to 10.06 percent. Never-married female heads of elite households were rare, and increased from zero households in 1765 to only one by 1836.

The heads of the most prosperous households of urban São Paulo in 1836 were a decidedly younger group than in 1765 or in 1802, following the same trend as urban heads of households in São Paulo in general. The proportion of elite married heads of households under the age of 44 increased from 21.4 percent in 1765 to 54.05 percent in 1836, while single male elite heads under age 44 increased even more significantly from 12.5 percent in 1765 to 57.97 percent by 1836. Comparison of the analysis of elite urban heads of household from 1765 to 1836 with that for urban heads of households as a whole lends further support for the hypothesis that growth in the never-married female head of household category basically implied an increase in urban poor. Households headed by never-married females were never an important element in the elite and became even less so between 1802 and 1836.

HOUSEHOLD COMPOSITION AND THE ECONOMIC TRANSFORMATION

The organization of the household economy in São Paulo in 1765 was almost wholly subsistence oriented. In such a non-market economy the household mode of production and distribution was relatively visible because all households regardless of wealth necessarily had to physically acquire, or else have a specific personal exchange agreement in terms of all the means of production of the goods and services required or desired for the running of the household. Households of the most wealthy residents were located in the urban area, though many of them also had rural estates. Involvement with the exchange economy (as many of the wealthy were businessmen) in no way divorced these individuals from a self-sufficient economy since it was common for the head of household in 1765 to have several professions (including that of subsistence farmer), and

TABLE VI:5

Composition of Elite Households by Age and Type of Head of Household in Urban São Paulo in 1765, 1802 and 1836

AGE	1765			1802			1836		
	1	2	3	1	2	3	1	2	3
15-29	0	0	1*	2	2	1	9	10	0
30-44	6	1	0	14	5	2	31	30	4
45-59	15	2	2	25	16	2	28	18	7
60+	7	5	3	12	5	8	6	10	5
Total	28	8	6	53	28	13	74	69	16
Percent	66.67	19.05	14.28	56.38	29.79	13.83	46.54	43.4	10.06
Prop.-44	21.40	12.50	16.67	30.19	25.00	23.08	54.05	57.97	25.00
Prop. 60+	25.00	12.50	50.00	22.64	17.86	61.54	8.11	14.49	31.25

NOTE: See note Table VI:6.

KEY: 1 = married heads of households with wife present
2 = single males heading households including never-married males, widowed males and married males whose wives are absent.
3 = single female heads of households including never-married females, widowed females and married females whose husbands were absent.

*This young woman--although listed as a separate head of household owning property--was also noted to "stay with her mother".

TABLE VI:6

Mean Elite Household Size and Household Composition in Urban São Paulo in 1765, 1802, and 1836

	1765	1802	1836
Total households	47	94	159
Mean size free household	5.57	5.99	4.96
Mean no. slaves household	N.A.	12.97	6.77
Mean size total household	N.A.	18.96	11.74
Mean children of head	2.71	2.33	2.25
(Percent free members)	(48.50)	(38.90)	(45.25)
Mean nuclear members	4.38	4.01	3.63
(Percent free members)	(78.30)	(66.96)	(73.13)
Mean kin-related members	.21	.54	.41
(Percent free members)	(3.80)	(9.06)	(8.24)
Mean non-related members	.98	1.45	.92
(Percent free members)	(17.40)	(23.98)	(18.63)

NOTE: The elite sample was chosen on the basis of attributes which carried privilege in São Paulo society, not on any more general theory of elites. The group with most access to economic and political resources, as determined from the census manuscripts, was defined as "elite." In 1765 the listing of wealth was the major criteria for elite membership, along with high military rank or a position in Royal government. In 1802, since neither wealth nor income was given, the sample was created primarily on the basis of ownership of ten or more slaves, or an appropriate occupation. The 1836 sample was based on a combination of some social characteristics (as in 1802) and an annual income of 400 mil reis or more.

it was also common to maintain both rural and urban residences.[17] In any case, the non-existence of any permanent urban marketplace in 1765 effectively prevented any real disconnectedness from subsistence living at that time.

The introduction of money and the market into a previously subsistence oriented economy would necessarily have resulted in a radical change in household organization and economy. Household production of certain goods potentially could be replaced by purchasing them, just as household slaves could alternatively have been replaced by day laborers for certain tasks. Similarly, personal exchanges of goods and assistance could have been replaced with the impersonal exchange of the marketplace. Money could substitute indirectly for the productive activities of certain household members which were needed in a non-market situation, as well as substituting the personal exchanges between households which supplemented household productions in the subsistence economy.

The move to a market economy affected household location and size, who worked away from home and who stayed, what was sold and what used, the actual productive basis of the household--in short, every aspect of the household economy and organization. The closer the household economy was to the subsistence situation, the less the members were forcibly affected by the market. That is to say, a household which continued to produce basic crops for home consumption and/or homespun clothes to wear retained more alternatives in the sense that there was always the possibility of returning to a self-sufficient existence. The further the household economy moved from that point, the more the internal functions of the household were dependent on the movement of wages and prices.

By 1802 the development of the external market and the urban marketplace had had strong effects on household organization in São Paulo.[18] Although the subsistence household economy continued to prevail or at least co-exist with market production in the rural <u>bairros</u>, agricultural activity had almost disappeared from the urban setting. Wealthy households continued to maintain both rural and urban residences, thus retaining their options in terms of market involvement. The increasing valorization of property and of labor was beginning to make the acquisition of marginal lands for farming difficult for low-income people on the one hand, and to attract them to a more exciting and remunerative employment in the urban area on the other. Unlike the wealthy households, the move of poor families to the urban situation did tend to restrict their subsistence alternatives--making them dependent on the market or else on rural relatives with surplus product.

The economic circumstances of São Paulo in 1836 were an extension or development of those of 1802. The city offered more employment in 1836 though

[17]The late eighteenth-century property inventories are a good source for the demonstration of ownership of several residences in the case of wealthy householders.

[18]See Elizabeth Kuznesof, "Household Composition and Headship Rates as Related to Changes in Mode of Production: São Paulo 1765 to 1836," <u>Comparative Studies in Society and History</u> 22, no. 1 (Jan. 1980):78-108.

housing and food were much more expensive.[19] Farm land was more difficult to find in the rural bairros than in 1802. Subsistence farming had been replaced by specialized crop production for the urban market in the rural bairros near São Paulo. Alternatives for housing and for acquiring the necessities of life had become highly constricted relative to the earlier period. The households of both the urban and the rural bairros were by this time involved in the market economy, for better or for worse. This basic transformation with respect to the domestic economy had important effects on the structure and composition of the household at all socio-economic levels, and in both the urban and the rural milieux.

Positive factors encouraging increased size and complexity of the rural household by 1802 were those related to the over-all improvement in the economy during the late eighteenth century.[20] Increase in mean number of children is the most obvious change which can be so interpreted, whether it is seen as a decline in infant mortality or as a conscious decision on the part of paulista families to have more children. For rural households, increased household size was also related to the new market opportunities, stimulating the addition of more labor to produce a marketable surplus.

In wealthy households, the increase of fixed relative to variable capital associated with the development of market production may have resulted in even greater concern with the disposition of the inheritances of a numerous group of siblings. Rather than make disadvantageous marriages, adult children would have been retained in the paternal home or else have joined the household of a married sibling, thus resulting in larger and more complex households. Rural households with small capital resources also took advantage of these to enter the market economy in the late eighteenth century, selling surpluses to the urban market, or growing cane for processing at a more wealthy neighbor's engenho. These households, too, probably increased in size and complexity. Times had improved and the young people who married began to marry earlier and to have more children. Since land was still relatively free and available in the final decades of the eighteenth century, both total population and number of households expanded rapidly in the rural bairros of São Paulo.

The 1836 census registered continued modifications in both rural household composition and rural household economy. Mean household size declined to about the 1765 level while mean number of children per head declined significantly below the 1765 level. The proportion of extended family members and non-related members in the average rural household declined slightly but continued much higher than in 1765. Composition of types of heads of households showed a continued decline in married heads and a rise in single male and single female heads of households.

---

[19]From 1798 the censuses have tables with them concerning food prices. Of course inflation was probably a factor. However, a few comparative prices for 1798 and 1836 will give some indication of the change: Rice: 1798--300 reis the alqueire; 1836--2000 reis the alqueire; Beans: 1798--560 reis the alqueire; 1836--2560 reis the alqueire; Manioc flour: 1798--640 reis the alqueire; 1836--1000 reis the alqueire; Corn: 1798--320 reis the alqueire; 1836--about 7-- reis the alqueire. The 1798 data comes from the "Mapa dos preços correntes da cidade de São Paolo e seu destríctos no mes de Dezembro do anno de 1798," AESP, Maços de população, caixa 32, no. ordem 32. The 1836 figures come from Daniel Pedro Muller, São Paulo em 1836 (São Paulo, 1923), Tabella No. 2, pages 122-23. Median prices were taken in each case.

[20]The positive correlation between household size and prosperity is fairly universal. See, for example, Chie Nakane, "An interpretation of the size and structure of the household in Japan over three centuries" in Laslett, Household, p. 521, "The more favourable the environment, such as a village on fertile land situated close to a commercial centre, the larger the mean household size."

While the wave of commercial prosperity which accompanied the Napoleonic wars had passed by 1820, the proportion of rural household economies committed to exchange production continued to grow. Land was no longer freely available, nor was wood for building or heating purposes. For poor households the ownership of the paternal homesite became a matter of extreme relevance. Middle-income small sugar producers were especially hard hit by the decline in the price of sugar. Since they paid 50 percent of their sugar for the use of a mill, and were faced by rapidly rising prices for slaves, these small producers were incapable of reproducing their initial capital in order to continue production.[21] Many of them sold some of their slaves to the large producers and transferred their investment into production for the less risky local urban market. By 1836 the rural landscape adjacent to the city of São Paulo was composed of a few large agricultural complexes with many slaves engaged primarily in production for the urban market. The middle-income small producers, so notable in the lists of 1802, had disappeared, as well as some of the larger producers, many of whom had sold out and moved to the more fertile and available lands of the paulista west.

The decline in both mean household and mean number of children per head of household by 1836 was a sign of decreasing prosperity in the rural milieu. In fact, decline in household size not directly attributable to decrease in number of children per head of household was significant only in the rural bairros. The decreased size of household is not apparently explicable in terms of lessened needs in the economy of the rural household itself which if anything would have increased with the decrease in proportion of households with slaves. Juxtaposition of the censuses of Penha and Nossa Senhora do O for 1836 with those of 1802 indicates a relative stagnation in total population and number of households over the period in the rural bairros. Migration to either the paulista west or else to the urban center of São Paulo is the probable explanation. Migration must have seemed preferable in many cases to the option of remaining as an agregado or dependent kindred resident in a household in which the economic base was deteriorating.

Within the urban area the changes in household economy over the period 1765 to 1836 were even more profound. Subsistence agriculture as well as domestic production of a wide range of household items was characteristic of the vast majority of urban households in 1765. Construction of the permanent urban marketplace in 1774, expanded several times before 1800, is indicative of the critical development of exchange and redistribution in the urban economy in this period. The fact that by 1802 only 10 percent of urban households were engaged in agriculture for either subsistence or sale is strong evidence that agricultural production for the urban market had developed sufficiently to allow a general reliance upon the marketplace for daily subsistence needs.

Household composition had also changed dramatically in the urban area by 1802. While mean household size increased inappreciably and mean number of children per head of household declined slightly, the proportion of members of the household made up by persons unrelated to the head of household rose from 4.67 percent in 1765 to an astounding 20.7 percent of household members by 1802. Proportion of households headed by women rose from 28.85 to 44.71 percent in the same period. There is evidence to suggest that low-income female-headed households were particularly likely to include non-related members.

---

[21] See the discussion in Sérgio Buarque do Holanda, ed., História geral da civilização, I (São Paulo, 1972), pp. 206-09 concerning the importance of sugar grown on lands adjacent to the engenho to the actual production of sugar. The Engênho Sergipe do Conde actually continued under full operation in the period 1622 to 1653 without growing any cane on the engênho's property.

The most surprising statistic is the proportion of female heads of households in urban São Paulo both in 1802 and in 1836.[22] Very likely most of these were a product of dissolved consensual unions which became increasingly common and less stable by 1802 as compared to 1765. These women were relatively unmarriageable next to their virgin sisters and therefore had to make lives for themselves. The commercial opportunities and potential profits of the new urban area was probably more attractive to them than was the prospect of remaining in the rural area where there was less market for the services and homemade products of single women. Whatever the interpretation, the proportion of female-headed households in urban São Paulo in 1802 and in 1836 was extraordinary--compared either to pre-industrial or nineteenth-century cities or to modern twentieth-century cities.

It is important to note that households headed by never-married females--the most numerous single type of head of household in urban São Paulo in 1836--were never a significant element in the elite household. The analysis of household composition based on inheritance also supports the contention that elite, never-married females would have been unlikely to head households. Some never-married females headed middle-income households, particularly those in charge of lodging houses, or who had taken over the management of a family business from a deceased brother or father. However, the vast majority of these households headed by never-married females were clearly in the low-income group and frequently had to depend upon the productive activities of several household residents, including other women, agregados and children for the maintenance of the household.

The steep rise in the agregado element in urban São Paulo to 20.7 percent of household members in 1802 and 26.9 percent by 1836 is understandable within the circumstances of early nineteenth-century São Paulo. The increase in land values and housing costs meant that housing had become an important expense, particularly for lower-income persons. Probably a high proportion of the agregados were also recent migrants who had no family in São Paulo or migrated with a child and possibly one other relative. For these persons the option of living as an agregado or a lodger or, if they found a house, to look for others to share their households, was very rational.[23]

Another factor which encouraged co-residence with non-related persons in the early nineteenth-century was the incomplete transition between the home as both residence and workplace, and the modern situation in which place of employment is external to the home. In urban São Paulo the domestic production of cloth, quilts, inexpensive apparel, sifters, whistles, candles, candies, and other articles was frequently organized in households where a number of women co-resided in order to co-operate in these productive activities. In 1836 many tradesmen's homes included live-in apprentices, while merchants often included clerks and cashiers in their households. The type of housing construction which included a "store" (loja) as the inferior level of the

---

[22]I have as yet found no comparable headship rates for non-Latin American societies. For comparative comments see Elizabeth Kuznesof, "The Role of the Female-Headed Household in Brazilian Modernization," The Journal of Social History 13, no. 4 (June 1980):589-613.

[23]For examples of other situations of early modernization which also exhibited crowded and expensive housing see Philip J. Greven, Jr., "The average size of families and households in the Province of Massachusetts in 1764 and in the United States in 1790: an overview," in Laslett, ed., Household, pp. 549-51, Chie Nakane, "An interpretation," pp. 519-21; Anderson, Family Structure, pp. 45-55 discusses the high frequency of non-related household residents in nineteenth-century Lancashire principally in terms of short-term residence for new migrants, and a means of housing for young adults or low-income persons needing an inexpensive alternative.

sobrado or a front room of the casa têrrea maintained the identification of home and workplace in the urban setting. The casa de porão alto, which came into style in the last half of the nineteenth century, was specifically built only for residential purposes and symbolized the divorce of productive activity from the home.

Occupational listings in 1802 show a considerable frequency of multiple occupations for the head of household, while other household members were seldom employed outside the home. Apparently many household heads found it necessary to pursue a number of occupations because demand in any one employment was still relatively weak and uncertain. By 1836 patterns of lower-class employment had changed in the sense that it had become common for several members of the household to work. Undoubtedly this was evidence of an increased exchange orientation within the domestic group. This change in employment patterns also indicates that the demand for goods and services within the city had strengthened, making possible the employment of a larger proportion of the population. Women and children are prominent in these lists. Both the larger number of such workers and their extremely weak earning power suggests that necessity played a major role in the entrance of women and children into the labor market in this period. If the development of commercial infrastructure and the expansion of the market brought prosperity for merchants, sugar planters, and bureaucrats, it was not at all clear that lower-income households were better off, or even as well off in 1836, as they had been in 1765.

Data on elite household size and composition in urban São Paulo in 1765, 1802, and 1836 is provided in Table VI:6. From 1765 to 1802 the change in household composition was effectively a slight increase in size of the free household combined with an increase in kin-related members from 3.8 to 9.06 percent and an increase in non-related members from 17.4 to 23.98 percent. From 1802 to 1836 the increase in proportion of nuclear family members to 73.17 percent reflected a decline in mean family size, a slight decline in kin-related members to 8.24 percent and a decline in non-related members to 18.63 percent. At the same time the mean number of nuclear family members in the elite household continued to decline--from 4.38 in 1765, to 4.01 in 1802, and 3.63 in 1836.

The elite household, like other households in São Paulo, increased in size and complexity from 1765 to 1802, responding to the general economic improvements of the period. By the census year of 1836 the worsening fortunes of the times had prompted different accommodations in the elite household than in the average urban household. Elite households in 1836 had reduced the dependent elements in the household compared to the earlier period--less children and less relatives. In the case of the elite household the decline in agregados was probably also a decrease in the dependent elements. Improvements in urban services and market may have also made a difference in the personnel desirable or useful in the elite household by that time. The elite household responded to a somewhat less optimistic economic situation by cutting the more superfluous expenses. The average urban household, on the other hand, not only needed to cut dependent elements, but to bring in new productive members to share household costs in order to be able to survive reasonably in the new situation.

CONCLUSION

In 1765 the household economy of São Paulo was characterized by a small, predominantly nuclear family unit, engaged in a seminomadic subsistence form of domestic production, with mutual assistance between households an important and integral aspect of the household economy. Land and housing materials were freely available and therefore presented no limitation to the setting up of new households, nor to inheritance or fertility considerations. The lack of any reasonably accessible market for produce in 1765 also meant that production of surpluses was relatively superfluous and wealthy households therefore did not invest in fixed capital in order to expand production in this period.

The transformation from the subsistence to the exchange mode of household production was already substantially accomplished by 1802. The attraction of a profitable market encouraged the development of complex agricultural establishments in the rural bairros, which likewise stimulated increased size and complexity in the wealthy rural household. New inheritance considerations related to fixed cost improvements on these properties acted to discourage marriages which might have had a diluting effect on the value of the undivided property. Since land was still relatively available, the first decade of the nineteenth century brought a kind of generalized prosperity to rural São Paulo which was likewise characterized by an increase in mean number of children per head of rural household and an increase in non-nuclear members in the household to assist in the increased effort necessary to produce a surplus for the market.

By 1836 land had been included in the general inheritance law and property ownership was being increasingly concentrated into the hands of a few planters. The decline in sugar prices and the rise in the cost of slaves both acted against the small producers who were forced out of the export market. The application of inheritance law to land was also having a morselization effect on all property, save that of those wealthy enough so that heirs could purchase their plots from each other. Mean household size decreased from 1802 to 1836, demonstrating the decline in prosperity in the rural area.

Urban household economy in São Paulo in 1765 was little different from that of the rural bairros. By 1802, however, a considerable differentiation had taken place. The transition in the productive base of the household was critical in this change because in the urban area not only was the subsistence mode being replaced by exchange production, but agriculture was also being substituted by other productive activities. In 1802 and in 1836 workplace continued to be identical with place of residence. In part this can be seen as a function of the small scale of production, in which domestic manufacture was still practicable. In part the high cost of housing in the urban area in this period and the difficulty of transport from more marginal areas explains the practice of including apprentices, cashiers, artisan's helpers, and co-workers in cloth and clothing and other types of manufacture within the domestic unit. Although non-related persons were commonly encountered in the urban household on all socio-economic levels in this period, agregados were clearly most significant in the composition of the low income, female-headed household. This latter type of household was also the kind which most approximated a domestic factory situation--with several women engaged in spinning, weaving, sewing, the making of quilts, sieves, whistles, candles, or sweets. In other cases co-residence was not linked to a common productive activity, but only to the need for sharing household expenses.

Like the rural bairros, the social ecology of the urban area of São Paulo in the first decades of the nineteenth century was markedly heterogeneous. Most elite households continued to locate in the urban bairros, and to maintain bigger households with larger proportions of nuclear family members and kin-related members than other urban households. Both female-headed households and agregados were much less significant for elite households than in other urban households. Whatever the true explanation for the enormous proportion of female-headed households and household agregado members in urban São Paulo in 1802 and 1836, it is clear that both were basically lower-class phenomena intimately related to the recent profound changes in the household mode of production, and that both were most likely a means of social and economic accommodation to the effects of these changes.

VII Conclusion

In the period from 1765 to 1836 the household economy in the city of São Paulo was transformed from that of a subsistence or domestic mode of production to one based on production for exchange. This fundamental change in the deep structure of the political economy was intentional, engineered by an interested elite who utilized local government bodies to promote the construction of a commercial infra-structure. Later changes in local administration and land law were also related to the interests of this group in monopolizing and controlling the resultant commerce in sugar and coffee. The story of how this happened provided the first major theme of this study. Accommodations to this fundamental economic change on the individual and household levels in terms of marriage, fertility and household economy, composition and size was the second major topic of analysis. This chapter will integrate these themes in the light of a more general historiography and sociology of the city and the household.

Within the context of eighteenth- and nineteenth-century São Paulo, the two major transformations analyzed in this study were inextricably related, the political and economic parameters acting on and reacting to those related to the individual and the household. The change in mode of production would not have occurred without concomitant changes in the household economy and composition, nor would the latter have changed without the former. However, it does not follow that change in household economy and structure would occur only in conjunction with the totally basic substitution of an exchange for a subsistence household economy. To the contrary, there is reason to believe that the domestic group has much greater plasticity in any given society, in terms of composition and size, than has generally been recognized. Household, as it emerged in this study, was a basically accommodationist unit, mobilizing kindred, non-kindred, productive resources, choosing and changing location depending upon personal needs or opportunities with respect to the economy and society, and upon available resources. Although the domestic group was an essentially responsive or dependent variable, the modifications in the household economy and organization provided strong reinforcement and were in fact necessary to the development of trade on the community level. Changes in household mode of production and organization facilitated and continued articulation of the exchange economy and the development of a more refined division of labor in society.[1]

The dominance of the city government of São Paulo in the eighteenth century by merchants and businessmen who directed and largely financed the construction of the commercial infra-structure is reminiscent of the classical studies of the nature of the city by Max Weber and Henri Pirenne.[2] For both Weber and Pirenne trade in general and the marketplace in particular was the quintessential characteristic of the city. Nevertheless, the colonial Brazilian city differed in several important ways from the medieval towns of Europe. The latter acquired recognition as corporate persons and their recognized citizens, the burghers, became a legal class with their own laws.[3] These towns were often largely autonomous, a "state within a state," and were little affected by decisions of any more central authority.[4] Brazilian towns, on the other hand, were born with a municipal organization prescribed by Portuguese law. No special law code was allowed, nor were the citizens a special legal class, though the homens bons were allowed the privilege of voting and participating in municipal

---

[1]Most of the literature has not attempted to inter-relate changes in political economy with modifications in household structure and/or family size. An important exception is Michael Anderson, Family Structure in Nineteenth Century Lancashire (Cambridge, 1971), who explicitly utilized an "actor-based perspective" to analyze modifications in household structure in Lancashire. J.A. Banks, Prosperity and Parenthood (London, 1954) and Chie Nakane, "An interpretation of the size and structure of the household in Japan over three centuries," in Peter Laslett, ed., Household and Family in Past Time (Cambridge, 1972), pp. 517-44 also tried to explain change in terms of the particular political economy of the households affected.

[2]For Pirenne, the town or "portus" was "a permanent commercial center. . . . Its existence depended upon an unbroken commercial activity. It grew spontaneously out of exchange between districts." Early Democracies in the Low Countries: Urban Society and Political Conflict in the Middle Ages and the Renaissance (New York, 1963), p. 16. Max Weber, on the other hand, has stated that, "Economically defined, the city is a settlement the inhabitants of which live primarily off trade and commerce rather than agriculture," and later, "Thus, we wish to speak of a "city" only in cases where the local inhabitants satisfy an economically substantial part of their daily wants in the local market, and to an essential extent by products which the local population and that of the immediate hinterland produced for sale in the market or acquired in other ways. In the meaning employed here the "city" is a marketplace. The local market forms the economic center of the colony in which, due to the specialization in economic products, both the non-urban population and urbanites satisfy their wants for articles of trade and commerce." The City, translated and edited by Don Martindale and Gertrud Neuwirth (New York, 1958), p. 67.

[3]Pirenne. Ibid., p. 34; Weber, Ibid., pp. 80-82.

[4]Pirenne, Ibid., p. 181, "In all the countries of western Europe, the governing bodies of the municipalities of the Middle Ages were animated by a more or less active republican sentiment. It could not well have been otherwise. For the economic exclusiveness of the burghers, as well as their social development, necessarily drove them to achieve complete autonomy, to deal with their affairs in their own way and, in short, to transform themselves into a state within a state.

government.[5] Brazilian municipal governments could be taxed by the crown and sometimes were, though collection of the tax was not easy. For practical reasons crown officials acted less as authorities with relation to the local city council than as interested and influential parties to municipal business. As Richard Morse concluded, "These municipal functions frequently originated beyond reach of effective imperial control, developed within an aramature of local interests and stubbornly resisted royal encroachment. The colonial Latin American town is therefore sometimes more appropriately conceived as a semiautonomous, agrourban polis, than as an outpost of empire."[6]

The economic position of European cities of the eleventh and twelfth centuries provides an interesting parallel. Max Weber interpreted the political takeover of the nobility in 1141 as having been necessitated by the financial requirements of the militant colonial and commercial policy of the city, which only the wealth of patriciates could support.[7] In eleventh- and twelfth-century Saint-Omer, Arras, Lille, Tournai, and Cambrai merchants used their fund collectively and individually for the "common good"--that is, for the building and maintenance of roads, gates, town fortifications and bridges and "their use of (their wealth) justified the influence they enjoyed."[8]

In each town a group of merchant patriciates undertook the direction of government. Town fortifications and the protection of order, "liberty," property and the marketplace were likewise necessities of mercantile society and explain the interest of the merchants in establishing the towns.[9] The "social unrest" which eventually led to the development of "plebian cities" to replace the "patrician cities" came only after the city economy had developed sufficiently that a large proportion of public income was being levied from the nongoverning group.[10] It does not seem too much to suggest that the period of patrician government was in some sense necessitated by the non-taxability of the general population at that time. Similarly, the semi-autonomous, self-financed government of the paulistano merchants of the eighteenth century was in

[5]The citizens of Porto (Portugal) theoretically enjoyed a special legal status which Brazilian towns frequently asked the crown to extend to them also but the privileges were not granted.

[6]Richard Morse, "A Prolegomenen to Latin American Urban History," HAHR, 52, no. 3 (August, 1972), p. 369.

[7]Weber, Ibid., pp. 125-26, "It cannot be too emphatically stressed that it was the financial needs of a militant colonial and commercial policy which made the participation of the patriciate in administration unavoidable. In the same manner, the financial needs of princely wars under conditions of a money economy established the growing power of the estates on the continent." "Public debts and permanent financial expenditures by the commune were self-evident concomitants of this foreign policy. These financial obligations, in turn, could only be covered through the means of the patriciate. . . . The patriciate, thus, was able to concentrate both monetary wealth and political power in their hands."

[8]Pirenne, Ibid., pp. 24-26.

[9]Ibid., pp. 34-54.

[10]Weber, Ibid., suggested the terms "patrician cities" and "plebian cities." See pages 161-64 for a discussion of the rise against the nobility.

part a function of the subsistence level of production of the city of São Paulo and its hinterland.[11]

The transition of São Paulo from a subsistence household mode of production to one in which exchange was predominant was neither trivial nor automatic. It involved the disruption of a non-monetary economy based on domestic production and neighborhood exchanges of goods and services negotiated through systems of kinship and ritual kinship on a principal of generalized reciprocity. Patterns of residence, work, marriage, fertility, mutual aid, crops grown, domestic industry, and even political office and road building were integral aspects of this system. In 1765 the sale of surpluses was a relatively unimportant and a highly undependable aspect of the subsistence economy which was basically production for use by the producer. Officials from the captain-general to the city council repeatedly attempted to legislate farmers into producing crop surpluses for sale in the urban market and to encourage the commercial production of particular crops such as sugar and rice. Most members of paulista society had little use for money, with barter and reciprocation forming the basis for most exchanges, and therefore they also had little real need or desire to produce products for sale. The non-monetary character of the economy and the fact that few people produced crops or other goods beyond those needed for subsistence also meant that eighteenth century São Paulo had few shops where such goods could be purchased. In fact the community even lacked a marketplace until 1773.

Most significant for the development of an exchange economy in São Paulo was the development of an infra-structure, particularly a road over the Serra do Mar usable by mule teams. An elite group of merchants and businessmen allied with the most powerful members of the family clans promoted and financed these improvements, utilizing their positions as militia officials, city council members and members of the board of the Santa Casa de Misericórdia. This conscious effort to promote infrastructural development prior to the emergence of an exchange economy or the development of a significant export runs counter to most literature on the relationship of transport to modernization. In most cases the development of an exchange economy and of markets is seen by scholars to precede significant infrastructural and transport developments. The function of transport development within the historiography is always to expand an already developed exchange economy, rather than to itself serve as a transforming agent.[12]

Even the specific case of the paulista road over the Serra do Mar has been interpreted by Odilon Nogueira de Matos as occurring because the development of sugar cane cultivation in the eighteenth century created "the necessity of improving

---

[11]See Susan Migden Socolow, "Economic Activities of the Porteño Merchants: The Viceregal Period," HAHR, 55, no. 2 (May, 1975):2, "These numbers of merchants suggest that it was the growth of a merchant group which spurred the creation of a new economic and political status for Buenos Aires and not the status of the city which created a merchant group."

[12]I wish to acknowledge my debt in this paragraph to discussions with Robert B. Oppenheimer. A discussion of much of the literature may be found in John H. Coatsworth, Growth against Development: The Economic Impact of Railroads in Porfirian Mexico (DeKalb, 1981), pp. 175-91 and in G.R. Hawke, Railways and Economic Growth in England and Wales 1840-1870 (Oxford, 1970), pp. 1-32.

transportation."[13] In fact sugar cane production on the plateau was insignificant prior to the completion of the road in 1790 as indicated in Chapter II. The creation of both a local exchange economy and an export economy was a conscious government policy as well as being a conscious effort and area of investment of private entrepreneurs.

These eighteenth century royal efforts toward development can be seen as an example of what Claudio Véliz has called "the centralist tradition"--the mercantilist ideal of an economy and polity integrated around and through the needs of the crown and the mother country.[14] The directive economic policies of the pombaline period contrast with the nineteenth century liberal ideal of laissez-faire economy in which the state provided the proper environment for the free functioning of the economy but did not involve itself in productive activity. In Portuguese America this took the form of specific efforts to stimulate new agricultural and extractive industries, to compel farmers to grow more of certain crops, to limit as much as possible colonial manufacturing which competed with production in Portugal, and to increase the collection of revenues for Portugal. What is remarkable, particularly as compared to Spanish America in this period, is that this "paternalism" was funded almost entirely by the colonials. In his study of royal government in Brazil during the pombaline period Dauril Alden concluded,

> And in return for its demands on the colonists for their obedience, their abstention from exercising any popular voice in the direction of the affairs of government, their enrollment in military levies, and above all their payment of taxes, the Portuguese regime provided fewer services than any other imperial government between the sixteenth and the early nineteenth centuries. In its orientation the Portuguese colonial bureaucracy was service-seeking rather than service rendering.[15]

Capital required for the construction of the needed infrastructure came--in the late eighteenth century--almost entirely from the private contributions of merchants and businessmen. Taxation on households--because of the subsistence mode of production and the difficulty of physically controllingg the population--did not yield significant revenues. It was the merchants who were most interested in the construction of commercial infra-structure and the merchants who essentially financed

---

[13]Odilon Nogueira de Matos, Café e Ferrovias (São Paulo, 1974), p. 123. In the case of the railroad linkage from São Paulo to Santos, Robert Mattoon in "The Companhia Paulista de Estradas de Ferro, 1868-1900: A Local Railway Enterprise in São Paulo, Brazil" (Ann Arbor, 1971), pp. 2-3, stated ". . . for São Paulo the railroad was less cause than result of economic activity and development. Coffee, with an assist from sugar, launched São Paulo on its modern course and created the need for railroads. Successful paulista lines stimulated but did not initiate the coffee industry. They answered demand functions in servicing existing markets rather than supply functions in creating new ones."

[14]Claudio Véliz, The Centralist Tradition of Latin America (Princeton, 1980).

[15]Dauril Alden, Royal Government in Colonial Brazil (Berkeley, 1968), p. 491. For examples of crown involvement in colonial road building in Chile see Santiago Marín Vicuña, Los Caminos de Chile (Santiago, 1930).

it. Once the roads, mule shelters, ports, and other facilities had been developed, capital investment in agricultural production began to be profitable.

Communications and transport improvements resulted in a parallel diminution in costs and a general facilitation of marketing procedures. High prices and demand for export products, especially sugar, stimulated a greater concentration on production for exchange, even among small producers. Concentration on exports, in turn, promoted the expansion of the urban market as more people began entering redistributive occupations and depending less on subsistence production. In the late eighteenth century efforts were made to protect the small producer and the urban consumer from commercial speculators in order to encourage production.[16] Production of foodstuffs for the market must have seemed like a profitable business at the end of the eighteenth century and in fact it was. However, the improvements in the export market were also having a valorizing effect on slaves and land, both perceptibly more expensive by 1802. At that point land, which had always been a free good in the district of the city of São Paulo, began to be relatively limited.

Many subsistence farmers lost their land holdings in the frequent litigations of the early nineteenth century. In other cases dispossession was accomplished illegally, through force or swindle. The purposes involved in these actions were 1) the monopolization of land for exports, 2) the elimination of small producers, and 3) the creation of a "free" labor force.[17] By 1836 the concentration of ownership of both slaves and land had resulted in many peasants being obliged to live as tenants, agregados, or otherwise as dependents to a fazendeiro who could force "rent" in kind or coin in return for the favor. For many low-income groups in 1836 the choice between a subsistence and an exchange mode of household production no longer existed. The lack of landed property and cash payments required for taxes or rents implied that it was no longer possible to live in a completely self-sufficient manner within the district of São Paulo.

Capitalization of agricultural estates in terms of engenhos and slaves was evident by 1802, at which time the visible wealth of merchant/businessmen and commercial farmers was approximately equal. A rapid concentration in the ownership of both slaves and land took place during the next three decades in the entire captaincy/province, and especially the sugar and cattle-producing areas. The size of land holdings was increased through legal dispossession, sale, or swindle. The prior owners became dependents of the new owners, moved farther into the interior where squatting lands could still be found, or joined the mass of urban poor in the city. By 1836 the commercial agriculturalists had become the dominant elite group in São Paulo. This subordination of the powers of the local municipal government to the authority of the new provincial assembly, as determined by the laws of 1828 and 1834, were also paralleled by the ascension of a provincial political and economic elite to replace the old municipally based merchant elite of the city of São Paulo. Many of the new agriculturalists, however, had begun their careers as merchants, just as much of the capital invested in agriculture in 1836 had been acquired in business.

---

[16]RGCMSP, XI, 15 janeiro 1783, 13 outubro 1783, 20 novembre 1798, 13 outubro 1798; ACMSP, XVII, 26 agosto 1780; 20 janeiro 1781.

[17]The stated purpose of the Lei das Terras of 1850 was to create a "free" (not encumbered by land) labor supply. RGCMSP, XI, 11 outubro 1800 is a letter from Captain-General Mello Castro e Mendonça complaining of all of the litigations with respect to land ownership, the legal moves against persons with doubtful title, and the many "squatters" who were being prosecuted.

Accommodations on the individual and household levels to the deep structural changes which occurred in the city of São Paulo between 1765 and 1836 were dramatic. São Paulo in 1765 was a community whose crude birth and death rates were probably over 50 per thousand, with an infant mortality rate above 200 per thousand. The mean household size was 4.24 persons, with over 90 percent of members consisting of the head of household, his spouse (if a male), and children. About 55 percent of households were headed by a married pair. The period from 1765 to 1802--which was a time of economic quickening, demographic growth, and a substantial transformation in the household mode of production from subsistence to an exchange economy--witnessed more and earlier marriages, an increase in mean number of children per head of a household, and a significantly larger mean size of household (5.02), as well as a substantial alteration in household composition to include more extended family members and a four-fold increment of non-related or agregado members. Households headed by a married pair declined to 42 percent.

The portrait of the mean paulistano household in 1765 is obviously very different from that of the traditional Brazilian household as described by Gilberto Freyre.[18] More important, however, is the correlation between prosperity, the development in markets and the increased size and complexity of the mean household. The implication is that the extensive household arrangement outlined by Freyre in the sugar region of Pernambuco in the sixteenth century, and which apparently existed, also, in the coffee lands of late nineteenth-century São Paulo, was a type of household composition not "traditional" in the sense of being characteristic of a self-sufficient subsistence economy, but rather "early-mercantile"--characteristic of household economies producing agricultural crops for export in semi-isolated circumstances.[19] The extensive, highly-capitalized agricultural estate would not have been economically meaningful in the subsistence situation of São Paulo in 1765. Large-scale production was incompatible with costly and insecure means of transport and unstable or non-existent markets.

From 1802 to 1836 both the economic and the individual and household changes seem to have been more complex, harder to define and more difficult to interpret. It is clear that the increasing costs of housing and land in this period led to the abandonment of the semi-nomadic (slash and burn) residence patterns of the eighteenth century within the district of São Paulo. The household census manuscripts in the rural bairros gave a vivid impression of concentrated and capitalized dwellings in 1836 as compared with 1802. Available evidence--admittedly spotty--leads to the

---

[18]The "ideal" Brazilian family appears to have been extrapolated from Gilberto Freyre's and Oliveira Vianna's depictions of upper-class patriarchal families of the landed aristocracy. See Gilberto Freyre, Casa grande e senzala (Rio de Janeiro, 1933) and Oliveira Vianna, Instituições políticas brasileiras, 2 vols. (Rio de Janeiro, 1949).

[19]Lucila Herrmann, "Evolução da estrutura social de Guaratinguetá num período de trezentos anos," Revista de Administração (março-junho 1948), p. 79, found the identical transformation in household size and composition between the subsistence period (census of 1775) and that of the engenhos (1805). She said, "O cicle dos engênhos não somente enriquece a base demográficia, com fortes entradas de indivíduos brancos e do cor, a econômica com a intensifição de produção e saida do produto, como permite, pelo aumente das posses, o alargamento das famílias, retenda no casal os filhos casados, addicionando parentes mais afastados, aumentando o número dos agregados e dos escravos...." Peter Laslett, op. cit., p. 49 and Chapter IV also found that for England, "...the onset of industrialization actually led in our country to a clear movement in the direction of more complex domestic groups."

hypothesis that many low-income domestic units were forced into a dependency relationship with respect to other affluent households because of the problem of available land. For those poor who moved to the urban bairros of São Paulo, the housing problem was difficult, especially as income distribution may have become more unequal between 1802 and 1836.

One of the most important types of accommodation in this period was living in rented rooms, renting out rooms and simply multiple-living arrangements to alleviate the housing difficulties.[20] By 1836 the percentage of urban household members not related to the head of household had risen to 26.6 percent of total members. These living arrangements were developed not only because of housing difficulties but also to improve the general income level of the household. The importance of the agregado element in the São Paulo household in the first decades of the nineteenth century cannot be divorced from the preponderance of the female-headed household in the same period. The female-headed household was more often poor and more frequently included agregados than did other types of households in São Paulo at the time.[21] Living as an agregado and accepting agregados into the household appear to have been major means of alleviating difficult financial circumstances in early nineteenth-century São Paulo.[22]

Another dimension of the presence of the agregado in the household was a specific attribute of the effective transition in the household mode of production. It became common to include apprentices, clerks, cashiers, and other helpers in the productive base of the household within its actual residential arrangements. Since the mode of exchange production generally required somewhat specialized skills--unlike the rudimentary understanding necessary for subsistence production--frequently the new work partners were only encountered among non-relatives. The common use of

[20]Modern-day urban "solutions" in Brazilian cities to housing for the poor include the favela (make-shift houses built illegally on marginal land), the cortiço (a large house with partitioned rooms and many resident families), and the casa de cómodos (rented rooms).

[21]The decline in the importance of female-headed households between 1836 and 1972 provides a particular explanation for the near-disappearance of the agregado element by 1972 (2.78 percent of household members). Edward T. Pryor, Jr., "Rhode Island family structure: 1875 and 1960," in Laslett, ed., op. cit., p. 586, also noted a relationship between houses headed by single persons and the presence of non-related members. However, in the case of Rhode Island, although the proportion of non-related household members declined dramatically over the period 1875 to 1960, the composition of heads of households by type of head did not change significantly. Pryor concluded that, "...the structural change of the household does demonstrate a changing economic organization which has made the presence of non-relatives in the household economically infeasible and/or unnecessary," p. 587.

[22]For examples of other situations of early modernization which also exhibited crowded and expensive housing and a high frequency of non-related persons in households see Philip J. Greven, Jr., "The average size of families and households in the Province of Massachusetts in 1765 and in the United States in 1790: an overview," in Laslett, ed., op.cit., pp. 549-55; Chie Nakane, op. cit., pp. 519-21; Pryor, op. cit., pp. 585-86. Anderson, op. cit., pp. 45-55 discusses the high proportion of non-related household residents in nineteenth-century Lancashire principally in terms of short-term residence for new migrants, and a means of housing for young adults wishing to leave home as well as an inexpensive alternative for low-income persons.

the downstairs portion of the sobrado or the front room of the casa têrrea as a store contributed to the incomplete separation of residence from workplace in this period.[23]

In some sense the most fascinating and perplexing phenomenon of the time was the extraordinary increase in female-headed households from 27 percent in 1765 (already very high) to 44 percent in urban São Paulo in 1802. Households headed by a married pair included only 29.2 percent of households in the urban area by 1836. Clearly, these are most unusual statistics, characteristic neither of a subsistence society nor of a twentieth-century city. Compared to the metropolitan district of São Paulo in 1972, for example, 77.95 percent of households were headed by a married pair, only 12.18 percent being headed by females.[24] Perhaps these curious figures for early nineteenth-century São Paulo can be best understood as short-term consequences of radical changes in occupation and place of residence.[25] Migration is most feasible for young, unmarried adults--precisely the type of population which came to predominate in São Paulo by 1836. The very flux of circumstances may have also reinforced the paulista reluctance to marry, have tended to make the consensual union even less stable, as well as provoking a short-term decline in fertility.[26]

Studies on the relationship of the family to modernization--which normally includes the process of monetarization and urbanization--have generally emphasized that the nuclear family is the residential unit most appropriate or convenient to an urbanized situation. Demographic transition theory suggests that as the economy moved from a pre-industrial to an industrial level, so would the organization of the residential group move from whatever traditional--often extended--form it had taken in

---

[23]John Demos, A Little Commonwealth: Family Life in Plymouth Colony (London, 1971), p. 187 concluded that the major reason for the change in household composition in Plymouth from 1689 to the present was "...the separation of work from the individual household, in connection with the growth of an urban, industrial system."

[24]IBGE, Grupo Executivo de Pesquisas Domiciliares, Pesquisa Nacional por amostra de Domicílios (4 trimêstre 1971-1972) Regiões Metropolitanas (Rio de Janeiro, São Paulo), pp. 228-29.

[25]Curious though these figures are, they are not unique. Lucila Herrmann, op. cit., pp. 72-73 also noted a very significant increase in female heads of households in 1805 compared to earlier figures and a considerable development in textile occupations, all of which were dominated by females. Donald Ramos, "Marriage and the Family in Colonial Vila Rica," HAHR, 55, no. 2 (May 1975), p. 220 shows that households headed by females included 45 percent in 1804 in Vila Rica (Ouro Preto). High numbers of female headed households have also been noted in eighteenth and nineteenth century Latin America by Ann Hagerman Johnson, "The Impact of Market Agriculture on Family and Household Structure in 19th Century Chile," HAHR 58, no. 4 (1978), pp. 625-48; Silvia M. Arrom, "Marriage Patterns in Mexico City, 1811," Journal of Family History 3, no. 4 (Winter 1978), pp. 376-91; and Kathy M. Waldron, A Social History of a Primate City: The Case of Caracas 1750-1810 (Ann Arbor, 1977).

[26]See Chapter III. Clearly the dramatic increase in proportion of unwed mothers from 6.02 percent of mothers in 1765 to 34.3 percent of mothers in 1836 had much to do with the decline in mean number of children per mother, as unwed mothers generally have fewer children.

the pre-industrial era towards a residential unit more and more dominated by the nuclear family.[27]

On the basis of this household analysis of São Paulo, the suggested relationship of domestic group to the economy or even to the urbanized situation is not observable. The dominance of the nuclear family within the residential group was a fact of pre-industrial subsistence society of São Paulo of 1765. Alterations in the early mercantile period were toward more household complexity and decreased importance of the nuclear members in the domestic group. By 1972 household data on the metropolitan area of São Paulo indicated a household composition very little different from that of 1765. In 1972, 89.31 percent of the household members were nuclear, 7.91 percent kin-related members, and 2.78 percent agregados. Mean household size for urban São Paulo was 4.32.[28] The composition of the domestic group of São Paulo in 1765 was much closer to that of 1972 than was the case for either 1836 or 1802. That the processes of industrialization and urbanization have important indirect effects on the family economy and organization is certain. However, it appears that the domestic unit had more flexibility to adjust rapidly and frequently to new circumstances than social scientists have previously believed.

Much of the literature on the demographic transition and on the relationship of the family and household to economic development implicitly equates the strength of kinship in personal life with the size and complexity of the household. It is clear from this study that no such relationship exists. Household size and complexity are closely associated with mode and locus of production, occupational structure, and consumption variables such as housing availability and cost, childcare, and the existence of urban services. Kinship was arguably most central in the lives of paulistas in the late eighteenth century subsistence economy when so many services and exchanges were based on a principal of generalized reciprocity. However, household structure at that time was simpler and smaller, on average, than it was to be for at least another hundred years.

The relationship of kinship to household and family structure in the nineteenth century exchange economy in urban São Paulo is less obvious. The marketplace effectively reoriented patterns of production and exchange away from their prior logic of personal exchange. Household composition in this period also often seemed to reflect the productive necessities of a household workshop more than they did domestic units of reproduction, socialization, and consumption. However, it would be as inappropriate to announce the demise of kinship as a dimension of social life for the nineteenth century based on household structure as it would have been to view the eighteenth-century nuclear household as evidence that the kindred did not exist. Kinship is organized as importantly among households as within them and may

---

[27]William J. Goode, The Family (Englewood Cliffs, 1964), p. 108 says, "Family research in the post-World War II period has documented one gross empirical regularity whose processes are not yet clearly understood--that in all parts of the world and for the first time in world history all social systems are moving fast or slowly toward some form of the conjugal family system and also toward industrialization. In agreement with the intuition of social analysts for over a century is the finding that with industrialization the traditional family systems--usually, extended or joint family systems, with or without lineages or clans--are breaking down..."

[28]IBGE, Pesquisa Nacional por amostra de Domicílios, op. cit., pp. 228-29.

continue to be functional even over great distances as research in other areas for the twentieth century suggests.[29]

Some researchers on Latin America have suggested that kinship in the modern period has continued to be important principally for the affluent, who continue to use it as a basis of business association, property accumulation, and political alliance.[30] Others point out that kinship and ritual kinship for rural lower classes and urban shanty towns function for the purposes of mutual help and exchange in a way almost as fundamental as that of eighteenth-century São Paulo.[31] Studies on rural-urban migration also emphasize the significance of help from kin at the point of destination for housing, money, and jobs.[32] The family and kindred in Brazil was always a system of mutual support as well as a system of economic and political alliance. In the subsistence economy that system was important to protect against shortages, to support members in times of emergency or economic failure, to share in important mutual tasks, to provide a place within a community and household, to identify a member as trustworthy to the larger community. Today the insecure, underpaid, underemployed, and unemployed lower classes living without property of their own in a society with little welfare support would seem to have all the more need for the personal support and economic and social insurance provided by the traditional systems of kinship and ritual kinship that have always underlaid the family and the household in Brazilian society.

---

[29]Linda Greenow argues the spatial dimension in, "Micro-Geographic Analyses as an Index to Family Structure and Networks," Journal of Family History 10, no. 3 (Fall 1985, in press). For the importance of kinship in twentieth century America see Eugene Litwak, "Extended kin relations in an industrial democratic society." In: Shanas, Ethel and Streib, Gordon F. (eds.), Social Structure and the Family: Generational Relations (Englewood Cliffs, 1965).

[30]See, for example, Donna Guy, "Latin American Family History: The Family as a Business and Corporation in Argentina," World Conference on Records, Vol. 9 (Salt Lake City, 1980).

[31]See Helen Icken Safa, "Class Consciousness among Working Class Women in Latin America: Puerto Rico," in June Nash and Helen Safa (eds.), Sex and Class in Latin America (Brooklyn, 1980), p. 79, Larissa A. Lomnitz, Networks and Marginality, Life in a Mexican Shanty Town (New York, 1977).

[32]Robert Kemper, Migration and Adaptation; Tzintzuntzan Peasants in Mexico City (Beverly Hills, 1977) and Lourdes Arizpe, Migración, Etnicismo y Câmbio Económico: Un Estudio Sobre Migrantes Campesinos a la Ciudad de Mexico (Mexico, 1978).

Appendix IV:1

Street Names and Numbers of Households in the Urban and Rural Districts of São Paulo According to the Censuses of 1765, 1802, and 1836

Recenseamento de 1765: Listas da gente que compreende a cid. de S. Paulo e todo o seu têrmo de que he Cap. Mor Manuel de Oliveira Cardoso[1]

I. Streets and households ascribed to the First Company[2]

1. No street listed (HH 1-7); Total 7 HH.
2. Rua do canto da Sé té o Rosário (Boavista included), HH 8-60, Total 53 HH.
3. Rua de S. Bento e Anhangabaú (HH 61-122); Total 62 HH.
4. Rua do canto da Lapa até a Mizericórdia (Rua do Comércio), HH 123-152; Total 30 HH.
5. Rua Direita (HH 153-194); Total 42 HH.
6. Canto de Santo Antônio e Anhangabaú grande até a cadeya (São Jose), HH 195-213; Total 19 HH.
7. Rua da cadeya (Ouvidor; José Bonifácio), HH 214-231; Total 18 HH.
8. Rua do canto da Mizericórdia pa o campo da fôrça e suas travessas (Principe), HH 232-249; Total 18 HH.
9. Rua da freira (HH 250-279); Total 30 HH.
10. Rua de S. Gonçallo até o largo da Sé (HH 280-299); Total 20 HH.

Total Households--299

II. Streets and households ascribed to the Second Company[3]

1. Bayrro de Ambuassaba (HH 407-411); Total 5 HH.
2. Bayrro de Pirayossara (HH 412-420); Total 9 HH.
3. Bayrro dos Pinheros (HH 421-430); Total 10 HH.
4. Bayrro de Jaraguá e Aricanduba (HH 584-599); Total 16 HH.
5. Bayrro de Tremembé athé a cachoeira inclusive (HH 572-583); Total 12 HH.
6. Bayrro de Cagoassú e seus distritos (HH 600-671); Total 72 HH.
7. Bairro de Cagoassú (HH 840-862); Total 23 HH.

Total Households--147

III.Streets and households ascribed to the Third Company[4]

1. Rua do canto do Cirurgião Fonseca até o beço de Sta Theresa e travessas (Rua das flores), HH 300-392; Total 93 HH.
2. Bayrro do Parí quaze todos gente bastarda (HH 393-406); Total 14 HH.
3. Bayrro de Tatuapé e Ancanduba (HH 672-686); Total 15 HH.

Total Households--122

Total households in all the urban militia companies--568

IV. Households and <u>bairros</u> ascribed to rural area[5]

1. Bayrro de Nossa Senhora do O (HH 431-488); Total 57 HH.
2. Bayrro de Sta. Anna (HH 489-571); Total 83 HH.
3. Bairro de S. Miguel (HH 777-839); Total 63 HH.
4. Bairro de Nossa Senhora da Penha e França (HH 863-899); Total 37 HH.

Total households in four rural <u>bairros</u>--240

.

<u>Maços de População (Capital, 1802)</u>

I. A Primeira Companhia de Ordenanças da Cidade de Sm Paulo[6]

1. Rua de São Bento (HH 1-76); 76 HH.
2. Rua da Boa Vista (HH 77-123); 47 HH.
3. Rua do Rosário (HH 124-185); 62 HH.
4. Rua da Quitanda (HH 186-242); 57 HH.
5. Rua de S. Francisco (HH 243-276); 34 HH.
6. Rua de Gabriel Antunes (HH 277-339); 63 HH.
7. Arrebaldes de S. Gonzalo (HH 340-404); 65 HH.
8. Rua da Freira (HH 405-423); 19 HH.
9. Rua do Coronel Mexia (HH 424-438); 15 HH.
10. Pateo da Sé (HH 439-443); 5 HH.
11. Arrebaldes de S. Bento (HH 444-472); 29 HH.
12. Rua da Sé Pa S. Gonçalo (HH 473-504); 32 HH.

Total Households--504

II. A Segunda Companhia de Ordenanças da Cidade de Sm Paulo7

1. No street listed (HH 1-48); 48 HH.
2. Rua de S Francisco (HH 49-70); 22 HH.
3. Rua de S Antônio (HH 71-153); 83 HH.
4. Rua de S. Efigênia (HH 154-286); 133 HH.
5. Bairro de Inbuasava (HH 287-302); 16 HH.
6. Bairro de Pirajocara (HH 303-323); 21 HH.

Total Households--323

III.A Terceira Companhia de Ordenança da Cidade de Sm Paulo[8]

No street names are given in this list. The Palácio do Episcopal, the Convento do Carmo, and the Convento Santa Theresa are all present in the listing.

Total Households--242

Total Households in Three Urban Companies--1,069

IV. Household and Bairros in Rural Area

1. A Companhia de Ordenanças do Bairro de Nossa Senhora do O (HH 1-157); 157 HH.
2. A Companhia de Ordenanças do Bairro de Santa Ana (HH 1-134); 134 HH.
3. A Companhia de Ordenanças que compreende os Bairros de Nossa Senhora da Penha e França e São Miguel (HH 1-168); 168 HH.

Total Households in Four Rural Bairros--459

Maços de População (Capital, 1836)

I. A Freguesia da Sé[9]

1. Quarteirão #1; no street given; 50 HH, 5 HH vacant.
2. Quarteirão #2; Rua de São Bento; 40 HH.
3. Quarteirão #3; no street given; 42 HH, 10 HH vacant.
4. Quarteirão #4; Rua Direita; 36 HH.
5. Quarteirão #5; no street given; 36 HH, 1 HH vacant.
6. Quarteirão #6; part of Rua Direita and Rua Rosário (21 HH); Travessa do Colégio (10 HH); Rua do Carmo (3 HH); total 34 HH.
7. Quarteirão #7; Rua do Comércio (HH 1-9; 33-40); 17 HH; Travessa das Casinhas; 26 HH; total 43 HH.
8. Quarteirão #8; no street given; 26 HH; Travessa do Comércio (13 HH); total 39 HH.
9. Quarteirão #9; Rua da Boa Vista; 56 HH, 2 HH vacant, 1 store. Rua do Thamadathehei; 48 HH, 8 vacant. Rua da Constituição, 31 HH, 7 vacant, 1 venda seguros. Total 135 HH.
10. Quarteirão #10; missing from the collection. Estimate 50 households (average number households in this district).

Total inhabited households listed--455
Total estimated households--505

II. Distrito do Juizo d'Paz do Sul da Sé, Município da Imperial Cidade de São Paulo

1. Quarteirão #1; Largo da Bichiga; Estrada que Legue para Sto. Amaro; 13 HH.
2. Quarteirão #2; no street given; 19 HH.
3. Quarteirão #3; missing from the collection. Estimated 30 households.
4. Quarteirão #4; Pateo da Sé (HH 1-6); 6 HH; Rua da Fundição (HH 1-14); 14 HH; total 24 HH. Four households listed without street.

5. Quarteirão #5; Rua de Santa Thereza; 7 HH; Travessas de S. Thereza; 33 HH; Total 40 HH.
6. Quarteirão #6; Rua das Flores; 61 HH.
7. Quarteirão #7; missing from the collection. Estimated 30 HH.
8. Quarteirão #8; Ladeira do Carmo (HH 1-20); 20 HH.
9. Quarteirão #9; no street given; 40 HH.
10. Quarteirão #10; no street given; 31 HH.
11. Quarteirão #11; missing from the collection. Estimated 30 HH.
12. Quarteirão #12; Rua da Esperança e parte da de Santa Thereza; 41 HH.
13. Quarteirão #13; Rua de S Gonçalo, Travessa do Príncipe e Jogo da Bola, 46 HH.
14. Quarteirão #14; no street given; 40 HH.
15. Quarteirão #15; Rua da Freira (HH 1-23); 12 HH; Fím Travessa da Casa Santa; 33 HH, 8 vacant.
16. Quarteirão #16; Príncipia na Rua atrás da cadeia e Largo de São Gonçalo; 38 HH.
17. Quarteirão #17; no street given; 32 HH; 6 vacant; Travessa denominada Monteiro 5 HH; total 37 HH.
18. Quarteirão #18; no street given; 13 HH, 1 vacant; 13 HH.
19. Quarteirão #19; Bairro de Ipiranga; 18 HH.

Total inhabited households listed--516
Total estimated households--576

Total inhabited households listed for Freguesia da Sé--971
Total estimated households for Freguesia da Sé--1,081

III. Distrito do Juiz do Paz da Freguesia de Santa Efigênia do Município da Cidade, Anno 1836[10]

1. Quarteirão #1; no street given; 33 HH, 7 vacant. Rua Alegre, 21 HH, 5 vacant; total 54 HH.
2. Quarteirão #2; Bairro da Luz, 41 HH; Convento Recolhidos da Luz (not included analysis); Hospital dos Lázaros (not included analysis); no street given, 2 vacant; Total 39 HH.
3. Quarteirão #3; missing from collection; estimated 44 HH.
4. Quarteirão #4; no street given; 32 HH.
5. Quarteirão #5; missing from collection; estimated 44 HH.
6. Quarteirão #6; no street given; 28 HH.
7. Quarteirão #7; no street given; 50 HH.
8. Quarteirão #8; no street given; 26 HH.
9. Quarteirão #9; Bairro dos Pinheiros; 24 HH.
10. Quarteirão #10; Bairros de Pirajocara; 27 HH.
11. Quarteirão #11; Bairros de Pirajocara e Jaguará; 34 HH.
12. Quarteirão #12; Guapira; 84 HH.
13. Quarteirão #13; Caxoeira; 49 HH.

Total inhabited households listed--447
Total estimated households for Santa Efigênia--535

IV. Distrito do Juiz do Paz da Freguesia do Senhor Bom Jesus de Mattos--Senhor do Brás

The lists of the four quarteirõens of this Freguesia are all missing from the collection. An 1842 listing of active citizens for Brás indicates that in that year

Brás included a total of 185 households. Both the Freguesia da Sé and the Freguesia de Santa Efigênia increased in numbers of households by 14 percent from 1836 to 1842. If the same was true for Brás, the total number of households in 1836 was 162.

Total estimated households for Brás--162

V. Households and Bairros Ascribed to Rural Area

1. Distrito do Juiz do Paz da Freguesia de Nossa Senhora do O.
   Quarteirão #1; missing from collection, estimated 32 HH.
   Quarteirão #2; missing from collection, estimated 32 HH.
   Quarteirão #3; (HH 1-27); 27 HH.
   Quarteirão #4; (HH 1-27); 27 HH.
   Quarteirão #5; (HH 1-35); 35 HH.
   Quarteirão #6; (HH 1-28); 28 HH.
   Quarteirão #7; (HH 1-38); 38 HH.
   Quarteirão #8; (HH 1-40); 40 HH.

Total households listed--195
Total estimated households--259

2. Distrito do Juiz do Paz da Freguesia de Nossa Senhora da Penha e França e São Miguel.
   Quarteirão #1; (HH 1-31); 32 HH.
   Quarteirão #2; (HH 1-28); 28 HH.
   Quarteirão #3; (HH 1-28); 28 HH.
   Quarteirão #4; (HH 1-37); 37 HH.
   Quarteirão #5; (HH 1-39); 39 HH.
   Quarteirão #6; (HH 1-51); 51 HH.

Total households listed--214

Total households listed for rural area--409
Total estimated households for rural area--473

---

[1]The original spelling is retained for all Portuguese words as found in the document.

[2]These households represent the beginnings of the area to be designated the First Company of the urban militia in 1795, keeping that designation until 1818. After 1818 the First Company was called the Sé in the censuses with quarteirõens as subdivisions. The name the Sé actually referred to the parish which, in 1747, encompassed sixteen leagues from east to west, and eight and a half leagues from north to south. See Marcílio, La ville de São Paulo (Rouen, 1970), pp. 54-61 for a detailed discussion of the territorial changes in the parish of the Sé. The Sé was gradually diminished in area as the population grew and other parishes were created. The two parishes of Santa Efigênia (the Second Company) and Brás (the Third Company) were created in 1809 and 1818 respectively. After that time the Sé included only the triangular center area of the city which, from 1795 to 1818, had been designated the First Company. The choice of the area to be included in the First Company, taken from the 1765 listing (which was not divided into companies) was done by comparisons of areas, streets, and changes in street names with later census lists and with maps. For this purpose the maps of most importance were "Planta da cidade de S. Paulo levantada em 1810 pelo engenheiro Rufino João Felisardo e Costa," "Planta da imperial cidade levantada em 1841 com todas as alterações" and an informative map noting dates of the erection of

important buildings and public works and some name changes by Affonso A. de Freitas, "Plan histórico da cidade de São Paulo, 1800-1874." These maps were consulted in the map section of the Instituto Histórico e Geográfico de São Paulo. A good collection of historical maps of São Paulo is Affonso de E. Taunay, Velho São Paulo ((São Paulo, 1954). Other sources important in identifying streets and bairros were Paulo Cursino Moura, São Paulo de outrora (São Paulo, 1943) passim, Antônio Egydio Martins, São Paulo antigo, 1554-1910 (São Paulo, 1911), 2 vols, and Marcílio, La ville de São Paulo, pp. 27-70. The decision to put "Rua Direita" in the First Company, rather than the Second, was based on the fact that the "Rua Direita" was normally included in the First Company in the militia censuses. The 1802 census does not list "Rua Direita" in any company, but does list "Rua S. Antônio" in the Second Company, a name sometimes substituted for "Rua Direita." The question turns on whether the "Rua Direita" in the 1765 census was to the east or to the west of the Anhangabaú. The continuation of "Rua Direita" east of the Anhangabaú pertained to the Second Company. West of the Anhangabaú Rua Direita was clearly in the First Company.

[3]The area which was designated as the Second Company in 1795, and as Santa Efigênia in 1809 was the part of the city east of the Anhangabaú, and included the Bairro do Guaré or Luz, the Santa Efigênia area, Consolação, and the southeastern section of Caguassú. Marcílio, La ville de São Paulo, pp. 23-27 was very helpful in locating the smaller bairros within this area. The "Bayrro de Tremembé athé a cachoeira inclusiva" through encountering that designation in other early nineteenth-century censuses in the Second Company.

[4]The Third Company was the most difficult of the areas to define. In the 1802 census there were no streets listed for this company, but the landmarks of the Palácio de Episcopal, the Convento do Carmo and the Convento Santa Theresa were included. These three landmarks were all placed slightly to the east of the Tamanduateí river, in the southwest corner of the triangle. The relatively large section of 93 households described by "Rua do canto do Cirurgião Fonseca Até o beço de Sta Theresa e travessas" in the 1765 census would clearly fall into it. However, the district called Brás, created in 1818, apparently did not include this section to the east of the Tamanduateí. The streets in this section were included in the Sé in the 1836 census lists. Other sections on the other side of the Tamanduatemeí which were included in the 1802 listing for the Third Company were designated as part of Brás in 1818. This, of course, makes the growth rates for the sections of the city difficult to calculate, but since these parts all ultimately are included within the urban area, the difference is not that important. The important thing is being sure that all parts are accounted for, and that extra areas have not been included.

[5]Included in the 1765 lists were households for the "Bayrro de S Bernardo e borda do campo" (HH 687-753, the "Bairro do N. Sra do Merces" (HH 754-765), and the "Bairros de S Caetano" (HH 766-776), none of which were included in this study. The parish of São Bernardo, created in 1812, included the bairro of São Caetano, and was not defined as a part of the city in 1836, nor was São Bernardo included in the listings of 1802. Therefore I thought it best to exclude these households from the analysis. The ten households of the "Bairro de N. Sra do Merces" were also excluded because I could not lcoate the bairro nor any church, convent, or brotherhood by that name in any of the sources I consulted. The "Bairro de N. Sra do Merces" could possibly be part of São Bernardo, in that the listing was physically located between São Bernardo and São Caetano which is part of São Bernardo. In any case the ten households in

question would not have a significant effect on the ennumeration of any of the three companies.

[6]The Ruas Direita, Comércio, São José, Ouvidor, and Príncipe--all present in the 1765 census under some recognizable heading with a total of 127 households--were not easily identifiable listings in the 1802 census. The Rua do Comércio may have been included in the listing for the Rua Quitanda. The Rua do Rosário, which in 1765 included the listing for the Boa Vista (in 1802 listed separately) may have included the Rua Direita in this listing. On that hypothesis, the sum of the households for the three streets Boa Vista, Rosário, and Direita grew from 95 households in 1765 to 109 in 1802, a reasonable possibility. The S. Francisco (a name which I have not been able to identify as the earlier name for any known street) must have been either the early São José, which in 1765 began at Santo Antônio and continued to the convento de São Francisco, or else possibly the S. Francisco was the Jogo da Bola, which also terminated at the largo São Francisco. I tend to think it was the São José because the number of households was greater than that given for Jogo da Bola in 1836, and because the São José was listed in 1765. The other street names given in the 1802 census which I have been unable to trace were the Rua do Coronel Mexia (15 HH) and the Rua do Gabriel Antunes (63 HH). The Rua do Coronel Mexia may have been an earlier version of the "Rua do Quartel." Another possibility would be the Rua da Esperança, given by that name in the 1836 listing. The Rua de Gabriel Antunes (63 HH) could have been the "Rua do Príncipe" or the "Ouvidor" or even both of these and Jogo da Bola as well. Gabriel Antunes may refer to Gabriel Antunes de Fonseça who was a public figure in the late eighteenth century. While much of this argument is conjecture based only on a knowledge of what had already existed, and which streets seem to have usually been listed together, it seems to be the best which can be offered.

[7]The Rua de S. Francisco in this case must refer to the street later known as the Rua da Palha which continued east from the largo São Francisco east of the Anhanguabaú. The Rua de S Antônio most probably was the continuation of Rua Direita east of the Anhangabaú (and the church of Santo Antônio), today known as the Barao de Itapetininga. The Rua de S. Efigênia is the same as the street by that name today.

[8]Little can be said about the area of Company Three since no actual streets were named. The listing of the Palácio do Episcopal, the Convento do Carmo and the Convento Santa Theresa indicate that some percentage of the households listed were located east of the Tamanduatheí. Another indication of the spreading of this Company on both sides of the Tamanduatheí river is that the 1836 District of Brás--the later descendent of Company Three but restricted to households west of the Tamanduatheí--included a total of only 162 households in 1836--indicating that the area covered had significantly decreased. The section of Company Three not included in Brás was transferred to the District of the Sé--or Company One.

[9]The districts and street names in the 1836 census lists are eaily identifiable. The Norte do Sé included all the streets in the triangle from the junction of the Anhangabaú and the Tamanduatheí into the Tieté south to the Largo da Sé. The Sul to Sé included those streets to the south of the Sé and between the two rivers to the level of the Largo da Força. The streets, with the exception of the "Travessa denominada Monteiro" (Sul do Sé, 5 HH), can be readily located since the names are either unchanged, or else are names known in the literature and maps as predecessors of present names. Names which have changed since 1836 include the Rua das Casinhas (today Senador Feijó), Constituição (Florencio de Abreu), Cargo da Bichiga (Largo do Piques, or Capim), the Rua da Fundição (Floriano Peixoto), Príncipe (Quintino Bocaiuva), Jogo da Bola

(Benjamin Constant), Rua atrás da Cadeia (Rodrigo Silva). The Bairro de Ipiranga was the most southerly district in the freguesia, located in the area of the little river by the same name which branched off of the Tamanduateí.

[10]One of the two missing quarteirõens may have been Santana, which according to a Mapa geral of 1827 had been included in the Freguesia of Santa Efigênia. Unfortunately, numbers of households were not given.

Appendix V:1
Occupational Distributions

Occupational distributions were developed from each of the three São Paulo censuses, in the years 1765, 1802, and 1836. There were several problems involved in the working out of these distributions.

In the 1765 census, over 70 percent of households did not specify occupations. Those who did provide occupations sometimes listed more than one. The fact that agriculture was not included as an occupation in the 1765 census made it seem likely that its omission meant that the household economy was based on subsistence agriculture. This hypothesis was confirmed by evidence in the 1767 and 1774 censuses, in which agriculture was the indicated occupation for a majority of households.

The 1802 census listed occupations for practically all households, up to three occupations for the head of household, and as many as five occupations for the household as a group. The 1836 census usually specified only one occupation per head of household, but it became very common, especially among low-income households, for other members of the household to also list occupations.

In order not to lose track of these transformations in the organization of household economy, I decided to use household as the basic unit for analyzing occupations, rather than number of occupations or total number of workers. The multiple occupations of heads of households were coded with reference to the worker's position in the household, as were the multiple-worker households. The distributions were worked out in terms of the principal occupation of the head of household, with the other effects being noted but not included in the distributions. The only exception to this was the occupational distribution for 1836 based on the mapa geral, which was apparently based on registered occupations.

Appendix V:2

Income Distribution Estimates for 1836

The estimated income distribution for 1836 for the districts of the Sé and Santa Efigênia was made in the following manner. Annual incomes were given in the census lists for a sizable proportion of the population. All of these incomes were collected according to occupation and the income data for each occupation were analyzed to make an income distribution for that particular occupation. For example, the occupation "lavrador" (agriculturalist) was listed by 101 heads of households in these two bairros, of which 59 also included income. The range of incomes for those 59 was from twelve to four thousand mil reis annually, the total income being 9,138 mil reis for the 59 agriculturalists. The average income was thus 145.05 mil reis per year. A distribution was made on the assumption that the distribution of the specified incomes corresponded to the actual distribution of incomes in the population. By this means I estimated, for example, that 33.33 percent of the agricultural heads of household with annual income below 50 mil reis received a total income equal to 7.15 percent of the total income realized among agriculturalists.

In order to generalize the estimate for agriculturalists, I multiplied the average income (145.05 mil reis) by the total number of agriculturalists (101) for an estimated total income of 14,650.05 mil reis annually. Then I distributed both the income and the agriculturalists among the income categories in the same proportions as they were distributed in the population of those heads of household in agriculture indicating incomes.

I proceeded in this manner for each occupation within each sector, and the totals in the general distribution, as well as the sector totals, are simply sums of these amounts. In some cases all members of the particular occupation listed incomes in which case no estimate was needed. In other cases the incomes were so well set that there was little chance of a mistake as long as the numbers within occupations (that is the population) were correct. Categories such as "capital" or "rents" obviously could not be included in the estimate.

I suspect, as stated in the text, that the greatest omissions were in the lower income occupations--that is the actual number of those in the occupations. This method applied to the data of the mapa geral would undoubtedly produce a more unequal distribution than that from the census lists. Other omissions were sometimes made in the case of some personnages like Daniel Muller and Antônio da Silva Prado whose qualifications for public office were commonly known, and who appeared in the census lists without a given income. In general, all of the biases tend to go in the same direction--that of a more equal distribution. Thus the estimate produced can be considered highly optimistic in that sense.

Glossary

AGREGADO--A person unrelated to the head of a given household, who lives as a member of the household, often as an unofficial servant.

ALQUEIRES--A grain measure during the colonial period, though the unit varied somewhat according to time and place. Dauril Alden suggests that an alqueire of rice weighed 72 pounds. In modern Brazil an alqueire is usually a unit of agricultural land varying in size according to region.

ARROBA--Unit of weight equivalent to 14 kilos, 688 grams, or between 25 and 32 pounds.

BAIRRO--A major division of a city. A neighborhood.

BANDEIRANTES--Prospectors and slave-raiders. Especially applied to seventeenth century paulistas who went out in groups, each with a flag (bandeira) searching for Indians and gold.

BEXIGAS--Colonial term for smallpox, more correctly known as variola.

CAMARA--City council.

CAMINHO DO MAR--Road from the city of São Paulo to Santos, originating from an Indian path over the same route.

CANADAS--A liquid measure with varying value, usually one twelfth of a liquid alqueire or 1.41 liters.

CASA DE PORAO ALTO--Type of house intended only for family residence which became popular among the Brazilian elite about 1850. The basement (posporão) separated the floor of the house from the ground. It was like the casa têrrea but with a raised floor.

CASA TERREA--One-story house with beaten earth floor, predominant for all classes in the colonial period, but gradually associated with the lower classes in the nineteenth and twentieth centuries.

COMARCA--A district; administrative division of a captaincy in the colonial period.

COMPADRIO--Ritual kinship. Compadres were selected for the occasions of christening, baptism and marriage.

CORONELISMO--Exercise of power by local magnates.

EMBOABAS--Term by which paulistas referred to non-paulistas who came to the mines in search of gold in the first years of the eighteenth century.

FAZENDEIRO--Farmer or rancher, usually owner of a large estate.

FREGUESIA--Parish; administrative division of a city.

HOMENS BONS--"Men of quality"; the electors of the electors of the city council.

JUIZ DE FORA--Royal judge appointed by the crown to certain city councils in the eighteenth century to restrict the autonomy of the councils.

JUIZ ORDINARIO--Justice of the peace; a member of the city council; handled disputes over small property claims and taxes in the colonial period.

JUIZ DOS ORPHAOS--Municipal judge who managed the property and tutorage of orphaned minors in the colonial period.

LANCO--Group of rooms in a house beside a corridor. A house with two lancos had rooms on both sides of a corridor. It was a means of suggesting the size of a house in colonial property inventories.

LAVRADORES A FAVOR--Farmers living on lands belonging to others who usually had to work a given number of days per week on the estate of the owner.

MAMELUCO--A persons of Portuguese and Indian blood.

MASCATES--Travelling salesmen of cloth, jewels, pans, and other products.

MATO--Jungle, brush, or wild growth.

MEIOS DIREITOS--A municipal tax on river crossings, established in the captaincy of São Paulo in 1747, farmed out to private citizens in the colonial period.

MESTRE DE CAMPO--Coronel who commanded first-line militia regiments (auxiliarios) in the colonial period; an important administrative officer.

MORGADO--The one next in line to an entailed estate.

MUTIRAO--Voluntary collective work meeting, as to raise a house or clear land; an important aspect of Brazilian colonial society and economy.

OUVIDOR--Royal circuit judge whose jurisdiction extended over a large territory.

PANELINHA--Royal circuit judge whose jurisdiction extended over a large territory.

PARCEIROS--Sharecroppers; farmers who live and work on land owned by someone else with the obligation to give some portion of the crops to the owner of the land.

PARDO--Mulatto.

PATRIMONIO--Property belonging to someone or some institution.

PAU-A-PIQUE--Type of popular housing construction also known as wattle and daub. A frame of wicker or pliable branches is plastered with mud to build walls. This construction was common throughout the colonial period and is still found in rural bairros of Brazil today.

PAULISTA--Resident of the captaincy/province/state of São Paulo.

PAULISTANO--Resident of the city of São Paulo.

POUSO--Open shelter or lean-to along a road for the use of mule teams and travelers in the eighteenth and nineteenth centuries; also called rancho.

PROCURADOR--Procurator or people's lawyer. Heard public complaints and inspected roads, bridges, fountains and the like. A member of the city council.

PROVEDOR--A person of special social status to whom is given the administration of a public institution, especially a charity. The administrator of the Santa Casa de Misericórdia.

ROCA--Farmland on which subsistence crops are grown.

SENHOR DE ENGENHO--Owner of a sugar plantation complex.

SERTAO--The interior.

SESMARIA--Grant of uncultivated land for the purpose of cultivating and populating the area. Sesmarias were given in Brazil throughout the colonial period.

SITIANTES--Owner or renter of a sítio or small farm.

SOBRADO--House with more than one story, which became popular in Brazil in the nineteenth century for elite families. The family lived on the upper floor or floors while the lower floor was reserved for a carriage, slaves, a store or animals.

TAIPA DE PILAO--Type of house construction common in colonial Brazil and still found today. Parallel supports of posts or wicker were filled with moistened earth and rammed down hard. Dried by the sun these usually thick walls would last for centuries.

TERMO--Official territory belonging to a town.

TROPEIRO--Mule driver; buyer and seller of livestock.

VEREADOR--Alderman, city councilmember and administrator of a municipality.

Bibliography

I. MANUSCRIPT MATERIALS

Arquivo da Curia Metropolitana de São Paulo

Regístros das freguezias do destrito da cidade de São Paulo (1730-1850).

Livro do tombo, Freguezia da Sé, 1747.

Arquivo do Estado de São Paulo: Secção histórica

No. ordem 30-37A, caixa 30-37A; População, capital (1765-1846).

No. ordem 235, no. caixa 9; Ofícios de Mogi Mirím, Parnaiba, capital, Jundiaí, Campinas (1721-1822).

No. ordem 239, caixa 13; Contas das camaras municipais (1802-1821).

No. ordem 241, caixa 14; Ofícios dos engenheiros sobre estradas e jardins (1747-1822).

No. ordem 296, caixa 57A; Ordenanças da Capital (1721-1821).

No. ordem 313, caixa 72; Poder judiciário ouvidor, juízes da Capital de Parnaiba.

No. ordem 338-343, caixa 91-94; Requerimentos sobre dívidas, heranças, queixas, licenças, relaxação de prisões (1721-1820).

No. ordem 344-345, caixa 95-95A; Requerimentos sobre dívidas, heranças, queixas, licenças, relaxação de prisões e permissões para engenhos (1821-1822).

No. ordem 346, caixa 96, Físico-Mor, botica real, Santa Casa de São Paulo, dívidas diversas e carta da tia do marquês de S. Vicente (1709-1839).

No. ordem 347, caixa 97, Papeis referentes as minas de ouro e ferro de diversas localidades, casa de fundição e almoxarifado de São Paulo e Paranagua (1721-1815).

No. ordem 362-373, caixa 4-15, Sesmarias, Patentes, Provisoõs (1734-1810).

No. ordem 543-572, caixa 66-95, Inventários naõ publicados (1765-1851).

No. ordem 599-604, caixa 1-6, Inventários e testamentos (1770-1799).

No. ordem 5331-5332, caixa 1-2, Juíz de orfaõs da capital (1720-1800).

Arquivo Nacional

Caixa 748, pacote 2, Correspondência da capitania de São Paulo, 1762-1796, 1802-1807.

Biblioteca Nacional: Manuscriptas

Coleção Morgado de Matheus:

Lista 1, documentos 299-307, cartas a Bento Lopes de Leão Taubaté por fazendeiros locais, 1769.

Lista 1, documentos 414-431, documentos relacionados a administração da capitania de São Paulo, 1767.

Lista 1, documentos 907-916, documentos sobre a exploração de ferro e lavoura do algodaõ em São Paulo, 1765-1770.

Lista 1, documentos 1087-1166, documentos vários, 1770-1774.

Unpublished Papers and Dissertations

Davidson, David. "Rivers and Empire: The Madeira Route and the Incorporation of the Brazilian Far West 1737-1808" (University Microfilms, Yale, 1970).

Fernandes, Heloisa Rodrigues. "A força pública de São Paulo: origem, determinações e fundamentos históricos, 1831-1926," Dissertação de mestrado em sociologia na Universidade de São Paulo (São Paulo, 1972).

Fukuí, Lia Freitas Garcia. "Parentesco e família entre sitiantes tradicionais," Tese de doutoramento em ciencias sociais na Universidade de São Paulo. São Paulo, 1972.

Kiernan, James P. "The Manumission of Slaves in Colonial Brazil: Parati 1789-1822" (Ann Arbor, 1976).

Levi, Darrell. "The Prados of São Paulo: An Elite Brazilian Family in a Changing Society, 1840-1930" (University Microfilms, Yale, 1974).

Lisanti Filho, Luis. "Comércio e capitalismo: O Brasil e a Europa entre o fim do século xviii e o ínicio do século xix," Tese de doutoramento na história na Universidade de São Paulo. São Paulo, 1962.

Marcílio, Maria-Luiza. "Crescimento demográfico e evolução agraria paulista 1700-1836," Tése de livre docência no história na Universidade de São Paulo. São Paulo, 1974.

Mattoon, Robert. "The Companhia Paulista de Estradas de Ferro, 1868-1900: A Local Railway Enterprise in São Paulo, Brazil" (Ann Arbor, 1971).

Mesgravis, Laima. "A 'roda' da Santa Casa de São Paulo: a assistencia social aos enjeitados no século xix." Paper presented at the I Congresso de História de São Paulo in Campinas, July 1972.

Mulvey, Patricia. "The Black Lay Brotherhoods of Colonial Brazil: A History" (Ann Arbor, 1976).

Nazzari, Muriel. "Women and Property in the Transition to Capitalism: Decline of the Dowry in São Paulo, Brazil (1640-1870)." Paper presented at the American Historical Association Meeting in Chicago, December 1984.

Ramos, Donald. "A Social History of Ouro Preto: Stresses of Dynamic Urbanization in Colonial Brazil, 1695-1726" (Ann Arbor, 1972).

Smith, David Grant. "The Mercantile Class of Portugal and Brazil in the Seventeenth Century: A Socio-Economic Study of the Merchants of Lisbon and Bahia, 1620-1690" (University Microfilms, Austin, 1975).

Waldron, Kathleen. "A Social History of a Primate City: The Case of Caracas 1756-1810" (Ann Arbor, Bloomington, 1977).

II. PRINTED MATERIALS

Published Documents

Coleção das leis do Brasil, 1810 (Rio de Janeiro, 1880-1946).
Instituto Brasileiro de Geografia e Estatística. Pesquisa nacional por amostra de domicílios; Regiões Metropolitanas Rio de Janeiro e São Paulo, 4 trimestro 1971-1972 (Rio de Janeiro, n.d.).
Repertório das ordenações e leis de reino do Portugal. 4 vols. (Coimbra, 1795).
Rio de Janeiro. Instituto Histórico e Geográfico Brasileiro, Revista do Instituto Histórico e Geográfico Brasileiro. I- (Rio de Janeiro, 1839-).
__________. Tomos especiais. 15 vols. (Rio de Janeiro, 1956-1959).
São Paulo (state), Arquivo do Estado de São Paulo. Cartas de datas terras. I (São Paulo, 1937-).
__________. Documentos avulsos de interêsse para a história e costumes de São Paulo (São Paulo, 1952-1954).
__________. Inventários e testamentos. I- (São Paulo, 1920-).
__________. Publicação official de documentos interesantes para a história e costumes de São Paulo. I- (São Paulo, 1895-).
São Paulo, Arquivo Municipal de São Paulo. Actas da camara municipal de São Paulo (São Paulo, 1918-1939).
__________. Regístro geral da camara municipal de S. Paulo (São Paulo, 1919-1941).
São Paulo, Assembleia Legislativa. Annaes da assembleia legislativa provincial de S. Paulo: reconstituição desde 1835 a 1861. 30 vols. (São Paulo, 1925-1927).

Coeval or Near Contemporaneous Works

Abreu, Manoel Cardoso de. "Divertimento admirável para os historiadores observarem as machinas do mundo reconhecidas nos sertões da navegação das minas de Cuiabá e Mato Grosso," RIHGSP, VI (1900-1901), pp. 253-90.
Alincourt, Luis d'. "Memória sobre a viagem do porto d Santos a cidade de Cuiabá," Anais do Museu Paulista. XIV (São Paulo, 1950), pp. 253-381.
Almeida, Francisco José do Lacerda e. Roteiro da viagem pelos capitanias do Pará, Rio Negro, Mato Grosso, Cuiabá e São Paulo nos anos de 1780 a 1790 (São Paulo, 1841).
Andrada, Martim Francisco Ribeiro do. "Jornais das viagens pela capitania de São Paulo," RIHGB, XLV (1882), pp. 5-47.
Beyer, Gustavo. "Ligeiras notas de viagem do Rio de Janeiro a capitania de São Paulo, no Brasil, no verão de 1813," translated by Alberto Lofgren, RIHGSP, XII (1908), pp. 275-311.
Carvalho, Theophilo F. de. "Caminhos e roteiros nas capitanias do Rio de Janeiro, São Paulo e Minas," Anais do Museu Paulista, IV (São Paulo, 1931).
Chichorro, Manoel da Cunha de Azevedo. "Memória em que se mostra o estado económico militar e político da capitania de São Paulo, em 1814," Revista do Instituto Histórico, XXXVI (1873), pp. 197-232.
Davatz, Thomas. Memórias de um colono no Brasil, 1850, translated by Sérgio Buarque de Holanda (São Paulo, 1972).
Florence, Hercules. Viagem fluvial do Tieté ao Amazonas de 1825 a 1829, translated by the Visconde do Taunay (São Paulo, n.d.).
Henderson, James. A History of Brazil (London, 1921).
Karasch, Mary C. Slave Life in Rio de Janeiro, 1808-1850 (Ann Arbor, 1982).

Kidder, Daniel P. Reminiscências de viagens e permanência no Brasil: províncias do Sul, translated by Moacir N. Vasconcelos. 2 vols. (São Paulo, 1972).

Luccock, John. Notas sobre o Rio de Janeiro e partes meridionais do Brasil tomadas durante uma estada de dez anos nesse pais, de 1808 a 1818, translated by Milton da Silva Rodriquez (São Paulo, 1951).

Mawe, John. Travels in the Interior of Brazil (London, 1812).

Mawe, John. Viagens aõ interior do Brasil principalmente aõs districtos de ouro e dos diamantes, translated by Salina Benevides Viana (Rio de Janeiro, 1944).

Mendonça, Antônio Manuel de Mello Castro e. "Memória económico-política da capitania de São Paulo," Anais do Museu Paulista, XV (São Paulo, 1961).

__________. "Memória sobre a communicação da villa de Santos com a cidade de São Paulo," DI, XXIX, pp. 112-13.

Muller, Daniel Pedro. Ensaio de um quadro estatístico da província de São Paulo (São Paulo, 1923).

Oliveira, Antônio Rodrigues Veloso. Memória sobre melhoramento da província de S. Paulo (Rio de Janeiro, 1822).

Rendon, José Arouche de Toledo. "Reflexões sobre o estado em que se acha a agricultura na capitania de São Paulo (1788)," DI, XLIV (1930), pp. 195-215.

Rugendas, João Maurício. Viagem pitoresca através do Brasil, translated by Rubens Borba do Morães (São Paulo, 1972).

Sainte-Hilaire, Auguste de. Viagem a província de São Paulo e resumo das viagens ao Brasil, província cisplatina e missões do Paraguaí, translated by Rubens Borba de Morães (São Paulo, 1972).

Later Works

Abreu, Joao Capistrano de. Capítulos de história colonial, 1500-1800 (Brasilia, 1963).

Albornoz, Nicholás Sánchez. The Population of Latin America: A History, translated by W.A.R. Richardson (Berkeley, 1974).

Alden, Dauril. Royal Government in Colonial Brazil (Berkeley, 1968).

Allan, William. Studies in African Land Usage in Northern Rhodesia, Rhodes-Livingstone Papers No. 15 (Livingstone, 1949).

Allan, William. The African Husbandman (Edinburgh, 1965).

Almeida, Aluisio. O tropeirismo e a feira de Sorocaba (Sorocaba, 1968).

Almeida, Jr., Joao Mendes de. Monographia do município da cidade de S. Paulo (São Paulo, 1882).

Amin, Samir. Accumulation on a World Scale (New York, 1974).

Anderson, Michael. Family Structure in Nineteenth-Century Lancashire (Cambridge, 1971).

Arizpe, Lourdes. Migración, Etnicismo y Cámbio Ecónomico: Un Estudio Sobre Migrantes Campesinos a la Ciudad de Mexico (Mexico, 1978).

Arriaga, Eduardo E. New Life Tables for Latin American Populations in the Nineteenth and Twentieth Centuries. Population Monograph Series, No. 3 (Berkeley, 1968).

Arroyo, Leonardo. Igrejas de São Paulo (São Paulo, 1966).

Azevedo, Aroldo de (ed.). A cidade de São Paulo: estudos de geografia urbana. 4 vols. (São Paulo, 1956).

________. Vilas e cidades de Brasil colonial (São Paulo, 1956).

Banks, J.A. Prosperity and Parenthood (London, 1954).

Barros, G. Leite de. A cidade e o planalto (São Paulo, 1967).

Bastide, Roger and Florestan Fernandes. Brancos e negros em São Paulo (São Paulo, 1959).

Bastos, Humberto de Oliveira Rodrigues. O pensamento industrial no Brasil (São Paulo, 1952).

Boserup, Ester. The Conditions of Economic Growth (Chicago, 1965).

Boxer, Charles R. The Golden Age of Brazil 1695-1750 (Berkeley, 1962).

__________. Portuguese Society in the Tropics: The Municipal Councils of Goa, Mação, Bahia and Luanda, 1510-1800 (Madison, 1965).

Brading, David. A. Miners and Merchants in Bourbon Mexico, 1763-1810 (Cambridge, 1971).

Brookfield, Harold. Interdependent Development (London, 1975).

Brown, Paula and W.C. Brookfield. Struggle for Land (Melbourne, 1963).

Bruno, Ernani Silva. História do Brasil geral e regional: São Paulo e o Sul, V (São Paulo, n.d.).

__________. Viagem aõ pais dos paulistas (Rio de Janeiro, 1966).

Campos, Pedro Dias de. O espírito militar paulista: na colonia, no império, na republica (São Paulo, 1923).

Candido, Antonio. Os parceiros do Rio Bonito (Rio de Janeiro, 1964).

Cardim, Fernao. Tratado da terra e da gente do Brasil (São Paulo, 1939).

Cardoso, Fernando Henrique and E. Faletto. Dependencia e desenvolvimento na América Latina (Rio de Janeiro, 1970).

Castro, Jeanne Berrance do. A Milicia Cidadá: A Guarda Nacional de 1831 a 1850 (São Paulo, 1977).

Chayanov, A.V. The Theory of Peasant Economy (Homewood, 1966).

Coale, A.J. et al. (eds.). Aspects of the Analysis of Family Structure (Princeton, 1965).

Coale, Ansley J. Methods of Estimating Basic Demographic Measures from Incomplete Data. United Nations Organization, Manuals on Methods of Estimating Population, ST/SOA/Series A/42 (New York, 1962).

Coale, Ansley J. and Paul Demeny. Regional Model Life Tables and Stable Populations (Princeton, 1966).

Coatsworth, John H. Growth against Development: The Economic Impact of Railroads in Porfirian Mexico (DeKalb, 1981).

Connell, K.H. The Population of Ireland, 1750-1845 (Oxford, 1950).

Costa Pinto, Luiz Aguiar de. Lutas de famflias o Brazil (São Paulo, 1949).

Cox, Peter R. Demography (Cambridge, 1970).

Dean, Warren. The Industrialization of São Paulo, 1880-1945 (Austin, 1969).

Delson, Roberta Marx. Town Planning in Colonial Brazil (Ann Arbor, 1980).

Demos, John. A Little Commonwealth: Family Life in Plymouth Colony (London, 1971).

Dobb, Maurice. Studies in the Development of Capitalism (London, 1946).

Duarte, Raul da Gama. São Paulo de ontem e do hoje (São Paulo, 1941).

Egas, Eugenio. Galeria dos presidentes de São Paulo. 3 vols. (São Paulo, 1926-1927).

__________. Os municípios paulistas (São Paulo, 1925).

Ellis, Alfredo, Jr. A economia paulista no século XVIII (São Paulo, 1950).

__________. Capítulos da história social de São Paulo (São Paulo, 1944).

Faoro, Raymundo. Os donos do poder. 2 vols. (São Paulo, 1975).

Fernandes, Florestan. Aspectos do povoamento de São Paulo no século xvi (São Paulo, n.d.).

Ferreira, Tito Livio. Génese Social da Gente Bandeirante (São Paulo, 1944).

Franco, Francisco de Assis Carvalho. Bandeiras e Bandeirantes de São Paulo (São Paulo, 1940).

Franco, Maria Sylvai de Carvalho. Homens livres na ordem escravocrata (São Paulo, 1969).

Frank, Andre Gunder. Capitalism and Underdevelopment in Latin America (New York, 1969).

Freitas, Affonso A. de. Diccionário histórico, topográphico, ethnográphico, illustrado do município de São Paulo (São Paulo, 1929).

__________. Tradições e reminiscências paulistanas (São Paulo, 1921).

Freyre, Gilberto. Casa grande e senzala (Rio de Janeiro, 1933).

__________. Sobrados e mucambos. 2 vols. (Rio de Janeiro, 1961).

Furtado, Celso. The Economic Growth of Brazil, translated by Ricardo W. de Aguiar and Eric Charles Drysdale (Berkeley, 1965).
Garcez, Martinho. Dos testamentos e successões (Rio de Janeiro, 1917).
Glass, D.V. and D.E.C. Eversley (eds.). Population in History (London, 1965).
Goode, William J. The Family (Englewood Cliffs, 1964).
__________. World Revolution and Family Patterns (New York, 1963).
Graham, Richard. Britain and the Onset of Modernization in Brazil 1850-1914 (Cambridge, 1968).
Greene, Jack P. and David W. Cohen. Neither Slaves nor Free: the freedmen of African descent in the slave societies of the New World (Baltimore, 1972).
Guimaraes, Alberto Passos. Quatro seculos de latifúndio (Rio de Janeiro, 1968).
Harris, Marvin. Town and Country in Brazil (New York, 1956).
__________. Moncões (Rio de Janeiro, 1945).
Hawke, G.R. Railways and Economic Growth in England and Wales 1840-1870 (Oxford, 1970).
Henry, Louis. Anciennes familles genevoises (Paris, 1960).
Holanda, Sergio Buarque de (ed.). História geral da civilização brasileira. 6 vols. (São Paulo, 1973).
Kemper, Robert. Migration and Adaptation: Tzintzuntzán Peasants in Mexico City (Beverly Hills, 1977).
Keynes, J.M. A Treatise on Money. 2 vols. (London, 1950).
Laslett, Peter (ed.). Household and Family in Past Time (Cambridge, 1972).
__________. The World we have Lost (London, 1965).
Leal, Vitor Nunes. Coronelismo, enxada e voto (Rio de Janeiro, 1948).
Leme, Pedro Taques de Almeida Paes. Nobilarquia paulistana: história e genealogia. 3 vols. (São Paulo, 1954).
Leme, Luiz Gonzaga da Silva. Genealogia paulistana. 9 vols. (São Paulo, 1954).
Lisanti Filho, Luis. Negócios Coloniais: Uma Correspondência Comercial do Século XIII. 5 vols. (São Paulo, 1973).
Lloyd, Cynthia (ed.). Sex, Discrimination and the Division of Labor (New York, 1975).
Lobo, Eulalia Maria Lahmeyer. História do Rio de Janeiro. 2 vols. (Rio de Janeiro, 1978).
Lomnitz, Larissa A. Networks and Marginality, Life in a Mexican Shanty Town (New York, 1977).
Luis, Washington. A Capitania de São Paulo: Govêrno de Rodrigo Cesar de Menezes (São Paulo, 1938).
Luz, Nícia Vilela. A luta pela industrialização do Brasil (1808-1930) (São Paulo, 1961).
Machado, Alcantara. Vida e morte do bandeirante (São Paulo, 1930).
Magro, Omar Simoes. Mulheres perigrosas: crónicas da história paulista (São Paulo, 1937).
Manchester, Alan K. British Pre-eminence in Brazil: Its Rise and Decline (Chapel Hill, 1933).
Marcílio, Maria-Luiza. La ville de São Paulo: peuplement et population, 1750-1850 (Rouen, 1970).
Martins, Antonio Egydio. São Paulo antigo, 1554-1910. 2 vols. (São Paulo, 1911).
Martíns, José de Souza. A imigração e a críse do Brasil agrária (São Paulo, 1973).
Marqués, Manoel Eufrásio de Azevedo. Apontamentos históricos, geográficos, biográficos, estatistícos e noticiosos da província de São Paulo. 2 vols. (Rio de Janeiro, 1879).
Marx, Karl. Capital. 3 vols., translated from the third German edition by Samuel Moore and Edward Aveling (London, 1967).
Mattoso, Katia M. de Queiros. Bahia: A cidade do Salvador e seu mercado no século XIX (São Paulo, 1978).
McCaa, Robert. Marriage and Fertility in Chile (Boulder, 1983).
Menucci, Sud. Cem anos de instrução pública (São Paulo, 1932).

Merrick, Thomas W. and Douglas H. Graham. Population and Economic Development in Brazil (Baltimore, 1979).
Mesgravis, Laima. A Santa Casa de Misericórdia de São Paulo 1599?-1884 (São Paulo, 1974).
Mintz, Sidney. Worker in the Cane (New Haven, 1964).
Miranda, Dr. Pontes de. Fontes e evolução do direito civil brasileiro (Rio de Janeiro, 1928).
Monberg, Pierre. La croissance de la ville de São Paulo (Grenoble, 1953).
__________. Pionniers e planteurs de São Paulo (Paris, 1952).
Moog, Clodomiro Vianna. Bandeirantes and Pioneers, translated by L.L. Barett (New York, 1965).
Morse, Richard M. (ed.). Las ciudades latinoamericanas. 2 vols. (Mexico, 1973).
__________. From Community to Metropolis: a biography of São Paulo, Brazil (Gainesville, 1958).
__________. (ed.). The Bandeirantes: The Historical Role of the Brazilian Pathfinders (New York, 1965).
Moura, Paulo Cursino. São Paulo de outrora (São Paulo, 1943).
Nogueira, Oracy. Família e comunidade: um estudo sociológico de Itapetininga. 2 vols. (Rio de Janeiro, 1962).
Nogueria de Matos, Odilon. Café e Ferrovias (São Paulo, 1974).
Oliveira, José Joaquim Machado d'. Quadro histórico da província de São Paulo até o anno de 1822 (São Paulo, 1897).
Penteado, Nicanor. Reformas e innovações feitas pelo código civil (São Paulo, 1918).
Pestana, Paulo R. A expansão económica do estado de São Paulo num século, 1822-1922 (São Paulo, 1923).
Petrone, Maria Thereza Schorer. A lavoura canavieira em São Paulo (São Paulo, 1968).
Petrone, Pasquale. A baixada paulista (São Paulo, 1965).
Pierson, Donald. Cruz das Almas (Rio de Janeiro, 1966).
Pinchbeck, Ivy. Women Workers and the Industrial Revolution (New York, 1969).
Pirenne, Henri. Early Democracies in the Low Countries: Urban Society and Political Conflict in the Middle Ages and the Renaissance (New York, 1963).
__________. A History of Europe (New York, 1955).
Pombo, José Francisco da Rocha. História de S. Paulo: resumo didáctico (São Paulo, 1925).
Portella, Joaquim Pires Machado. Constituição política do império do Brasil (Rio de Janeiro, 1876).
Prado, J.F. de Almeida. D. Joao VI e o ínicio da classe dirigente do Brasil, 1815-1889 (São Paulo, 1968).
Prado, Paulo. Paulística (Rio de Janeiro, 1934).
Prado Junior, Caio. Evolução política do Brasil e outros estudos (São Paulo, 1969).
__________. História económica do Brasil (São Paulo, 1974).
__________. The Colonial Background of Modern Brazil, translated by Suzette Macedo (Berkeley, 1967).
Queiroz, Maria Isaura Pereira de. Bairros rurais paulistas (São Paulo, 1972).
__________. O mandonismo local na vida política brasileira (São Paulo, 1969).
Reis Filho, Nestor Goulart. Quadro da arquitetura no Brasil (São Paulo, 1970).
__________. A Evolução urbana do Brasil, 1500-1720 (São Paulo, 1968).
Rey, P. Les alliances de classes (Paris, 1973).
Robinson, David J. (ed.). Social Fabric and Spatial Structure in Colonial Latin America (Ann Arbor, 1979).
Ruí, Afonso. História da camara municipal da cidade do Salvador (Salvador, 1953).
Russell-Wood, A.J.R. The Black Man in Slavery and Freedom in Colonial Brazil (New York, 1982).

__________. *Fidalgos and Philanthropists: The Santa Casa da Misericordia of Bahia, 1550-1755* (London, 1968).
Sahlins, Marshall. *Stone Age Economics* (Chicago, 1972).
Saia, Luis. *Fontes primárias para o estudo das habilitações, das vias de comunicação e dos aglomerados humanos em São Paulo, no século xvi* (São Paulo, 1948).
__________. *Notas sobre a evolução da morada paulista* (São Paulo, 1957).
Salvador, José Gonçalves. *Os transportes em São Paulo no período colonial* (São Paulo, 1959).
Sant'Anna, Benevenuto Nuto. *São Paulo histórico*. 6 vols. (São Paulo, 1937-1944).
Santos Filho, Lycurgo. *História da medicina no Brasil*. 2 vols. (São Paulo, 1947).
Schwartz, Stuart. *Sovereignty and Society in Colonial Brazil: The High Court of Bahia and its Judges, 1609-1751* (Berkeley, 1973).
Shirley, Robert W. *The End of a Tradition: Culture Change and Development in the Municipio of Cunha* (New York, 1971).
Singer, Paul. *Economia Política da Urbanização* (São Paulo, 1973).
Sodre, Nelson W. *As classes sociãis no Brasil* (Rio de Janeiro, 1957).
Taunay, Affonso d' Escragnolle. *Colectanea de mapas de cartografia paulista antiga abrangendo nove cartas, 1612-1837* (São Paulo, 1922).
__________. *História do cafe no Brasil*. 15 vols. (Rio de Janeiro, 1927-1937).
__________. *História da cidade de São Paulo no século xviii*. 2 vols. (São Paulo, 1949).
__________. *História geral das bandeiras paulistas*. 11 vols. (São Paulo, 1924-1950).
__________. *História siescentista da ville de São Paulo*. 4 vols. (São Paulo, 1926-1929).
__________. *Velho São Paulo* (São Paulo, 1954).
Tilly, Louise A. and Joan W. Scott. *Women, Work and Family* (New York, 1978).
Torres, Maria Celestina Teixeira Mendes. *O bairro de Santana* (São Paulo, 1970).
Tripoli, Cesar. *História do direito brasileiro*. 3 vols. (São Paulo, 1936).
United Nations. *The Population Debate: Dimensions and Perspectives. Papers of the World Population Conference Bucharest 1974* (New York, 1975), 2 vols.
Uricoechea, Fernando. *The Patrimonial Foundations of the Brazilian Bureaucratic State* (Berkeley, 1980).
Vasconcellos, Diogo de. *Linhas geraes da administração colonial* (n.p., n.d.).
Veliz, Claudio. *The Centralist Tradition of Latin America* (Princeton, 1980).
Vianna, Oliveira. *Instituições políticas brasileiras*. 2 vols. (Rio de Janeiro, 1949).
__________. *Populações meridionaes do Brasil* (São Paulo, 1922).
Vicuna, Santiago Marin. *Los caminos de Chile* (Santiago, 1930).
Vieira, Hermes. *História da polícia civil de São Paulo* (São Paulo, 1955).
Wallerstein, Immanuel. *The Modern World System: Capitalist Agriculture and the Origins of the European World Economy in the Sixteenth Century* (New York, 1974).
Weber, Max. *The City*, translated and edited by Don Martindale and Gertrud Neuwirth (New York, 1958).
Willems, Emilio. *Cunha: tradição e transição* (São Paulo, 1947).
Zenha, Edmundo. *O município no Brasil (1552-1700)* (São Paulo, 1948).

Articles

Alden, Dauril. "Black Robes Versus White Settlers: The Struggle for 'Freedom of the Indians' in Colonial Brazil," in Howard Peckham and Charles Gilson (eds.), *Attitudes of Colonial Powers Toward the American Indian* (Salt Lake City, 1969), pp. 19-45.
__________. "The Population of Brazil in the Late Eighteenth Century: A Preliminary Survey," *HAHR* XLIII, No. 2 (May 1963): 173-205.

Araripe, Tristão de Alencar, "O paterfamílias no Brasil colonial," Revista do Instituto Histórico LV, No. 2 (1892):15-23.
Arriaga, Eduardo E. "A New Approach to the Measurements of Urbanization," Economic Development and Cultural Change 18, No. 2 (1970):206-218.
________. "The Nature and Effects of Latin America's Non Western Trend in Fertility," Demography 7 (1970), pp. 483-501.
________. and Kingsley Davis, "The Patterns of Mortality Change in Latin America," Demography 6 (1969), pp. 223-42.
Arrom, Silvia M. "Changes in Mexican Family Law in the Nineteenth Century: The Civil Codes of 1870 and 1884," Journal of Family History (Fall 1985, in press).
________."Marriage Patterns in Mexico City, 1811," Journal of Family History, 3:4 (Winter 78): 376-91.
Azevedo, Thales de, "Família, casamento e divórcio no Brasil," in Thales de Azevedo (ed.), Cultura e situação racial no Brasil (Rio de Janeiro,1966).
Barbier, Jacques A. "Elite and Cadres in Bourbon Chile," HAHR 52, No. 3 (1972):417-35.
Barth, Fredrik, "On the Study of Social Change," American Anthropologist 69, No. 6 (December 1967):661-69.
Blake, Judith. "Family Instability and Reproductive Behavior in Jamaica," Current Research in Human Fertility (New York, 1955), pp. 24-41.
Borah, Woodrow Wilson, "European Cultural Influence in the Formation of the First Plan for Urban Centers That Has Lasted to our Time," Actas y Memórias del XXXIX Congreso Internacional de Americanístas, II (Lima, 1970), pp. 35-54.
Brass, W., "Methods of Obtaining Basic Demographic Measures Where Data Are Lacking or Defective," World Population Conference, 1965 (New York,1967).
Brown, Paulo and W.C. Brookfield, "Chimbu Land and Society," Oceania 30 (1959-60), pp. 1-75.
Burch, Thomas, "The Size and Structure of Families, a Comparative Analysis of Census Data," American Sociological Review 32:3 (1967):347-63.
Burkholder, Mark A. "From Creole to Pensinsular: The Transformation of the Audiencia of Lima," HAHR 52, No. 3 (August 1972):395-415.
Campbell, Leon G. "A Colonial Establishment: Creole Eighteenth Century," HAHR 52, No. 1 (1972):1-25.
Canabrava, Alice P. "Uma economia de decadência: os níveis de riqueza na capitania de São Paulo, 1765/67," Revista Brasileira de Economia 26, No. 4 (out./dez., 1972):95-123.
________. "A repartição da terra na capitania de São Paulo, 1818," Estudos Econômicos II, No. 6 (1972):77-130.
Cancian, Francesca M., Louis W. Goodman, and Peter H. Smith, "Capitalism, Industrialization and Kinship in Latin America: Major Issues," Journal of Family History 3:4 (Winter 1978):319-36.
Candido, Antônio, "The Brazilian Family," in A. Marchand and T. Lynn Smith (eds.), Brazil, Portrait of Half a Continent (New York, 1947), pp. 291-312.
Cardoso, Fernando Henrique. "As condições sociais da industrialização de São Paulo," Revista Brasiliense (marco-abril 1960), pp. 31-46.
Carneiro, Robert L. "Slash and Burn Agriculture: A Closer Look at its Implications for Settlement Patterns," in A.F.C. Wallace (ed.), Men and Cultures (Philadelphia, 1960), pp. 229-34.
________. "Slash and Burn Cultivation among the Kuikuru and its Implications for Cultural Development in the Amazon Basin," in Y. Cohen (ed.), Man in Adaptation: The Cultural Present (Chicago, 1968), pp. 131-45.
Castells, Manuel. "La urbanizacíon dependiente en América Latina," in Castells (ed.), Imperialismo y urbanizacíon en América Latina (Barcelona, 1972), pp. 7-26.

Coale, Ansley J. "How the Age Distribution of a Human Population Is Determined," Cold Springs Harbor Symposia on Quantitative Biology XXII (1957): 83-89.

________. "The Demographic Transition," in United Nations, The Population Debate, Vol. 1, pp. 347-55.

Couturier, Edith. "Women and the Family in Eighteenth Century Mexico: Law and Practice," Journal of Family History (Fall 1985, in press).

Davis, Kingsley. "Colonial Expansion and Urban Diffusion in the Americas," International Journal of Comparative Sociology I (1960), pp. 43-66.

________. "The Theory of Change and Response in Modern Demographic History," Population Index (October, 1983), pp. 345-66.

________. "The Urbanization of the Human Population," in Kingsley Davis (ed.), Cities (New York, 1965), pp. 3-24.

________. and Judith Blake. "Social Structure and Fertility: An Analytic Framework," Economic Development and Cultural Change IV, No. 3 (April 1956): 211-35.

Deffontaines, Pierre. "The Origin and Growth of the Brazilian Network of Towns," The Geographical Review XXVIII (1938), pp. 379-99.

Ellis, Myriam Austregesilio. "Contribuição ao estudo do abastecimento das zonas mineradoras do Brasil no século XVIII," Revista de História XVII (1958), pp. 429-67.

Flory, Rae and David Grant Smith. "Bahian Merchants and Planters in the 17th and early 18th Centuries," HAHR 58, no. 4 (1978): 571-94.

Flory, Thomas. "Judicial Politics in Nineteenth-Century Brazil," HAHR 55, No. 4 (November 1975): 664-92.

Fonseca, Luiza de. "Bachareís Brasileiros: Elementos Biográficos, 1635-1830," Anais do IV Congresso de História Nacional II (Rio de Janeiro, 1951), pp. 109-405.

Fourastie, Jean and Rene Grandamy. "Remarques sur les prix salariaux des cereales et la productivité du travaill agricole en Europe du XVe au XXe siècle," Third International Conference of Economic History, Munich, 1965, I (Paris, 1968), pp. 647-56.

French, John D. "Riqueza, Poder e Mão de Obra Numa Economia de Subsistencia: São Paulo 1596-1625," Revista do Arquivo Municipal 195 (1982), pp. 79-107.

Fukuí, L.F.Q. "Riqueza do pobre; relações país e filhos entre sítiantes tradicionais brasileiros," Revista do Instituto de Estudos Brasileiros 14 (1973), pp. 67-77.

Greenow, Linda. "Micro Geographic Analysis as an Index to Family Structure and Networks," Journal of Family History (Fall 1985, in press).

________. "Spatial Dimensions of Household and Family Structure in Eighteenth Century Spanish America," Discussion Paper, No. 35 (Department of Geography, Syracuse, July 1977).

Greven, Philip J., Jr. "The Average Size of Families and Households in the Province of Massachusetts in 1764 and in the United States in 1790: an overview," in Laslett, ed., Household, pp. 545-60.

Gross, Daniel R. "Factionalism and Local Level Politics in Rural Brazil," Journal of Anthropological Research 29, No. 2 (1973): 123-44.

Guy, Donna. "Latin American Family History: The Family as a Business and Corporation in Argentina," World Conference on Records, Vol. 9 (Salt Lake City, 1980).

Habakkuk, H.J. "Family Structure and Economic Change in Nineteenth-Century Europe," Journal of Economic History XV, no. 1 (1955): 1-12, reprinted in Norman W. Bill and Ezra F. Vogel (eds.), A Modern Introduction to the Family (Glencoe, 1960), pp. 163-72.

Hagerman Johnson, Ann. "The Impact of Market Agriculture in Family and Household Structure in 19th Century Chile, HAHR 58, no. 4 (1978): 625-48.

Hajnal, John. "Age at Marriage and Proportions Marrying," Population Studies 7, no. 2 (1953): 111-32.

__________. "European Marriage Patterns in Perspective," in Glass and Eversley (eds.), Population in History (Chicago, 1965), pp. 101-43.

Hamilton, Earl J. "American Treasure and the Rise of Capitalism," Economica IX, no. 27 (1929): 338-57.

Harevan, Tamara K. "Postscript: The Latin American Essays in the Context of Family History," Journal of Family History 3, no. 4 (1978): 454-57.

Herrmann, Lucila. "Evolução da estrutura social de Guaratinguetá num período do trezentos anos," Revista de Administração II (março/junho 1948), pp. 3-333.

Hoberman, Louisa Schell. "Merchants in Seventeenth Century Mexico City: A Preliminary Portrait," HAHR 57 (August 1977), pp. 479-503.

Holanda, Sérgio Buarque de. "Movimentos da população em São Paulo no século xviii," Revista do Instituto de Estudos Brasileiros, No. 1 (1966), pp. 55-111.

Hoselitz, Bert F. "The Role of Urbanization in Economic Development: Some International Comparisons," in R. Turner (ed.), India's Urban Future (Berkeley, 1962), pp. 157-81.

Jardim, Caio. "São Paulo no século xviii," Revista do Arquivo Municipal XLI (1937), pp. 149-80.

Kaplan, Marcos. "La ciudad latinoamericana como factor de transmision de control socioeconómico y político externo durante el périodo contemporaneo." Paper presented for the 39th Congress of Americanists, Aug. 2-9, 1970, Lima.

Kennedy, John. "Bahian Elites 1750-1822," HAHR 53, no. 3 (August 1973): 415-39.

Kirk, Dudley and Frank Oeschli. "Modernization and the Demographic Transition in Latin America and the Caribbean," in Economic Development and Cultural Change, Vol. 23 (1975), pp. 381-417.

Kuznesof, Elizabeth. "Clans, the Militia and Territorial Government: the Articulation of Kinship with Polity in Eighteenth-Century São Paulo," in David J. Robinson (ed.), Social Fabric and Spatial Structures in Colonial Latin American (Ann Arbor, 1979), pp. 181-226.

__________. "Household Composition and Headship as Related to Changes in Mode of Production: São Paulo 1765 to 1836," Comparative Studies in Society and History 22, no. 1 (January 1980): 78-108.

__________. "The Role of the Female-Headed Household in Brazilian Modernization," The Journal of Social History 13, no. 4 (June 1980): 589-613.

__________. "The Role of the Merchants in the Economic Development of São Paulo: 1765-c 1850," HAHR (November 1980), pp. 571-92.

Lampard, E.E. "The History of Cities in the Economically Advanced Areas," Economic Development and Cultural Change III, no. 2 (January 1955): 81-136.

Lavrin, Asuncion and Edith Couturier. "Dowries and Wills: A View of Women's Socioeconomic Role in Colonial Guadalajara and Puebla 1640-1790," HAHR 59, no. 2 (1979): 280-304.

Leeds, Anthony. "Brazilian careers and social structure, a case history and model," in D.B. Heath and R.N. Adams (eds.), Contemporary Cultures and Societies of Latin America (New York, 1965).

Lewin, Linda. "Some Historical Implications for Kinship Organization for Family based Politics in the Brazilian Northeast," Comparative Studies in Society and History 21, no. 2 (April 1979): 262-92.

Litwak, Eugene. "Extended kin relations in an industrial democratic society," in Ethel Shanas and Gordon F. Streib (eds.), Social Structure and the Family: generational relations (Englewood Cliffs, 1965).

Luz, Nicia Vilela. "A administração provincial de São Paulo em face do movimento abolicionista," Revista de Administração II, no. 8 (1948): 80-100.

Martinho, Lenira Menezes. "Organização do trabalho e relações sociais nas firmas comerciais do Rio de Janeiro: primeira metade século XIX," Revista do Instituto de Estudos Brasileiro 18 (São Paulo, 1976), pp. 41-62.

McKenna, Edward E. "Marriage and Fertility in Postfamine Ireland: A Multivariate Analysis," American Journal of Sociology LXXX, no. 3 (1974): 688-705.

McKeown, Thomas and R.G. Brown. "Medical Evidence Related to English Population Changes in the Eighteenth Century," Population in History (Chicago, 1965), pp. 285-309.

Medik, Hans. "The Proto-Industrial Family Economy: The Structural Function of Household and Family during the Transition from Peasant Society to Industrial Capitalism," Social History, 3 (1976), pp. 291-315.

Mesquíta, Eni de. "O papel do agregado na região de Itu, 1798-1830," Coleção Museu Paulista, serie de História, VI (São Paulo, 1977), pp. 1-105.

Monbeig, Pierre. "Aspectos geográficos do crescimento da cidade de São Paulo," Boletim Paulista de Geografia XVI (marco 1954), pp. 3-29.

Morães, Rubens Borba de. "Contribuições para a história do povoamento de São Paulo ate fins do século xviii," Geografia Ano I, no. 1 (1935): 69-87.

Morse, Richard. "A Prolegomenon to Latin American Urban History," HAHR 52, no. 3 (August 1972): 359-94.

________. "The Development of Urban Systems in the Americas in the Nineteenth Century," Journal of Inter-American Studies and World Affairs 17, no. 1 (1975): 4-26.

________. "São Paulo: Case Study of a Latin American Metropolis," in Francine F. Rabinovitz and Felicity M. Trueblood (eds.), Latin American Urban Research (Beverly Hills, 1971), pp. 151-86.

________. "Trends and Issues in Latin American Urban Research," Latin American Research Review (Part I), VI, no. 1 (Spring 1971): 3-52; (Part II), VI, no. 2 (Summer 1971): 19-75.

________. "Trends and Patterns of Latin American Urbanization, 1750-1920," Comparative Studies in Society and History 16, no. 4 (1974): 416-47.

Moura, Américo Brasiliense Antunes de. "Govêrno do Morgado de Matheus," Revista do Archivo Municipal LII (1938), pp. 5-155.

Nakane, Chie. "An Interpretation of the Size and Structure of the Household in Japan over Three Centuries," in Laslett, ed., Household, pp. 517-44.

Petrone, Maria Theresa Schorer. "Um comerciante do cíclo do açucar paulista: Antônio da Silva Prado (1817-1829)," Revista de História 36, no. 73 (1968): 115-38;

Phelps-Brown, E.H. and Sheila V. Hopkins. "Builders Wage-rates, Prices and Population: Some Further Evidence," Economica XXVI, no. 101 (February 1959): 18-38.

Pleck, Elizabeth. "Two Worlds in One: Work and Family," Journal of Social History 10 (Winter 1976), pp. 178-95.

Prado, Caio, Jr. "O fator geográfico na formaçáo e no desenvolvimento da cidade de São Paulo," in Evoluçáo política do Brasil e outros estudos (São Paulo, 1969).

Preston, Samuel H. "The Changing Relation between Mortality and level of Economic Development," Population Studies 29 (1975), pp. 231-48.

Quijano, Anibal. "The Urbanization of Latin American Society," in Jorge E. Hardoy (ed.), Urbanization in Latin America: Approaches and Issues (Garden City, 1975), pp. 109-53.

Ramos, Donald. "Marriage and the Family in Colonial Vila Rica," HAHR 55, no. 2 (May 1975): 200-25.

Ridings, Eugene W. "Interest Groups and Development: the Case of Brazil in the Nineteenth Century," Journal of Latin American Studies 9, no. 2 (1977): 225-50.

Rocha Filho, Gustavo Neves de. "Casas de residência no Brasil do século xix," Bem Estar 2 (1958), pp. 3-7.

Safa, Helen Icken. "Class Consciousness among Working Class Women in Latin America: Puerto Rico," in June Nash and Helen Safa (eds.), Sex and Class in Latin America (Brooklyn, 1980), pp. 69-85.

Saia, Luis. "Notas sobre a arquitetura rural paulista do segunda século," Revista do Serviço de Património Histórico e Artístico Nacional No. 8 (1944), pp. 211-75.

Smith, David Grant. "Old Christian Merchants and the Foundation of the Brazil Company, 1649," HAHR 54, no. 2 (May 1974): 233-59.

Smith, Raymond T. "The Family and the Modern World System: Some Observations from the Caribbean," Journal of Family History 3, no. 4 (1978): 337-57.

Socolow, Susan Migden. "Economic Activities of the Porteño Merchants; The Viceregal Period," HAHR 55 (1975), pp. 1-24.

Sousa, Antonieta de Paulo. "Expansão da propriedade rural paulista," Anais do Nono Congresso Brasileiro de Geografia III (1940), pp. 710-14.

Spengler, Joseph J. "Demographic Factors and Economic Development," Daedalus (Spring 1968), pp. 433-46.

Taunay, Afonso de Escragnolle. "Ensaios de história economica e financeira," Anais do Museu Paulista XV (São Paulo, 1961), pp. 3-81.

Teitelbaum, Michael S. "Importancia de la téoria de la transición demográfica para paises en desarrollo," Demografía y Economía 10 (1976), pp. 54-67.

Thompson, Warren S. "Population," American Journal of Sociology, Vol. 34 (1929), pp. 959-75.

Turner, Ralph E. "The Industrial City: Center of Cultural Change," in Caroline Ware (ed.), The Cultural Approach to History, pp. 228-42.

Wagley, Charles. "Kinship patterns in Brazil: the persistence of a cultural tradition," in Wagley (ed.), The Latin American Tradition (New York, 1968), pp. 175-93.

Willems, Emilio. "Social Differentiation in Colonial Brazil," Comparative Studies in Society and History 12, no. 1 (January 1970): 31-49.

__________. "The Structure of the Brazilian Family," Social Forces XXXI, no. 4 (1953): 341-45.

Wirth, Louis. "Urbanism as a Way of Life," American Journal of Sociology 44 (1938), pp. 1-24.

Index

Dellplain Latin American Studies
Published by Westview Press

No. 8 *Studies in Spanish American Population History,* edited by David J. Robinson

No. 9 *The People of the Colca Valley: A Population Study,* Noble David Cook

No. 10 *Tierra Adentro: Settlement and Society in Colonial Durango,* Michael M. Swann

No. 11 *Andean Reflections: Letters from Carl O. Sauer While on a South American Trip Under a Grant from the Rockefeller Foundation, 1942,* edited by Robert C. West

No. 12 *Credit and Socioeconomic Change in Colonial Mexico: Loans and Mortgages in Guadalajara, 1720–1820,* Linda Greenow

No. 13 *Once Beneath the Forest: Prehistoric Terracing in the Rió Bec Region of the Maya Lowlands,* B. L. Turner, II

No. 14 *Marriage and Fertility in Chile: Demographic Turning Points in the Petorca Valley, 1840–1976,* Robert McCaa

No. 15 *The Spatial Organization of New Land Settlement in Latin America,* Jacob O. Maos

No. 16 *The Anglo-Argentine Connection, 1900–1939,* Roger Gravil

No. 17 *Costa Rica: A Geographical Interpretation in Historical Perspective,* Carolyn Hall

No. 18 *Household Economy and Urban Development: São Paulo, 1765 to 1836,* Elizabeth Anne Kuznesof

Previous Dellplain Studies
Available from University Microfilms International

No. 1 *Social Fabric and Spatial Structure in Colonial Latin America,* edited by David J. Robinson

No. 2 *New Towns for Colonial Brazil: Spatial and Social Planning of the Eighteenth Century,* Roberta Marx Delson

No. 3 *Carl Sauer's Fieldwork in Latin America,* Robert C. West

No. 4 *Studying Latin America: Essays in Honor of Preston E. James,* edited by David J. Robinson

No. 5 *First Among Equals: Great Britain and Venezuela, 1810–1910,* George E. Carl

No. 6 *Amazon Economics: The Simplicity of Shipobo Indian Wealth,* Roland W. Bergman

No. 7 *The Mining Society of Potosí, 1776–1810,* Rose Marie Buechler